Essential Guide to Managed Extensions for C++

SIVA CHALLA AND ARTUR LAKSBERG

Essential Guide to Managed Extensions for C++

ISBN (pbk): 1-893115-28-3

Printed and bound in the United States of America 12345678910

Editorial Directors: Dan Appleman, Peter Blackburn, Gary Cornell, Jason Gilmore, Karen Watterson

Managing Editor: Grace Wong

Project Manager: Tracy Brown

Copy Editors: Ami Knox, Nicole LeClerc

Production Editor: Kari Brooks

Compositor: Impressions Book and Journal Services, Inc.

Indexer: Ann Rogers

Cover Designer: Tom Debolski

Marketing Manager: Stephanie Rodriguez

Distributed to the book trade in the United States by Springer-Verlag New York, Inc.,175 Fifth Avenue, New York, NY, 10010 and outside the United States by Springer-Verlag GmbH & Co. KG, Tiergartenstr. 17, 69112 Heidelberg, Germany.

In the United States, phone 1-800-SPRINGER, email orders@springer-ny.com, or visit http://www.springer-ny.com. Outside the United States, fax +49 6221 345229, email orders@springer.de, or visit http://www.springer.de.

For information on translations, please contact Apress directly at 901 Grayson Street, Suite 204, Berkeley, CA 94710. Phone 510-549-5938, fax: 510-549-5939, email info@apress.com, or visit http://www.apress.com.

The source code for this book is available to readers at http://www.apress.com in the Downloads section.

To my daughter, Ramya, whose smile lights up the whole world.
— Siva Challa

Contents at a Glance

Contents

Part Two: Interoperability

Foreword by Mark L. Hall

A FEW YEARS AGO, a small team of Microsoft engineers was assembled to design the software development tools for a revolutionary new platform that would later be unveiled to the world as Microsoft .NET.

The first goal of the Managed C++ design team was to "bring forward" the vast array of successful C++ applications and components that had been written for the native Windows platform. This would greatly accelerate the availability of critical technology on .NET, thereby shifting its adoption curve. To accomplish this task, the team implemented what it called "It Just Works" (IJW) technology. This technology allows any preexisting C++ program to be compiled directly to the .NET platform. Once there, it can be made available to any new application written for .NET through the use of simple wrapper classes.

The second goal for the team was to allow existing C++ programs to seamlessly avail themselves of the wide array of services being developed for .NET. A host of upward-compatible extensions was devised to make it easy to use the new .NET Framework classes without altering the preexisting C++ code. This extends the useful life of preexisting applications, protecting the investment developers have made in C++ and Windows over the years.

The third goal for the team was to maintain the C++ ethos of *power* through access to the underlying platform. Here are some examples:

- It provides seamless access to the entire Windows API by a simple `#include` of the `windows.h` header file.

- The concept of boxing is explicit in the language, so the user can control when it happens.

- Full indexed properties are supported.

- All of the combinations of member visibility within and across assemblies are exposed.

- Interior pointer variables are supported.

- The get and set methods for properties can have different visibilities.

Managed C++ is the only .NET language that provides any of these features.

Given the scope of its capabilities, understanding Managed C++ in its entirety can be a daunting challenge. This book is an excellent companion to the specification available in the Visual C++ .NET product. It provides detailed examples of how Managed C++ can be used to achieve the goals of its design. The book is written by two of the compiler's principal implementers, Artur Laksberg and Siva Challa. They were witness to, and participated in, all of the countless hallway discussions and design-room debates that have occurred since the conception of Managed C++. They are uniquely qualified to write this book, and I highly recommend it.

Mark L. Hall
Compiler Architect
Microsoft Corporation

Foreword by
Stanley Lippman

C++ IS A MULTIPARADIGM LANGUAGE invented at Bell Laboratories in the late 1970s. While it supports object-oriented programming, it is not an object-oriented programming language—at least not in the way C# or Java is. It is still not all that unusual to find thousands of lines of C++ code that neither use inheritance nor the strict encapsulation of a class. This was one of the complaints Bill Joy cited in a keynote speech he delivered at the 1988 Usenix C++ Conference. (Joy was one of the individuals at Sun Microsystems shaping Java.)

The multiparadigm nature of C++ is largely responsible for its somewhat imposing complexity. In part, this was a side effect of meeting the initial requirement to provide both source and binary compatibility with C. For example, the fact that C allowed a declaration of the form

```
int ( i );
```

although the parentheses are absolutely superfluous, introduced ambiguities in the parsing of a local C++ function-style cast:

```
PFI( *r )(); // declaration or expression?
```

The function-style cast was introduced into C++ to provide support for casts (constructors) of user-defined types that require more than a single argument. For example:

```
z = complex( x, y );
```

Using C-style casting is not possible because the following:

```
z = (complex)( x, y );
```

would be interpreted as casting the result of the comma operation (x,y).[1]

Way back when, disallowing superfluous parentheses in a declaration was not an option since that would have broken syntactic compatibility with C.

---

[1] For a full discussion, see Lippman, Stan, and B.E. Moo. "C++: From Research to Practice." Usenix C++ Conference Proceedings, Denver, 1988.

Syntactic compatibility with C, however, is not always the same as semantic compatibility. For example, in order to allow overload function matching on a character literal, the rules for expression evaluation were bent slightly. This allowed the following statement in cfront Release 1.1:

```
cout << 'a' << endl;
```

to print a on the user's terminal rather than 97. That was not the case with the original cfront Release 1.0.

For safety reasons, C++ chose to disallow the implicit cast of a void* pointer to a pointer to an actual type, although that was the C language behavior.

Support for overloaded operators required the introduction of the reference type in order to provide object syntax with the efficiency of pass by reference semantics. I still find pockets of C++ programmers unsure when to declare a class member as either a pointer or reference, or what the difference in copy semantics is between the two.

So, right from the beginning, there was this sort of faceted brain mode (FBM) required of the working C++ programmer.

With the release of Visual Studio .NET, Microsoft has provided a series of extensions to standard C++ to allow it to serve as a .NET language, called Managed Extensions for C++ (MC++). In one sense, this builds on the tradition of extending the multiparadigm nature of C++—in this case, into the managed component .NET paradigm. That paradigm, however, is a very different object and programming model. To paraphrase Dorothy when she wakes up in OZ, *I don't think we're in Kansas any longer*. Think of MC++ as super FBM, or FBM++.

The *managed extensions* to C++ allow for three primary application strategies that are unique to C++:

- Providing a .NET managed wrapper class to an unmanaged API, thereby exposing existing C++ classes to the .NET platform.

- Making use of the .NET class framework and intermixing it with unmanaged C++. There are three aspects to the framework: core language support, such as collection classes and system I/O; foundation programming classes, such as support for threading, network sockets, and regular expressions; and application domain support, such as XML, ASP.NET and Web services, Windows Forms, ADO.NET, and so on.

- Writing directly in the .NET environment the same as you might do in C# or Visual Basic, but with more access to the underlying .NET architecture.

Siva Challa and Artur Laksberg are members of the Visual C++ compiler development team, and they are well equipped to jump-start your entry into this new technology. They build on yet another tradition—that of language implementers authoring a book on the language. Siva and Artur provide essential insider knowledge on both how MC++ behaves on the .NET platform and the thinking that went into its design.

Stanley Lippman
Architect, Visual C++ Team
Microsoft Corporation

Preface

WELCOME TO *Essential Guide to Managed Extensions for C++!*

Managed Extensions for C++ (Managed C++ or MC++ for short) are extensions added to C++ in the Microsoft Visual C++ compiler to enable access to the functionality provided by the .NET Framework.

While MC++ is a general-purpose programming language, its key benefit is the fine-grain control over the interaction between managed and unmanaged (native) code. No other language targeting the .NET platform supports mixing managed and unmanaged code better than MC++.

This book will show you how to use MC++ to write managed applications and port existing applications to the .NET platform.

Written by members of Microsoft Visual C++ development team, this book focuses on MC++ as a language and by no means claims to be a thorough guide to the .NET Framework. All major .NET concepts relevant to MC++ are introduced in this book.

For a deeper understanding of the functionality provided by the .NET Framework and tutorials on how to write Web services, you should consult the online documentation for Visual Studio .NET or the .NET Framework SDK, or other .NET books available on the market.

Organization of the Book

This book is divided into two parts. Part One starts with an introduction to the .NET Framework (brief descriptions of relevant tools, namespaces, and types from the .NET Framework base class library are provided as needed throughout the book). The early chapters discuss managed classes, value types, and managed interfaces. Following chapters shed light on how garbage collected pointers work and how to use managed arrays and managed operators. The book then moves on to properties, followed by custom attributes, delegates, events, and exceptions.

All topics in Part Two focus on the techniques used for interoperability between managed and native code. Part Two starts with a discussion on how MC++ can be used to mix managed and native code. This discussion is followed by chapters on the Platform Invoke service, .NET and COM interoperability, and managed wrappers.

Throughout the book, you will see code samples. Unless otherwise mentioned, you need to use the /clr compiler option to compile the code.

Target Audience

You don't have to be a C++ expert to be able to read and understand this book. However, we expect you to have a working knowledge of C++ and experience with the Visual C++ compiler in particular. A good understanding of the principles of object-oriented programming is essential. Experience with COM programming will help you understand the COM and .NET interoperability concepts explained in Part Two.

Having some familiarity with other .NET languages, specifically Microsoft Visual C# and Microsoft Visual Basic, is not mandatory but it will help you get up to speed with MC++ faster.

From the Authors

Thank you for choosing this book. We hope that it will provide you with a solid understanding of how to write managed code using the Visual C++ .NET compiler, and that it will help you write interoperable code between native and MC++ as well as between MC++ and other .NET languages.

We appreciate your feedback about the book. Please send us your suggestions and comments.

Siva Challa (siva_challa@apress.com)
Artur Laksberg (artur_laksberg@apress.com)
Redmond, Washington
November 2001

Acknowledgments

THIS BOOK COULDN'T HAVE BEEN WRITTEN without the help of our friends and colleagues. It was a long journey from the beginning to the end.

We want to thank all of the reviewers for helping us make the content of this book presentable. We would also like to thank Microsoft and our managers for letting us work on such a unique project. Thanks to Ronald Laeremans for igniting our interest in writing the book by forwarding an e-mail from Apress' cofounder, Gary Cornell.

We would like to thank all of the following folks (in alphabetical order) for helping us: Dan Appleman, Andrew Brown, Jonathan Caves, Eric Gunnerson, Mark Hall, Habib Heydarian, Jim Hogg, Sonja Keserovic, Jagadish Kurma, Ronald Laeremans, Rose Lam, Stan Lippman, Shahrokh Mortazavi, David Mortenson, Grant Richins, Paul Ringseth, Dario Russi, and Steven Toscano.

Thanks to Gary Cornell for constant encouragement throughout this project. The editorial team at Apress did a wonderful job of getting things in order. Thanks to Tracy Brown, Ami Knox, Nicole LeClerc, and Grace Wong. We would like to express our special thanks to the technical reviewer, David Schwartz.

Although our reviewers helped improve the content of this book, we take responsibility for any errors in the presentation.

Artur would like to thank Siva for his goodwill and the unshakable positive attitude he kept throughout the course of writing this book. It was a tough task. Siva had to put up with the impatience of his coauthor, who was eager to get the book out the door quickly.

Siva would like to profoundly thank his wife, Madhavi, and his daughter, Ramya, for their courage and patience during all those long and late hours. This book would not have seen daylight had it not been for their support and understanding.

About the Authors

Siva Challa is a software design engineer in the Visual C++ compiler development team at Microsoft. Siva has a master's degree in Artificial Intelligence from the University of Hyderabad and a Ph.D. in Computer Science from Virginia Tech. Although Siva works on compilers, he tries to interpret his one-year-old daughter's language and frequently recovers from errors by using his wife's knowledge base.

Artur Laksberg is a software design engineer in the Visual C++ development team at Microsoft. When not working, he can be seen cycling the backroads of the Puget Sound, reading books (military history being his latest passion), and programming.

Introduction

MODERN SOFTWARE IS BECOMING increasingly complex and expensive to develop and maintain. Trying to cope, developers are embracing a component-oriented engineering approach, in which applications are constructed by reusing existing pieces of software.

The Component Object Model (COM) has been successful in simplifying component-oriented software development. The central theme of COM is interoperability. COM components can "talk to each other" regardless of the language in which they were developed.

However, the cross-language interoperability of COM is rather incomplete. You cannot inherit a new COM type from an existing COM type, throw an exception from one object to another, or step between two COM objects written in two different languages in the debugger.

Furthermore, being just a binary standard for defining interfaces, COM itself does not provide any functionality, such as a set of libraries or a common runtime.

.NET aims to address these limitations. Not only does it provide for multi-language interoperability, but also the .NET Framework itself is a platform with its own class library (the *base class library*, or *BCL*) and execution environment (the *common language runtime*, or *CLR*).

Is the learning curve of .NET worth the climb? Yes it is, especially if you are a seasoned C++ developer. You will be surprised how easy it is to find your way in .NET and make use of your C++ knowledge with the help of Managed Extensions for C++.

What Are Managed Extensions for C++?

Managed Extensions for C++ are extensions added to C++ in the Microsoft Visual C++ compiler to enable access to the functionality provided by the .NET Framework. Several new keywords and the concepts they represent were added to the C++ language to make it managed.

We use the terms "Managed C++" and "MC++" to mean the Microsoft Visual C++ language with managed extensions. Similarly, we use the term "MC++ compiler" to mean the Microsoft Visual C++ compiler that is used with compiler options to generate code that targets the .NET Framework.

MC++ is so called because the code generated by the compiler is executed within the .NET execution environment, which provides many services, including automatic garbage collection and security restrictions. In other words, the code is managed by the .NET runtime. As an option, part of your code can still be *un*managed if you want to avoid the performance overhead imposed by the execution environment and you don't need your code to interoperate with other .NET applications.

Even though every C++ program can be compiled to target the .NET Framework, not every program can take full advantage of the functionality provided by the .NET Framework. For example, classes that use multiple inheritance cannot be exposed to other applications targeting the .NET Framework, because the Framework does not have the concept of multiple inheritance. That is one of the reasons that not all C++ classes are compatible with the .NET.

What Language Is Right for You?

Several programming languages already support the .NET Framework. Microsoft's Visual Studio .NET includes the languages Microsoft Visual C++ (which includes managed extensions), Microsoft Visual C#, Microsoft Visual Basic, and Microsoft JScript. Languages developed by other vendors are planned or already available.

Several languages are suitable for a particular task. The choice is often based on (or at least heavily influenced by) the programmer's experience and aesthetic preferences. This is not unreasonable. It takes years to master a programming language, not to mention the execution environment, libraries, and tools that come with it.

When implementing a component in a new language, you usually have to tackle two problems: learning the new language and making your old code work with the new component written in the new language. .NET eliminates both problems. If you are familiar with a language, stick with it. Chances are that this language targets .NET. Still, if you decide to use another language, integrating it with the existing software is straightforward.

Why Managed C++?

C++ is arguably the most powerful programming language ever invented. It is also one of the most commonly used. Billions of lines of C++ code exist, and millions more are written each year.

Because of the burden of the C++ legacy, MC++ might at first feel awkward. However, after you take a closer look you will realize that MC++ has its beauty, as does C++. And MC++ is as close to C++ as you can get.

You don't have to be a C++ guru to learn MC++—in fact, you just have to understand the most fundamental concepts. It is easy to start using MC++. Just learn the basics and discover new possibilities as you go. If you consider yourself a C++ expert and have come to appreciate the language, so much the better. You will feel right at home.

When to use MC++? The answer is simple: As in the case of any other language supported in .NET, use MC++ to expose your program to .NET or take advantage of the .NET Framework's functionality.

And this is not the only reason. One of the main design goals of MC++ is to bridge the gap between the managed and unmanaged worlds. MC++ makes it possible to expose all or part of your existing C++ program to the .NET Framework. Likewise, you can easily modify an existing C++ program to take advantage of the Framework.

MC++ is your language of choice if you need full control over your application and the flexibility of being able to switch between managed and unmanaged code, even within the same source file.

Part One

Basics

CHAPTER 1

Hello, World!

THIS CHAPTER IS YOUR starting point in learning MC++. Here you will see what managed code is, and how to write a simple managed program and a simple managed class that can be exposed to other languages.

Your First Program

When learning a new programming language, the first program a programmer sees often does nothing but print the phrase, "Hello, World!" We will follow the same tradition here—even though, strictly speaking, Managed C++ cannot be called a *new* language, being based as much as it is on C++.

Because any valid C++ program is a valid MC++ program, we will start with a simple C++ example and turn it into managed C++ code. Let's begin by creating a file called `Hello.cpp` with the following text:

```cpp
#include <iostream>
using namespace std;
int main()
{
    cout << "Hello, World!";
}
```

The same compiler is used to compile both unmanaged and managed C++ code. If you are working at the command line, use the `/clr` compiler option to tell the compiler you want your code to be managed. When working with the Visual Studio .NET integrated environment, enable the Use Managed Extensions property in the General property page of the project's Properties dialog box.

To compile `Hello.cpp` from the command line, enter the following:

```
cl hello.cpp /clr /EHsc
```

The compiler will create an executable file called `hello.exe`. When you run it, you will see that it does what you would expect it to do—print a message on the screen:

```
Hello, World!
```

That's it! You have created your first managed program—although it doesn't really use any functionality provided by the .NET Framework. Your first *truly* managed program would look like the following:

```
#using <mscorlib.dll>
using namespace System;
int main()
{
    Console::WriteLine( S"Hello, World!" );
}
```

The first statement of the program, the preprocessor directive #using <mscorlib.dll>, tells the compiler to find and load the file mscorlib.dll, which contains the .NET *base class library* (BCL). The directive #using is similar to the C++ #include directive except that the imported file contains definitions of the types and modules in special binary format that is available to programs written in any .NET language. Such files are called *assemblies* and *modules* (you can read more about these files in Chapter 2).

Similar to classes defined in the Standard C++ Library, BCL classes are enclosed in namespaces. The using namespace directive brings all symbols of the specified namespace into the current scope, so you can write Console::WriteLine instead of System::Console::WriteLine.

One of those symbols, class Console, provides functionality for basic textual input-output. Method WriteLine prints out a string and moves the caret position down to the next line.

Console::WriteLine expects a pointer to the BCL class System::String as an argument. The compiler allows you to create instances of this class by preceding a string literal with the prefix S—similar to how you would create a wide string with the prefix L.

Managed versus Unmanaged Code

What does it really mean for the code to be managed? The executable file produced by the MC++ compiler does not contain any x86 instructions, except for the startup stub. Instead, the code is compiled into an intermediate language called MSIL, which stands for Microsoft Intermediate Language (see Figure 1-1), and the *metadata*, which records the information about all objects that compose the module.

MSIL is then compiled into the native code at runtime by the Just In Time (JIT) compiler every time the program is executed. Alternatively, MSIL can be precompiled by JIT at the program installation time.

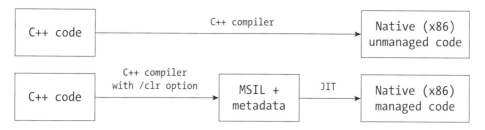

Figure 1-1. Managed code versus unmanaged code

The code produced by the JIT compiler (either at runtime or installation time) is managed by the .NET execution environment, which tracks pointers into the managed heap (to make automatic garbage collection possible), and provides security checks and other services.

Unmanaged code, however, does not and cannot use any services provided by the .NET Framework. Yet its advantage is the absence of the performance overhead imposed by the execution environment.

While developing the MC++ compiler, substantial effort was devoted to ensuring that all existing C++ programs work correctly when they are compiled into MSIL. This requirement was called IJW—short for "It Just Works." IJW is a fundamental necessity for enabling porting of existing C++ programs to .NET. Thanks to IJW, you don't have to change your code at all; compile it with the /clr compiler option, and it will "just work."

Even though the MC++ compiler tries to compile every C++ program into MSIL, it is not always possible to do this. For instance, a function containing inline x86 assembler instructions cannot be compiled into MSIL, simply because MSIL is a platform-independent language of higher level than the x86 assembler. Such a function has to be compiled into unmanaged code; it cannot use any functionality provided by the .NET Framework.

Fortunately, both managed and unmanaged code can coexist in the same compilation unit. This means you can create managed and unmanaged functions in the same source file. You can call an unmanaged function from a managed function, which is why it is possible to call C runtime functions, such as `printf`, or WinAPI functions, such as `CreateWindow`, from managed code.

Interoperability

Let's see how things work across different languages. We will create a simple MC++ function that generates Fibonacci numbers and call it from a C# program. Note that in C# all functions must be members of a class.

```
#using <mscorlib.dll>
public __gc class Fibonacci
{
public:
    static int GetNumber( int n )
    {
        int previous = -1;
        int result = 1;
        for( int i=0; i<=n; i++ )
        {
            int sum = result + previous;
            previous = result;
            result = sum;
        }
        return result;
    }
};
```

This program defines a managed class, Fibonacci, with a static method, GetNumber, that returns the *n*th Fibonacci number. Managed classes are described in detail in Chapter 3, but for now just remember that managed classes can be exposed to other languages.

As you might have noticed, there is no main function in this program. This is because the program is a library, not a standalone application; its sole purpose is to expose the functionality provided by the class Fibonacci. Usually, programs like this are compiled into DLLs, not executable files. Here is how to do so: call the source file Fibonacci.cpp and compile it like this:

```
cl Fibonacci.cpp /clr /LD
```

The resulting binary file will be called Fibonacci.dll.

Now create a C# file, TestFibonacci.cs:

```
using System;
class TestFibonacci
{
    public static void Main()
    {
        Console.WriteLine( "Fibonacci number 10 is {0}",
                                        Fibonacci.GetNumber(10) );
    }
}
```

Compile this C# program with a reference to the assembly `Fibonacci.dll`:

```
csc TestFibonacci.cs /reference:Fibonacci.dll
```

When executed, the resulting program `Fibonacci.exe` prints:

```
Fibonacci number 10 is 55
```

As you can see, it is easy to use a MC++ class in C#. It is also easy to consume an assembly in MC++. The following program imports `Fibonacci.dll` (the same one created before or written in some other language):

```
#using <mscorlib.dll>
using namespace System;
#using <Fibonacci.dll>
int main()
{
    Console::WriteLine( S"Fibonacci number 10 is {0}",
        Fibonacci::GetNumber(10).ToString() );
}
```

Writing a multilanguage application is easy—so is debugging. You will appreciate a feature of Visual Studio .NET debugger that allows you to step from a source written in one language to a source written in another language.

Summary

Managed code and interoperability are the cornerstone concepts of MC++, and as such are the main focus of this book. In this chapter, we looked at how to write managed code that can be consumed by programs written in other .NET languages.

In the next chapter, we will take a deeper look at the .NET Framework—the environment in which all managed programs operate.

CHAPTER 2
The .NET Framework

APPLICATION DEVELOPMENT on the Windows platform has traditionally been a tedious task due to the flat nature of the thousands of functions that are used to access system functionality, exposed via dynamic link libraries (DLLs). Also, reuse of software components written in other languages is typically cumbersome. For example, a Visual Basic (VB) developer may find it difficult to reuse a library component written with Visual C++. Although the Component Object Model (COM) addresses this issue, developers are still faced with the daunting task of rewriting code in the languages they are specialized in. Another serious problem facing software development on the Windows platform is known as DLL hell. A simple example of DLL hell is when a user upgrades to a newer version of an application that replaces an existing DLL, and as a result other applications that depend on the replaced DLL stop working.

The .NET Framework addresses all of these issues and much more. It is an object-oriented programming platform supported by several languages (at least 15[1]). The platform services are divided into various namespaces that have meaningful names. Each namespace defines types that allow access to the system services.

The .NET Framework provides a simpler programming model that is implemented by all participating languages. Any .NET-targeted language can be used to write .NET application components, which in turn can be used by any other .NET-targeted language. For example, if you have a C++ library, you can use it in VB and extend the functionality by inheriting the classes from the C++ library.

The .NET Framework solves the DLL hell problem by incorporating the version information into the applications themselves. The common language runtime of the .NET Framework can inspect the version information of the applications when loading them into memory for execution. Multiple versions of an application can coexist in the .NET Framework. So, an application requiring a specific version of a DLL is guaranteed to bind to that version of the DLL, even though different versions are available.

In this chapter, we discuss the .NET Framework architecture briefly and show how a managed application is compiled and executed. We also explain how garbage collection works.

---

[1]   One of the Web sites that maintains a list of language vendors is http://www.gotdotnet.com.

The .NET Framework Architecture

The .NET Framework architecture consists of a set of layers on top of the Windows operating system and COM+ Services (such as Threading, Queued Components, and Automatic Transactions). The first layer is the common language runtime.

Common Language Runtime

The common language runtime (CLR) is the most important component of the .NET Framework. It provides a secure execution and high performance environment (the latter comparable to the native execution environment) for applications. The services provided by the CLR include managing the code loading, verifying type safety, providing memory management through garbage collection, converting MSIL code to native code and execution of that native code, and supporting error handling that includes cross-language exceptions. The CLR provides interoperation between managed and native code (see Figure 2-1).

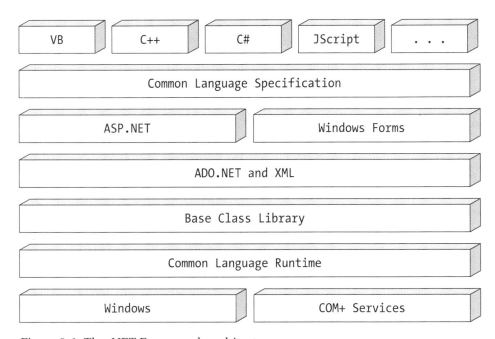

Figure 2-1. The .NET Framework architecture

The CLR includes the common type system (CTS), which provides a rich set of types equivalent to those found in many of today's programming languages. The CTS defines two kinds of types—value types and reference types. A *value type* represents a value that is a sequence of bits. A *reference type* is an address to a value that represents a sequence of bits. Value types and reference types together are called *managed types*. Any other type is called an *unmanaged type*.

There are three kinds of reference types: interface types, object types, and pointer types. An *interface type* is a partial description of a value and does not contain any data members. An *object type* is an address to a self-describing value, and it is a reference to a managed type. A *pointer type* is an address of a value, and it usually points to an unmanaged object.

Class Libraries

The .NET Framework defines a set of class libraries enclosed in namespaces. The class libraries expose the .NET Framework functionality.

Base Class Library

The base class library (BCL) provides support for exception handling, late binding, multithreading, and inspection of the type information at runtime (also known as *reflection*). It also provides support for constructs optimized for the CLR, such as strings and I/O streams. A majority of the base class libraries are implemented in the DLL file called `mscorlib.dll`.

The base class library supports a set of value types that map to the built-in types of the implementing languages. For example, `int` in C++ has a corresponding `System::Int32` in the base class library.

The CLR defines a special class called `Object` in the `System` namespace. This `System::Object` class is the base class for all managed classes and the root of all managed class hierarchies.

Other Rich Class Libraries

Built on top of the base class library is a set of class hierarchies that support data and Extensible Markup Language (XML). Windows Forms is a class hierarchy that provides support for rich Win32 applications.

ASP.NET

ASP.NET is an application development platform for Web Services that uses the .NET Framework components such as Windows Forms. For instance, you can use the Windows Forms class library API to provide graphical user interfaces for your applications. ASP.NET is an extension of Active Server Pages (ASP) and provides a new programming model to develop enterprise-level Web applications.

Common Language Specification

The common type system is a rich set of features that tries to support many programming paradigms, including object-oriented, functional, and logic. The common language specification (CLS) is a common subset of features that is usually present in all languages targeting the .NET platform. It specifies a subset of the common type system and a set of usage conventions. By supporting the CLS features, the languages can help build software components that can interoperate with the rest of the languages targeting the .NET platform. So, you need to make sure that your software components are CLS compliant (by using CLS-compliant features only) for them to be interoperable with all .NET-targeted languages.

To ensure maximum interoperability with clients written in other languages, the CLS specification must be applied to types that are accessible outside the assembly (assemblies are discussed later in this chapter). A type is CLS compliant if all of its publicly accessible members are made up of CLS-compliant types.

A language is a CLS-compliant consumer if it can completely use any CLS-compliant type. A language is a CLS-compliant extender if it can extend/implement any CLS-compliant type.

.NET-Targeted Languages

Visual Studio .NET includes several languages that target the .NET platform: Visual C++, Visual Basic, Visual C#, and JScript.

Since the compilers for all .NET-targeted languages generate MSIL and metadata, the common language runtime makes it very easy to interoperate between components written in different languages. All public types defined in a managed component can be imported into a program written in another managed language, with a single statement! So, the question of which language to develop an application in becomes largely a decision of which language you are most comfortable using. For example, if you are a C++ programmer, MC++ would be the language of choice for you.

When developing applications that interoperate with native components, you can use any .NET-targeted language because all of them can interoperate with native components. However, MC++ would be a preferred language for performance-critical applications because it allows mixing managed and native code in the same executable.

A Typical Managed Application

To understand how a managed application is translated from source code to machine code and how it is executed, you first need to understand the concept of an assembly.

Assemblies

An *assembly* is a set of one or more files used to run an application. It is a collection of types (in the form of a binary representation), executable code (in the form of MSIL), resources, and a description of the assembly (called *assembly manifest*). The assembly manifest information provides an identity, a list of files that constitute the assembly, a list of other assemblies referenced, a list of referenced types, and permission requests that are set by the author of the assembly. The permission requests include those required for the assembly to run, those that are preferred but not necessary for the assembly to run, and those that are not intended to be granted.

Assemblies are closely tied to CTS and CLR. They provide type, reference scope, and version boundaries. Each type's identity is associated with the assembly in which it is defined. Types have assembly visibility—a type is visible inside or outside the assembly.

An assembly is the smallest entity that is versionable in the .NET Framework. All types and resources in an assembly become part of a version of the assembly. In an assembly, the combination of metadata and MSIL can exist in one or more files called *netmodules*. Appendix C discusses assemblies in detail.

Metadata

Metadata is a binary description of assemblies and netmodules, types, and attributes of the types used in the assemblies. Metadata is represented by annotations added to the portable executable generated by the compilers that target the .NET Framework. When an assembly is loaded into memory, the metadata also gets loaded. The CLR uses metadata to gather details about the types used in the application.

The metadata for the types in an assembly contains a description of the types and their members, which includes definitions and references of types. Metadata also describes the information about internal implementation details and layout information of types.

Attributes are annotations added to an assembly and the types and their members in the assembly. They are used to modify the default behavior. Attributes can be built in or user defined.

Metadata eliminates the need for type description languages such as IDL. It combines the type description with the code in an assembly. This makes software components (assemblies) self-describing and language neutral.

Metadata generated for an application can be viewed using the .NET Framework's SDK tool ILDasm (`ildasm.exe`). Appendix B discusses metadata in detail.

MSIL

Microsoft Intermediate Language (MSIL) is a platform-independent intermediate language. All languages targeting the .NET Framework translate the source code into MSIL. The .NET Framework's SDK provides a compiler called Just In Time compiler (also known by the names JIT compiler and JITter) that translates MSIL code into native code specific to a particular platform (for instance, x86). This generated code is executed by the CLR. So, using the same assembly (which contains MSIL and metadata) generated by .NET-targeted languages, it is possible to execute the application on multiple platforms that have implemented the .NET Framework. The MSIL in an assembly can be viewed using ILDasm.

Translation and Execution of a Managed Application

As mentioned, compilers for all .NET-targeted languages translate source code into MSIL with annotations for types in the form of metadata. The MSIL and metadata are saved in an assembly along with the resources used by the application and a manifest. At execution time, the MSIL code is passed through a Just In Time compiler that generates native code for the specific machine architecture (see Figure 2-2).

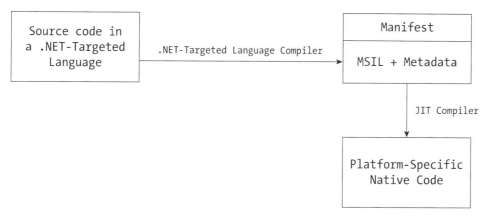

Figure 2-2. A managed application—from compilation to execution

Before executing the program, the CLR loads the assembly (MSIL and metadata) into memory. It makes use of the metadata to gather information about the types used in the application. Whenever a function is called, the CLR first generates native code for that function and executes it. When the same function is called again, the already-generated native code is reused.

Instances of the types are called *managed objects* and are created on a heap maintained by the CLR. This heap is called a *garbage-collected heap*. Garbage collection is discussed in the following section.

Garbage Collection

The memory management of all managed types is handled by the common language runtime. This is one of the major advantages of the .NET Framework because memory management is a complex task in the application development process. The CLR ensures that there are no memory leaks caused by managed objects in applications. Any unused memory is reclaimed by the runtime via the process called *garbage collection.*

The basic garbage collection mechanism employed by the CLR is called *mark and compact.* It is a highly optimized (with extensions such as generational garbage collection) and efficient memory management scheme.

Here briefly is how the garbage collector tracks managed objects in a program. The garbage collector has access to the list of storage locations for the managed objects used by the program. These locations are called *roots.* As new objects are created on the garbage-collected heap, the heap slowly becomes full. When there is not enough memory available for a new object, a garbage collection cycle starts. In the beginning, the garbage collector assumes that all objects are unused; that is, no object on the heap is reachable from any one of the roots. Then, the garbage collector navigates through the roots and starts building a graph of all reachable objects while avoiding circular references. After traversing through all roots, a graph of all reachable objects in the program is created. Any object not in this graph is considered garbage and is subject to reclamation.

All managed objects have a method called `Finalize` (referred to as a finalizer) defined. When the garbage collector identifies a managed object for reclamation, that object will be added to the queue of objects whose memory is to be reclaimed. The `Finalize` method of each one of the objects in the queue will be executed before the memory is reclaimed. All finalizers are executed in a separate thread dedicated to running finalizers.

After marking all reachable objects, the garbage collector walks through the heap linearly, finding contiguous blocks of memory occupied by unused objects. It reclaims their memory and shifts the live objects on the reachable graph to fill the gap. The garbage collector updates all roots to point to the modified locations along with any addresses in the objects on the heap that point to other objects. At the end of a garbage collection cycle, there will be one big unused chunk of memory and a linear list of compacted, reachable objects.

The garbage collector assumes that older objects live longer. The compacted objects during the first execution of a garbage collection cycle become members of generation 0. As new objects are created and the heap becomes full, the necessity for the garbage collector to run arises again. The reachable graph is formed again. Now, the members of generation 0 are compacted and they are moved to generation 1. The remaining newer objects are then compacted and moved to generation 0. The younger generations are always compacted first, which makes this an effective process because there will be less movement in the older generations, saving roots update time.

An application cannot stop a garbage collection cycle. However, it can initiate a garbage collection cycle. The BCL class `System::GC` is used to control the garbage collector programmatically. All members of this class, listed here, are static members:

- `Collect`: An overloaded method that forces the garbage collection to start

- `GetGeneration`: Returns the current generation of an object

- `GetTotalMemory`: Returns the amount of memory currently allocated

- `KeepAlive`: References a given object so that it won't be considered for garbage collection

- ReRegisterForFinalize: Requests the common language runtime to call the Finalize method on the object whose Finalize method has been previously suppressed using the SuppressFinalize method

- SuppressFinalize: Requests the common language runtime not to call the Finalize method on a given object

- WaitForPendingFinalizers: Suspends the currently executing thread until the thread executing the finalizers empties the queue

- MaxGeneration: Returns the maximum number of generations supported by the common language runtime

Summary

In this chapter, we introduced the .NET Framework and its architecture. We showed how a typical managed application is compiled and executed by explaining the concepts of assemblies, metadata, MSIL, and garbage collection.

In the following chapters, we describe various features of MC++ starting with managed classes.

CHAPTER 3

Managed Classes

THE CONCEPT OF A *class* is the basic building block of object-oriented programming. A class is an abstract data type (ADT) and it can have partial or full implementation. Partially implemented classes (abstract classes) cannot be instantiated. Instances of a fully implemented class are called *objects.* A class defines the state (data members) and behavior (member functions) of its objects.

In the context of MC++, the native C++ classes are called as *native classes* or *unmanaged classes.* The instances of unmanaged classes are called *unmanaged objects.* In this chapter, we introduce the concept of managed classes, and we show how to define and use managed classes. You will see how the base class library (BCL) class System::Object is used as a root class of all managed classes. We discuss the various access specifiers of managed classes and their members, and we explain how inheritance works with managed classes.

Native C++ Classes versus Managed Classes

You can create instances of unmanaged classes on the runtime stack or on the heap (also called the *C++ heap*). If an object of a class is created on the stack, its memory is automatically reclaimed (by adjusting the stack pointer value so that the memory can be used for other stack-based allocations) when the object goes out of scope. However, when an object of an unmanaged class is created on the C++ heap, the responsibility of freeing that memory lies with the application.

Managed classes (also known as *gc classes*) are annotated (with the keyword __gc) C++ classes whose objects are created on the garbage collected (GC) heap. An instance of a managed class is called a *managed object.* The memory management of managed objects is handled by the .NET Framework's common language runtime (CLR). An application can create and use a managed object, but it cannot explicitly free the memory allocated for that object. The garbage collector reclaims the memory occupied by the managed objects that are no longer needed by the application.

Why Managed Classes?

Managed classes have the following advantages over native C++ classes:

- By implementing a common object model supported by the .NET Framework, all .NET-targeted languages can inherit and create objects from the managed classes defined in a component created with any .NET-targeted language (for instance, a C# component can create an object of a gc class defined in an MC++ component). This is because the information about managed classes is represented in metadata (a binary representation) that all .NET-targeted languages understand. This is not possible with native C++ classes, because the object model of C++ is different from the object models of other languages.[1]

- It is possible to use cross-language inheritance of managed classes—you can define a managed class in MC++ and inherit from it in C#. This is not possible with native C++ classes and the classes from other languages due to the differences in the object model of native C++ and those of the other languages.

- It is possible to customize the behavior of managed classes using attributes. Attributes are discussed in Chapter 11. All .NET-targeted languages understand attributes on managed classes. The Visual C++ .NET compiler allows you to define attributes on native C++ classes, but this is limited to native C++ only. Other languages using native C++ components do not recognize these attributes.

- Instances of managed classes are garbage collected. The CLR maintains the management of their allocation and deallocation. For native C++ objects created on the C++ heap, it is the application's responsibility to manage their memory.

Defining Managed Classes

There are two categories of managed types in the .NET Framework: managed classes or gc classes (*reference types* in .NET terminology) and *value types* (also called *value classes*). As mentioned earlier, the instances of gc classes are managed objects that can only be created on the GC heap. Value type instances are short-lived objects that typically reside on the program stack. It is not possible to

---

[1]   Note that COM allows you to create instances of classes written in different languages, but the interaction between different COM components is limited to using interfaces.

create a value type instance on the GC heap directly. Value types are discussed in detail in Chapter 5.

The keyword __gc is used to define or declare gc classes. Here is an example of a gc class:

```
// sample.cpp
#using <mscorlib.dll>
using namespace System;
__gc class ManagedCpp {
public:
    void Hello() { Console::WriteLine(S"Hello, from gc class!"); }
};
int main() {
        ManagedCpp *pMCpp = new ManagedCpp();
        pMCpp->Hello();
}
```

The following command compiles the previous program and generates an executable:

```
cl /clr sample.cpp /out:sample.exe
```

The output of the program is as follows:

```
Hello, from gc class!
```

In this example, the class ManagedCpp is annotated with the __gc keyword to make it a gc class. The MC++ compiler automatically adds the class System::Object as the base class of all gc classes. The public member function Hello prints the string Hello, from gc class!. The prefix S before the string indicates that it is a managed string. More on different string notations later in this chapter.

Member functions can be defined inside the class (as shown in this example) as well as outside the class (shown in the next example).

The new operator creates an instance of ManagedCpp on the GC heap. Note that unlike with native C++ classes, it is not possible to create an instance of a gc class on the stack. This is because the garbage collector in the CLR can only track the objects allocated on the GC heap, and all managed objects are garbage collected. Any attempt to create a managed object on the program stack will result in a compiler error. For example, if the following statement were used instead of the new operator in the previous main function, you would see a compilation error:

```
ManagedC pMCpp; // error
```

21

There is no call to delete in the main function, yet there aren't any memory leaks. This is because all managed objects are garbage collected.

C++ classes that do not have the __gc or __value keyword are implicitly unmanaged or native classes. You can use the __nogc keyword to explicitly declare or define unmanaged classes. To illustrate the difference between the objects created on the C++ heap and those created on the GC heap, consider the following example:

```
#using <mscorlib.dll>
using namespace System;
__nogc class NoGCclass {
public:
    void Hello() { Console::WriteLine(S"Hello, from NoGCclass!"); }
};
__gc class GCclass {
public:
    void Hello();
};
void GCclass::Hello() { Console::WriteLine(S"Hello, from GCclass!"); }
int main() {
    NoGCclass *pNoGC = new NoGCclass(); // creates an object on the C++ heap
    pNoGC->Hello();
    delete pNoGC; // needed because unmanaged objects are not garbage collected

    GCclass *pGC = new GCclass(); // creates an object on the GC heap
    pGC->Hello();
    // delete not needed because the garbage collector reclaims the memory
}
```

In the preceding sample, the NoGCclass class is unmanaged because the __nogc keyword is used. The GCclass class is managed because the __gc keyword is used. Objects of NoGCclass are created on the C++ heap and objects of GCclass are created on the GC heap.

These concepts are illustrated in Figure 3-1. As you can see, the C++ heap and the GC heap are distinct from each other. As you know from Chapter 2, during program execution, the garbage collection cycle starts when there is no single contiguous block of memory available for creating a new managed object. The managed object pointed to by the gc pointer pGC is a potential candidate for relocation on the GC heap during garbage collection. If that happens, the CLR updates the corresponding pointer (pGC in this example) on the program stack to reflect the new pointer location.

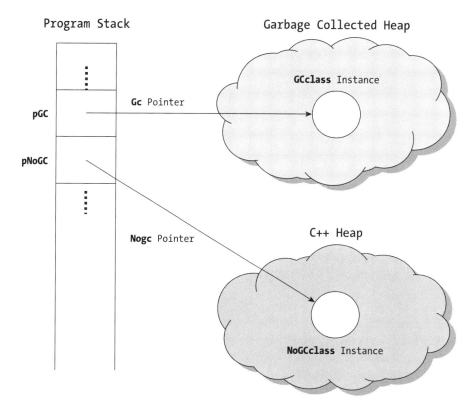

Figure 3-1.Garbage Collected heap and native C++ heap

Unlike managed objects, C++ objects do not change location after they are created; they stay at the same memory location until they are deleted from the C++ heap (with the delete keyword). You can see that the previous sample avoids memory leaks by deleting the object on the C++ heap pointed to by the pNoGC pointer.

The output of the previous program is as follows:

```
Hello, from NoGCclass!
Hello, from GCclass!
```

System::Object Class

We mentioned earlier that all gc classes inherit from the BCL class System::Object. The gc class Object is defined in the System namespace. This class is the root of the class hierarchy in the BCL.

Since the `Object` class is the base class of all gc classes, it's very convenient to write container classes that can hold objects of different types. You won't lose any type safety in the process because the `Object` class provides methods that can be used to inspect the types at runtime.

The MC++ declaration of the `System::Object` class is as follows:

```
__gc class Object {
  public:
    Object();
    bool Equals(Object*);
    virtual int GetHashCode();
    Type* GetType();
    virtual String* ToString();

    static bool Equals(Object*, Object*);
    static bool ReferenceEquals(Object*, Object*);
  protected:
    void Finalize();
    Object* MemberwiseClone();
};
```

The `System::Object` class has a constructor; four public, nonstatic member functions; and three static member functions. It also has two protected, nonstatic member functions. These functions are as follows:

- `Object` Constructor: This special member function initializes a new instance of `System::Object`.

- `Equals`: This method returns `true` if a given object is equal to the current object. For gc classes, the equality is "object equality," where a given reference and the current reference are checked to see if they point to the same object. Derived classes can override this method to implement different equality semantics other than comparing object identity. The following sample uses the `System::String` class, which overrides the `Equals` method of `System::Object`.

```
#using <mscorlib.dll>
using namespace System;
int main() {
    String* str1 = S"Hello";
    String* str2 = S"World";
```

```
      if (str1->Equals(str2)) {
        Console::WriteLine("strings {0} and {1} are the same", str1, str2);
      }
      else {
        Console::WriteLine("strings {0} and {1} are different", str1, str2);
      }
      String* str3 = S"Hello";
      if (str1->Equals(str3)) {
        Console::WriteLine("strings {0} and {1} are the same", str1, str3);
      }
      else {
        Console::WriteLine("strings {0} and {1} are different", str1, str3);
      }
    }
```

In this sample,[2] the string objects pointed to by str1, str2, and str3 are managed objects. The first call to the Equals function on str1 checks if str2 is the same as str1. The second call to the same Equals function on str1 checks if str3 is the same as str1.

The output of the program is as follows:

```
strings Hello and World are different
strings Hello and Hello are the same
```

- GetHashCode: This method returns the hash code of a managed object as an integer. The same instance is guaranteed to generate the same hash value whenever this function is called.

- GetType: This method returns an instance of System::Type corresponding to the current type. This sample shows how the member function GetType can be called:

```
#using <mscorlib.dll>
using namespace System;

__gc class Base {};
__gc class Derived : public Base{};
int main() {
```

---

[2]   In the WriteLine function, the numbers inside the curly braces represent the positions of the arguments that follow the string: –0 represents the first argument, 1 represents the second argument, and so on. Note that only managed objects of gc classes can be used this way.

```
    Base* pB = new Base();
    Base* pBD = new Derived();
    Object* pObj = pBD;

    Console::WriteLine("Type of pB object is {0}", pB->GetType());
    Console::WriteLine("Type of pBD object is {0}", pBD->GetType());
    Console::WriteLine("Type of pObj object is {0}", pObj->GetType());
}
```

The output of the program is as follows:

```
Type of pB object is Base
Type of pBD object is Derived
Type of pObj object is Derived
```

- ToString: This method returns an object of System::String that represents the current object's fully qualified name.[3] This sample shows the output of the ToString function when it is called on an instance of System::Object:

```
#using <mscorlib.dll>
using namespace System;

int main() {
    Object* pObj = new Object();
    Console::WriteLine("ToString() returned: {0}", pObj->ToString());
}
```

The output of the program is as follows:

```
ToString() returned: System.Object
```

Derived classes can override this method and provide a meaningful implementation. For instance, the BCL class System::Exception overrides this method to return information about the stack trace when the ToString method is called on an exception object.

- Equals: This static method determines if two managed objects are the same object. This method is different from the nonstatic Equals method in that it first checks to see if the objects are null and returns true if both of them are null.

---

[3] A fully qualified name of a type includes namespace names and enclosing class names attached to the name of the type.

- `ReferenceEquals`: This static method determines if two managed objects are the same object. This function returns `true` when two null gc pointers are passed as arguments.

- `Finalize`: This protected, nonstatic member function allows the current object to free any resources and allows any cleanup operations to be performed. This method is automatically called by the CLR when the object has no references. The exception to this is when the program explicitly requests the garbage collector not to call the finalizer using the `System::GC::SuppressFinalize` method. A derived class overriding the `Finalize` method must call the base class' finalizer in its implementation.

    To have explicit control over freeing unmanaged resources, the interface `IDisposable` must be implemented by a gc class. The implementation of the method contains code to free the unmanaged resources and a call to the `System::GC::SuppressFinalize` method. When a client of a managed object that implements the `IDisposable` interface calls the `Dispose` function on the managed object, the unmanaged resources are freed and the garbage collector is informed not to call `Finalize` method on the managed object.

- `MemberwiseClone`: This protected method creates a *shallow* or *bit-wise* copy of the current object. In other words, if there is a managed object of a gc class as a member of the current object, only the gc pointer (discussed in Chapter 6) is copied—the contents of the member object are not copied.

Class and Member Accessibility

A type is said to be accessible if other program elements, such as types or functions, can use the type. You already know that native C++ class members can have three levels of member accessibility: public, protected, and private.

Assembly Accessibility

In addition to the accessibility of C++ class members, a new accessibility is introduced for assemblies (discussed in Chapter 2 and Appendix C) in the .NET Framework. A member of a managed type is accessible inside the assembly, outside the assembly, or both. All managed types must be marked as `public` to be accessible outside of the assembly in which they are defined. A member of a managed class can have two accessibility modifiers associated with it. The more restrictive of the two modifiers becomes the accessibility of the type outside the assembly. The order of the access specifiers is irrelevant.

Table 3-1. Accessibility of Types and Members in Assemblies

MC++ SYNTAX	SEMANTICS	.NET EQUIVALENT
public or public public	Public inside, public outside	public
protected or protected protected	Protected inside, protected outside	family
private or private private	Private inside, private outside	private
public protected or protected public	Public inside, protected outside	famorassem
public private or private public	Public inside, private outside	assembly
protected private or private protected	Protected inside, private outside	famandassem

All the access specifiers in Table 3-1 are bounded by the access specifier of the class. For example, if the access specifier on the class is private, none of the members are accessible outside the assembly even though they are marked as public public. Consider the following example:

```
#using <mscorlib.dll>
public __gc class PublicC {
  public protected:
     int publicProtectedMember;
  protected private:
     int protectedPrivateMember;
};
private __gc class PrivateC {
  public protected:
     int publicProtectedMember;
  protected private:
     int protectedPrivateMember;
};
```

In the preceding sample, the PublicC class has the public access specifier. As a result, this class has public accessibility outside the assembly that contains it. The most restrictive access specifier on the member publicProtectedMember is protected, so this member has protected accessibility outside the assembly and public accessibility inside the assembly. The most restrictive access specifier on the member protectedPrivateMember is private. In this case, this member has private accessibility outside the assembly that contains its parent and it has protected accessibility inside the assembly.

The PrivateC class has the private access specifier, so this class is not accessible outside the assembly. The members of this type are not accessible outside the assembly because the class has the private specifier. The member `publicProtectedMember` has public accessibility inside the assembly, whereas the member `protectedPrivateMember` has protected accessibility inside the assembly.

Module Accessibility

You learned in Chapter 2 that an assembly can contain one or more netmodules. An important point to note is that a netmodule in an assembly can access types marked as `private` in the assembly. However, a type marked with a `private` access specifier in a netmodule is not accessible outside the assembly containing the module.

In this sample, the gc classes `PrivateType` and `PublicType1` have `private` and `public` accessibility outside the assembly:

```
// file: Module.cpp
#using <mscorlib.dll>
private __gc class PrivateType{};
public __gc class PublicType1 {
  private:
    void PrivateFunc() {
        PrivateType* p;
        // . . .
    }
};
```

The MC++ compiler generates a module DLL (`Module.dll`) when the preceding sample is compiled using the following command:

```
cl /clr:noAssembly /LD Module.cpp
```

When this module is imported into a source file that is used to create an assembly, the gc class `PrivateType` is accessible in that source file.

```
// file: MyAssembly.cpp
#using <mscorlib.dll>
#using "Module.dll"
public __gc class PublicType2 {
  private:
    void Func() {
        PrivateType* p; // okay
        // . . .
    }
```

```
public:
    void PublicFunc(){ /* ... */ }
};
```

When the code is compiled into an assembly DLL using the following command, the compilation succeeds and generates the assembly `MyAssembly.dll` without any errors because `Module.dll` is a module:

```
cl /clr MyAssembly.cpp /LD /out:MyAssembly.dll
```

In the assembly `MyModule.dll`, the types `PublicType1` and `PublicType2` have `public` accessibility outside the assembly, and the type `PrivateType` has `private` accessibility outside the assembly.

Inheritance

All gc classes inherit (directly or indirectly) from the `System::Object` BCL class. Only single inheritance of gc classes is allowed for gc classes in the .NET Framework, and MC++ supports single inheritance of gc classes. However, a gc class can inherit from any number of gc interfaces.

To become a concrete class (instantiable), a gc class that inherits from a gc interface must implement all methods of the interface. Otherwise, it becomes an abstract class and you cannot instantiate it.

Only public inheritance of a base class is allowed. This is because currently there is no matching representation for nonpublic inheritance in the metadata.

Similar to regular C++, a managed class can define virtual and pure member functions. The overloading rules of regular C++ apply to MC++. Similarly, the overriding and hiding rules also apply.

Gc classes can't inherit from unmanaged classes and vice versa.

In this sample, the class `UnmanagedDerived` tries to inherit from the gc class `ManagedBase` and the gc class `ManagedDerived` tries to inherit from the unmanaged class `UnmanagedBase`. Both attempts result in errors when compiled.

```
#using <mscorlib.dll>
using namespace System;
class UnmanagedBase {};
__gc class ManagedBase{};
class UnmanagedDerived : public ManagedBase {};  // error
__gc class ManagedDerived : public UnmanagedBase {};  // error
```

The following sample shows a gc class implementing two gc interfaces and inheriting from a gc class:

```
#using <mscorlib.dll>
__gc class CBase {
   public:
       void CbaseFunc(){};
};
__gc __interface IFace1 {
    void IFace1Func();
};
__gc __interface IFace2 {
    void IFace2Func();
};
__gc class Derived : public CBase, public IFace1, public IFace2 {
   public:
     void IFace1Func(){};
     void IFace2Func(){};
};
```

In the preceding sample, the gc class `Derived` inherits from the gc class `CBase` and implements the `IFace1` and `IFace2` interfaces. This is valid because there is a single inheritance of a gc class and multiple inheritances of gc interfaces.

Members of Gc Classes

Members of managed classes include function members, data members, properties (discussed in Chapter 9), events (discussed in Chapter 13), and a special member called the class constructor. The data members can be managed or unmanaged. For a detailed discussion on adding unmanaged types as members of managed types, refer to Chapter 15.

In this section, we discuss two special member functions: destructors and class constructors. We also present a list of restrictions imposed on gc classes.

Finalizers/Destructors

Managed classes can have destructors. Destructors in MC++ are conceptually equivalent to finalizers in the .NET Framework. You learned in Chapter 2 that during a garbage collection cycle the CLR calls finalizers on managed objects that do not have any references. It is valid to call `delete` on a managed object containing a destructor. When `delete` is called on a managed object, if the managed object's destructor contains code to free both managed and unmanaged resources, only the unmanaged resources of the managed object are freed. The managed resources are freed during garbage collection.

In MC++, you cannot define the `Finalize` method directly in a gc class. Instead, you must add the code for the `Finalize` method to the destructor of the gc class. If a base class happens to have the `Finalize` method defined (for example, by importing the base class from another .NET language), the derived class' destructor calls the base class' `Finalize` method by default. However, you cannot define a destructor for a derived class when there is no destructor defined for a base class of the derived class.

The destructor of a gc class is mapped to two member function in the metadata:

- A `Finalize` method, a renamed destructor with a call to the base class' `Finalize` method. The `Finalize` method has protected accessibility.

- A virtual destructor whose implementation calls the `System::GC::SuppressFinalize` method and the `Finalize` method on the same object. The destructor is virtual because when there is an explicit call to the destructor, the most derived class' destructor is called. As you know, this destructor call results in calls to the finalizers of all base classes starting from the closest. The call to `SuppressFinalize` ensures that the finalizer method of the object is not called again by the CLR, which would otherwise result in calling the finalizers of all base classes again.

The following sample illustrates how destructors/finalizers are called on managed objects:

```
#using <mscorlib.dll>
using namespace System;
__nogc struct Unmanaged {
  ~Unmanaged() { Console::WriteLine(S"Unmanaged::Destructor"); }
};
__gc struct Managed {
  ~Managed() { Console::WriteLine(S"Managed::Finalizer"); }
};
__gc struct Base {
  ~Base() { Console::WriteLine(S"Base::Finalizer"); }
};
__gc struct Derived : Base {
    Managed *m;
    Unmanaged *uM;
    Derived() {
        m = new Managed();
        uM = new Unmanaged();
    }
```

```
    ~Derived(){
        Console::WriteLine(S"Derived::Finalizer");
        delete uM;
    }
};
int main() {
  Base *pBase = new Derived();
  delete pBase;
  Console::WriteLine(S"Call to the delete operator returned");
}
```

In the preceding sample, the finalizer method is implemented as a destructor in all gc classes. The class Derived inherits from the class Base and has data member pointers to the gc class Managed and the unmanaged class Unmanaged. The output of the program is as follows:

```
Derived::Finalizer
Unmanaged::Destructor
Base::Finalizer
Call to the delete operator returned
Managed::Finalizer
```

When compiling this code, the MC++ compiler injects a virtual destructor for each of the gc classes and renames the existing destructors as the Finalize methods. You can see this when you use the ILDasm (ildasm.exe) tool on the application executable. The following listing shows partial output of ILDasm for the class Derived:

```
.class private auto ansi Derived extends Base {
  .field public class Managed m
  .field public valuetype Unmanaged* uM
  .method public specialname rtspecialname instance void  .ctor() cil managed {
    // code stripped
  } // end of method Derived::.ctor
  .method family virtual instance void  Finalize() cil managed {
    // code stripped
    // call to Unmanaged::Finalize on  Derived::uM
    // code stripped
    //call to  Base::Finalize()
  } // end of method Derived::Finalize
  .method public virtual instance void  __dtor() cil managed
```

```
  {
    // call to System.GC::SuppressFinalize(object)
    // call to  Derived::Finalize()
  } // end of method Derived::__dtor
} // end of class Derived
```

In this listing, you can see the `Finalize` method with `family` (`protected`) accessibility and a virtual `__dtor` method with `public` accessibility. Both methods are marked with `instance`, which indicates that they are nonstatic methods. Both methods are also marked with `cil managed`, which indicates that the code for these methods is managed code and is in MSIL. We deliberately ignore other details in this listing, as they are not important to understanding the concept of finalizers. The details on how to interpret the metadata output of ILDasm are discussed in Appendix B.

The call to the operator `delete` in the `main` function results in calling the injected virtual destructor of the `Derived` class. As you can see from the previous ILDasm listing, the call to the virtual destructor results in the finalizer of the derived class being called. This causes the chain of finalizers to be called in the base classes. In the current sample, the finalizer of the `Base` class is called. We mentioned that the user-defined destructors are renamed to `Finalize` methods. So, in the `Finalize` method of the `Derived` class, the unmanaged object is destroyed with the call to its destructor. However, at this time the managed object pointed to by the variable `m` of the `Derived` class is still alive and its memory has not been reclaimed. During the next garbage collection cycle, the `Finalize` method of the object of `Managed` is called.

Static Class Constructor

Unlike native C++ classes, managed classes can have a constructor marked as `static`. This constructor is called the *static class constructor* or simply the *class constructor*. This method is used to initialize static data members of a gc class. The CLR calls this method anytime between the application load time and the first reference to a static data member to initialize static data members before any instances of the class are created. It is not possible to accurately predict when this call is made by the runtime, but a class constructor is guaranteed to be called before any instance of the class is created.

There are a few restrictions on how to author a class constructor. These restrictions are as follows:

- The method is not allowed to take parameters.

- The method must be defined inside the class.

- Circular dependencies in class constructors are not allowed. For example, the static class constructor of gc class A should not call the static function in gc class B class that in turn calls the static method of gc class A.

- The method cannot refer to any nonstatic members of the class.

- The method cannot create an instance of its class directly using the new operator or indirectly as a function return type.

In the absence of a user-defined static class constructor for a managed class, the MC++ compiler generates the class constructor with the code to initialize the static data members of the class.

In this example, the constructor for the class C is marked as static. The static data member m_staticI is initialized in the static class constructor, but the member m_staticJ is not. The MC++ compiler inserts code to initialize m_staticJ to 0 before the initialization for m_staticI in the body of the class constructor.

```
#using <mscorlib.dll>
using namespace System;
__gc class C {
private:
    static int m_staticI;
    static int m_staticJ;
public:
    static C() { m_staticI = 10; }
    int GetStaticI() { return m_staticI; }
    int GetStaticJ() { return m_staticJ; }
};
int main() {
    C *c = new C();
    Console::WriteLine(c->GetStaticI());
    Console::WriteLine(c->GetStaticJ());
};
```

The program's output is as follows:

```
10
 0
```

Constraints on Gc Classes

When authoring members of gc classes, you need to be aware of the following restrictions:

- Gc classes cannot have copy constructors, assignment operators, and bit fields. Refer to Chapter 10 for a discussion on operators.

- Template members are not allowed. The current version of the .NET Framework does not support generic types.

- typedef inside a gc class is not allowed. This is a limitation in the current MC++ compiler.

- Friend functions and friend classes are not allowed inside gc classes. The current version of the .NET Framework does not support the concept of friends.

- Default arguments are not allowed for member functions. Not all .NET-targeted languages support default arguments. The current MC++ compiler restricts their use.

- Member functions with a variable number of parameters are allowed in native C++ classes using the . . . operator. In gc classes they are not allowed. The current version of the .NET Framework does not support the concept of methods with a variable number of parameters.

- It is an error to bring new names into the scope of a managed class via the using declaration. The current MC++ compiler restricts this usage.

- You cannot declare or define new or delete operators. This is because the memory management of gc classes is handled by the CLR.

- You cannot have const and volatile qualifiers on member functions of gc classes. This is a restriction in the current MC++ compiler.

Refer to the MC++ specification document for more details.

Nested Gc Classes

Similar to the nested types in native C++, gc classes can have nested gc classes. That is, a gc class can be defined inside another gc class. The nested gc classes are not allowed to have any access specifiers; they inherit the enclosing member access specifiers. A nested class must have one __nogc, __gc, and __value specifier. A nested class has access to the private members of the enclosing class.

In the following example, the class Inner is defined inside the class Outer. It has the same accessibility as the Outer class. As a result, the statement that creates an instance of the Inner class in the main function is allowed.

```
#using <mscorlib.dll>
using namespace System;

public __gc class Outer {
  public:
      __gc class Inner {
            public:
              void InnerFunc() {
                  Console::WriteLine(L"Outer::Inner::InnerFunc()");
              }
      };
      void OuterFunc() {
            Console::WriteLine(L"Outer::OuterFunc()");
      }
};

int main() {
    Outer *o = new Outer();
    Outer::Inner *i = new Outer::Inner();
    o->OuterFunc();
    i->InnerFunc();
}
```

The output of the preceding program is as follows:

```
Outer::OuterFunc()
Outer::Inner::InnerFunc()
```

Nested types can inherit from enclosing types. In this case, the nested types must be defined out of line with the enclosing class. The following code shows an example:

```
#using <mscorlib.dll>
using namespace System;
public __gc class Outer {
   int i;
   public:
        __gc class Inner;
        void OuterFunc() {
            Console::WriteLine(L"Outer::OuterFunc()");
        }
};
__gc class Outer::Inner : public Outer{
   public:
        void InnerFunc(Outer *o) {
            o->i = 10;
            Console::WriteLine(L"Outer::Inner::InnerFunc()");
        }
};

int main() {
    Outer *o = new Outer();
    Outer::Inner *i = new Outer::Inner();
    o->OuterFunc();
    i->InnerFunc(o);
}
```

In this sample, the member function of the nested class accesses the private data member of the enclosing class. This code compiles without any syntax errors reported from the MC++ compiler.

Abstract Classes

An *abstract class* is a gc class that cannot be instantiated—it can only be inherited by other gc classes. The keyword __abstract can be applied to a gc class. Note that a gc class becomes implicitly abstract if it contains a pure virtual member function. Using the __abstract keyword it is possible to provide implementation for all member functions of a gc class and still make it abstract (not instantiable).

In the following sample, the class Base is marked as __abstract, so it can only be inherited. An instance of Base cannot be created. The class Derived inherits from Base and it can be instantiated.

```
#using <mscorlib.dll>
__abstract __gc class Base {};
__gc class Derived: public Base {};
int main() {
   Base *b = new Base(); // compiler reports error here
   Derived *d = new Derived(); // okay
}
```

Sealed Classes

Sealed classes are managed classes that cannot be inherited by a derived class. The keyword __sealed can be applied to a managed class or its virtual member function. When applied to a managed class, it means that the class cannot act as a base class. When applied to a virtual member function, it means that the function cannot be overridden. Value types are implicitly sealed. Refer to Chapter 5 for a discussion on value types.

In the following sample, the __sealed keyword is applied to the gc class classA, making the class not inheritable by any derived class. The compiler reports an error when such a usage is detected.

```
#using <mscorlib.dll>
__sealed __gc class ClassA {
   public:
         void Func(){ /* ... */}
};
__gc class ClassB: public ClassA { // compiler reports error here
};
```

__typeof Keyword

The keyword __typeof is used to find the type of a managed type (a gc class, a value type, or a gc interface) at runtime. This keyword provides the functionality of the GetType method of System::Object class. Unlike the GetType method, __typeof can be applied to names of managed types.

In the following sample, the __typeof operator when applied to the BCL class System::String returns the type information as an object of the BCL class System::Type:

```
#using <mscorlib.dll>
using namespace System;
void main() {
    Type *t = __typeof(System::String);
    Console::WriteLine(t->ToString());
}
```

The output of the preceding program is as follows:[4]

```
System.String
```

Special gc Classes for Strings

From the BCL, two string-related classes are noteworthy: System::String and System::Text::StringBuilder.

System::String

The gc class System::String is a sealed class. It is a Unicode representation of a string in the .NET Framework. An instance of System::String class is immutable—it cannot be modified once it is created. If a function, for example, the string concatenation method, Concat of System::String, appears to modify the contents of a System::String object, but it is in fact creating a new object of System::String. Strings are represented in multiple ways in MC++. A C++ string literal with or without the L prefix can be assigned to an instance of type System::String. No explicit cast is required. The following code shows an example:

```
#using <mscorlib.dll>
using System::String;
int main() {
    String *str1 = "string";
    String *str2 = L"wide string";
    String *str3 = "string";
};
```

---

[4] Note that qualified names of types are represented in metadata with names separated by a period (.) rather than a double colon (::). For example, when you see the metadata for the Object class, you would see the name System.Object. When used in MC++, qualified names must use a double colon (::) to separate the namespace names and type names used in the qualified name. However, you need to be aware that when a method of a BCL class returns a qualified name, the name will have periods (.) separating the namespace names and type names used in the qualified name.

In the preceding sample, all assignments are valid. The compiler provides an implicit conversion from a narrow string literal or a wide string literal to `System::String*`. Note that there will be two copies of strings representing `"string"` pointed to by `str1` and `str3`. As a result, three different instances of type `String*` are created on the GC heap.

MC++ supports a third type of string provided by the .NET Framework. This string type contains the prefix S. Consider the following example:

```
#using <mscorlib.dll>
void main() {
    System::String *str1 = S"common language runtime string";
    System::String *str2 = S"common language runtime string";
};
```

In the preceding sample, only one instance of `String*` is created on the GC heap. Two identical strings with the prefix S will always point to the same instance in the GC heap. The string literals with the prefix S have better performance in the CLR compared to the strings that have no prefix or the prefix L. The `System::String` class has several members that can be used for string processing requirements. Refer to the .NET documentation on `System::String` for more details.

System::Text::StringBuilder

When you need to modify an existing string in an application without creating a new instance each time, you should use the class `System::Text::StringBuilder`. This is a sealed gc class.

The following code shows an example of how the `StringBuilder` class can be used:

```
#using <mscorlib.dll>
using namespace System;
using namespace System::Text;

int main() {
  String* hello = S"Hello ";
  String* world = S"Managed World!";

  // Work  with StringBuilder
  StringBuilder* strBldr = new StringBuilder(hello);
  StringBuilder* strBldrOld = strBldr;
  strBldr = strBldr->Append(world); // append a string
```

```
Console::WriteLine(strBldr->ToString());
if (strBldr->Equals(strBldrOld)) { // compare new and old pointers
  Console::WriteLine("New and old StringBuilder instances are the same");
}
else {
  Console::WriteLine("New and old StringBuilder instances are different");
}

// Work with String
String* str = hello;
String* strOld = str;  // save old pointer
str = String::Concat(hello, world); // concatenate two strings
Console::WriteLine(str);

if (str->Equals(strOld)) { // compare new and old pointers
  Console::WriteLine("New and old String instances are the same");
}
else {
  Console::WriteLine("New and old String instances are different");
}
}
```

In this sample, two CLR strings are created for hello and world. The System::Text::StringBuilder class is used to append two strings. The new and old System::Text::StringBuilder pointers are compared. The same procedure is repeated for the System::String class. The new and old pointers of System::Text::StringBuilder should be the same, whereas they are different for String. The output of the program is as follows:

```
Hello Managed World!
New and old StringBuilder instances are the same
Hello Managed World!
New and old String instances are different
```

Note that this sample is for illustration only. The StringBuilder class must be used when a managed component calls a function in a native component that returns a modified string. We discuss this in more detail in Chapter 16 and Chapter 19. For a detailed description on the gc class StringBuilder, refer to the .NET documentation.

Summary

In this chapter, we introduced the concept of managed classes (gc classes). You learned how to create and use managed classes. We discussed the BCL class `System::Object`, which is the root class of all managed class hierarchies and the base class of all managed classes. We showed the various accessibility options of gc classes and their members. You saw how inheritance works with managed classes. We described how the keywords `__abstract`, `__typeof`, and `__sealed` are used on gc classes. Finally, we discussed the special string classes `System::String` and `System::Text::StringBuilder`.

In the next chapter, we discuss interfaces and show how gc classes are used to implement interfaces.

CHAPTER 4

Interfaces

AN *INTERFACE* IS AN ABSTRACT data type that exposes a part or the entire functionality of an object, in that it contains the declarations of a subset of the methods implemented by the object. The implementation details of the methods declared in an interface are transparent to the users of that interface. An object can expose different facets of its behavior via multiple interfaces that declare different subsets of the object's methods. For example, an employee who is a manager in a company can have two interfaces—one that views him or her as an employee, and another that views him or her as a manager.

In C++ terms, an interface is an abstract class whose members are pure virtual functions that have public access. Interfaces are first-class citizens in the .NET Framework. In other words, interfaces are supported directly as a feature in the .NET Framework.

In this chapter, we discuss how to define and use managed interfaces through the keywords __gc and __interface. We briefly discuss the members of managed interfaces and explain the issues involved with interface inheritance and implementation.

Managed Interfaces

In MC++, interfaces are defined using the keyword __gc followed by the keyword __interface. The keyword __gc is required to distinguish between a native C++ (unmanaged) interface and a managed interface. A native C++ interface can be declared using the keyword __interface or the sequence of keywords __nogc and __interface. In the context of this book, when we use the term "interface," we are referring to a managed interface unless otherwise specified.

The following code shows how interfaces are defined:

```
#using <mscorlib.dll>
__interface IFace1 { /* declarations */ }; // unmanaged interface
__nogc __interface IFace2 { /* declarations */ }; // unmanaged interface
__gc __interface IFace3 { /* declarations */ }; // managed interface
```

The BCL class System::Object is the base class of all managed interfaces. So, methods defined in the System::Object class can be invoked on a managed object implementing an interface, via a pointer to the implemented interface.

A managed interface can only be implemented by a gc class or a value class. The access specifier for an interface in the implementing class must be `public`. A gc class or a value class can implement multiple interfaces. The following example shows a gc class implementing two interfaces:

```
#using <mscorlib.dll>
using namespace System;
__gc __interface IEmployeeFinances {
  void SetSalary(double salary);
  double GetSalary();
};
__gc __interface IEmployeeDetails {
  String* GetName();
  String* GetAddress();
};
__gc class CEmployee : public IEmployeeFinances, public IEmployeeDetails {
  int m_Id;
  double m_Salary;
  String* m_Name;
  String* m_Address;
public:
  CEmployee(int id) : m_Id(id) {
    // overly simplified
    if (id == 1) {
      m_Salary = 50000;
      m_Name = S"John";
      m_Address = S"1 Broadway St, NY, NY";
    }
  };
  void SetSalary(double salary) { m_Salary = salary; }
  double GetSalary() { return m_Salary; }
  String* GetName() { return m_Name; }
  String* GetAddress() { return m_Address; }
};
int main() {
  CEmployee* cEmp = new CEmployee(1);

  IEmployeeFinances *iEmpF = cEmp;
  iEmpF->SetSalary(100000);
  Console::Write(S"Salary is : ");
  Console::WriteLine(iEmpF->GetSalary());
```

```
  IEmployeeDetails *iEmpD = cEmp;
  Console::WriteLine(S"Name is : {0}", iEmpD->GetName());
  Console::WriteLine(S"Address is : {0}", iEmpD->GetAddress());
}
```

In this example, the declarations of interfaces IEmployeeFinances and IEmployeeDetails include the keyword __gc, which makes them managed interfaces. The gc class CEmployee implements the interfaces IEmployeeFinances and IEmployeeDetails. Note that in the definition of CEmployee the access specifier for the base class is public, which is required.

In the statement IEmployeeDetails *iEmpD = cEmp, the assignment of the CEmployee object pointer to iEmpD is allowed because the interface IEmployee is a base class of CEmployee. This is consistent with the semantics of assigning a derived class pointer to a base class pointer in native C++.

Note that the interface IEmployeeDetails must be a base class of the class CEmployee for the assignment to work; if the class CEmployee simply implements all members of the interface IEmployeeDetails without inheriting from it, then the assignment fails.

Here is the output of the preceding program:

```
Salary is : 100000
Name is : John
Address is : 1 Broadway St, NY, NY
```

Interface Members

An interface can only contain public, nonstatic member functions or properties. An interface cannot contain data members. It is an error to provide implementations to the interface methods in the interface itself. The managed classes that implement an interface must implement all methods of the interface.

```
#using <mscorlib.dll>
__gc __interface IfailsToCompile {
    void Func() {} // error, implementation not allowed
};
```

Interfaces can contain properties, as shown in the following example. (Properties are discussed in detail in Chapter 9.)

```
#using <mscorlib.dll>
__gc __interface Employee {
    __property int get_JobLevel();
```

```
        __property void set_JobLevel(int level);
};
__gc class Developer : public Employee {
    private:
        int m_level;
 public:
        __property int get_JobLevel() { return m_level;}
        __property void set_JobLevel(int level) { m_level = level;}
};
int main() {
   Employee *c = new Developer();
   c->JobLevel = 5; // set_JobLevel is called
   System::Console::WriteLine(c->JobLevel); // get_JobLevel is called
}
```

In the preceding code, the property JobLevel is defined in the interface
Employee. The class Developer implements the interface Employee. In the main
function, an instance of Developer is created on the GC heap. The method
set_JobLevel is invoked in the assignment statement for the property because
the property is assigned a value. As a result of the property value being
retrieved, the WriteLine function prints the value of the property by invoking
the method get_JobLevel.

Here is the output of the program:

5

Inheritance

An interface can inherit from more than one interface. Interfaces are not subject to
the problems that are caused with multiple inheritance because interfaces do not
have data members. A gc class can also inherit from more than one interface; however, a gc class can inherit from only one gc class. Similarly, a managed interface
can only inherit from another managed interface. As described in the previous
chapter, in MC++ there is no cross-inheritance between managed and unmanaged
objects—a gc class cannot inherit from an unmanaged class and vice versa.
Therefore, cross-inheritance of managed and unmanaged interfaces is not allowed.

```
#using <mscorlib.dll>
__gc __interface IParallelogram {
    int Side1();
    int Side2();
};
```

```
__gc __interface IRectangle : public IParallelogram {
      int Length();
      int Width();
};
__gc class TwoDimensionalSurface {
      public:
            void NumberOfSides() {}
};
__gc class Quadrilateral: public TwoDimensionalSurface, public IRectangle {
      int side1, side2;
      public:
            int Side1(){ return side1; }
            int Side2(){ return side2; }
            int Length(){ return side1; }

int Width() { return side2; }

/* other methods */
};
```

In this example, the class Quadrilateral inherits from the gc class TwoDimensionalSurface and the interface IRectangle. The derived class must provide implementations for all methods of the interfaces that are inherited; it becomes an abstract class otherwise. As mentioned previously, the inheritance access specifier must be public for gc class inheritance and interface inheritance.

Inheriting the Same Interface Multiple Times

In MC++, an interface can inherit from two interfaces, which in turn both inherit from the same interface. That is, an interface can be inherited by two interfaces that are themselves inherited by another interface. The following code clarifies this:

```
#using <mscorlib.dll>
using namespace System;
__gc __interface IEmployee {
      String* GetName();
};
__gc __interface IManager : IEmployee {
      int GetNumberOfReports();
};
```

```
__gc __interface IAdmin : IEmployee {
    int GetNumberOfEmpsSupported();
};
__gc class CSysAdmin : public IAdmin, public IManager {
    int m_Id;
    String* m_Name;
    int m_NumReports;
    int m_NumEmpsSupported;
public:
    CSysAdmin (int id) : m_Id(id) {
        // overly simplified
        if (id == 1) {
            m_Name = S"John";
            m_NumReports = 5;
            m_NumEmpsSupported = 0;
        }
    }
    String* GetName(){ return m_Name; }
    int GetNumberOfReports(){ return m_NumReports; }
    int GetNumberOfEmpsSupported() { return m_NumEmpsSupported;}
};
int main() {
    CSysAdmin *pCEmp = new CSysAdmin (1);
    Console::WriteLine(S"Name is {0}", pCEmp->GetName());
    Console::Write(S"Number of reports is ");
    Console::WriteLine(pCEmp->GetNumberOfReports());
}
```

In the preceding example, the interface IManager inherits from the interface IEmployee. The interface IAdmin also inherits from the interface IEmployee. The gc class CSysAdmin inherits from IAdmin and IManager. The class CSysAdmin provides implementation for the member methods of IEmployee, IAdmin, and IManager. Note that there is no ambiguity resulting from IEmployee being accessible in two ways from CEmployee—via IManager and via IAdmin. Virtual inheritance is implicitly realized in interface inheritance—there will only be one occurrence of an interface in the base class list even if it is multiply inherited.

Here is the output of this program:

```
Name is John
Number of reports is 5
```

Implementing Identical Methods from Two Inherited Interfaces

It is valid for a gc class to implement two different interfaces that have a method with the same name, return type, and parameter list, as demonstrated in the following code:

```
#using <mscorlib.dll>
__gc __interface IStudent {
     int GetId();
};
__gc __interface IProfessor {
     int GetId();
};
__gc class UniversityAffiliate: public IStudent, public IProfessor {
     int m_Id;
     public:
          int GetId(){ return m_Id; }
          // other methods
};
```

Here, the implementation of GetId in UniversityAffiliate works for the GetId member function in both interfaces—IStudent and IProfessor. A gc pointer to UniversityAffiliate can be cast to a pointer to either IStudent or IProfessor.

It is possible to provide implementations for methods with the same signature in two interfaces inherited by a gc class. The name of the implementation method must be qualified with the interface name. One limitation to note here is that a gc class implementing members with the same name from two or more interfaces cannot itself declare a member with that signature. In order to implement the same behavior for unmanaged interface inheritance in native C++, the implementations for both methods must be merged into one, and additional logic needs to be added to figure out which interface should be used. As this description indicates, the implementation in native C++ is very complicated compared to the implementation in MC++.

The following example shows how to implement identical methods from two inherited interfaces:

```
#using <mscorlib.dll>
__gc __interface ISecretary {
     int CalculateSalary();
};
__gc __interface IProfessor {
     int CalculateSalary();
};
```

```
__gc class UniversityEmployee: public ISecretary, public IProfessor {
    int m_salary;
    public:
        int ISecretary::CalculateSalary(){
            // code to calculate salary
            return m_salary;
        }
        int IProfessor::CalculateSalary(){
            // code to calculate salary
            return m_salary;
        }
        // other methods
};
```

In the preceding code, the interfaces ISecretary and IProfessor are implemented by the gc class UniversityEmployee. The UniversityEmployee class
implements two methods with the same name, but qualified with the two interfaces. When the method CalculateSalary is called via a pointer to the interface
ISecretary, the method ISecretary::CalculateSalary is called. When the same
method is called via a pointer to the interface IProfessor, the method
IProfessor::CalculateSalary is called. Calling the method CalculateSalary
without any qualification via a pointer to the instance of UniversityEmployee is
not allowed.

Default Implementation of Interface Methods

MC++ provides a convenient way to reuse the implementation provided by
a base class in a derived class when an interface method implemented
by the base class is identical to another interface method implemented by
the derived class.

Let's take a look at an example of default implementation of an interface
method. Imagine a hospital where some of the doctors are also professors.
Separate interfaces can exist for a doctor (IDoctor) and for a professor
(IProfessor). Suppose that the gc class CProfessor implements the IProfessor
interface. When implementing a gc class (CProfessorDoctor) that represents
a professor who is also a doctor, the class CProfessor can be inherited and the
interface IDoctor can be implemented.

```
#using <mscorlib.dll>
using namespace System;
__gc __interface IProfessor {
        String *Specialization();
};
__gc __interface IDoctor {
        String *Specialization();
};
__gc class CProfessor : public IProfessor{
    protected:
    String *m_Specialization;
      public:
      CProfessor(String *spl) : m_Specialization(spl) {}
      String* Specialization() { return m_Specialization;}
};
__gc class CProfessorDoctor : public CProfessor, public IDoctor {
    public:
    // no need to implement IDoctor::Specialization(),
    // the method CProfessor::Specialization() is reused.
    CProfessorDoctor(String *spl) : CProfessor(spl){}
};
int main() {
    CProfessorDoctor *pProfDoc = new CProfessorDoctor(S"Cardiology");
    IDoctor* pID = pProfDoc;
    Console::Write("Specialization is ");
    Console::WriteLine(pID->Specialization());

}
```

In this sample code, the gc class `CProfessorDoctor` implements `IDoctor` and inherits from the gc class `CProfessor`. The class `CProfessor` implements the method `Specialization` of `IProfessor`. The class `CProfessorDoctor` reuses this implementation for the method `Specialization` of `IDoctor`. To realize the same behavior in native C++ for unmanaged interface inheritance, the interface method must be implemented in the most derived class, and calls should be forwarded to the implementation in the base class. MC++ simplifies this by choosing the already implemented method as the default implementation.

Here is the output of this program:

```
Specialization is Cardiology
```

Summary

In this chapter, we have introduced the concept of managed interfaces. We explained what an interface is and what kind of members it can have. We also discussed issues related to inheritance. As you have seen, many problems attributed to multiple inheritance in C++ do not arise in the case of managed interfaces.

In the following chapter, we will talk about a special kind of managed class—value types. In particular, you will see how to use value types to implement interfaces.

CHAPTER 5
Value Types

As you may remember from the previous chapter, gc classes can only be instantiated on the GC heap. However, this is not always what you want. Creating an object on the heap is a costly operation and could trigger garbage collection. Further, accessing a gc object requires a pointer dereference, which doesn't come free either. Finally, having to use operator new every time you need to create an object would be a nuisance.

In MC++, classes that are meant to be created on the stack are called *value types*. In this chapter you will learn how to create value types, convert them to gc classes via boxing, and implement interfaces by deriving a value type from them.

Understanding Value Types

One of the first questions you face when designing a managed class is whether it should be a gc class or a value type. There is no "one-size-fits-all" answer, so usually you have to make a judgment call. Two important considerations affect your choice.

First, unlike gc classes, value types can be used as local variables, function parameters, or return values. They are usually small enough to be efficiently passed by a value, though they can also be passed by a pointer or a reference.

Second, value types usually represent small data items with short lifetimes. Because they exist on the stack, they are not garbage-collected—they can never become "garbage."

There are other things you need to know about value types—and this is what the rest of the chapter is all about.

Declaring Value Types

A value type is declared with the keyword __value followed by class or struct, for example:

```
#using <mscorlib.dll>
__value class Fraction
{
    int nominator_;
    unsigned int denominator_;
public:
    Fraction( int nominator, unsigned int denominator );
    // . . .
};
```

The value type Fraction can then be created on the stack:

```
int main()
{
    Fraction f(1, 2);
}
```

Primitive Types

The common language runtime defines frequently used value types that correspond to basic types such as System::Int32 and System::Byte. The MC++ compiler maps all primitive C++ types such as int and char to their managed counterparts so that they can be used interchangeably, as in the following example:

```
#using <mscorlib.dll>
int main()
{
    int i1 = 10;
    System::Int32 i2 = 20;
    i1 = i2;
    i2 = i1;
}
```

The complete list of the C++ primitive types and corresponding CLR equivalents are presented in the following table.

C++ PRIMITIVE TYPE	SIGNED TYPE	UNSIGNED TYPE
char	SByte	Byte
short	Int16	UInt16
int, __int32	Int32	UInt32
long int	Int32	UInt32
__int64	Int64	UInt64
float	Single	N/A
double	Double	N/A
long double	Double	N/A
bool	Boolean	N/A

C++ includes the keywords `signed` and `unsigned`, which can be applied to a primitive integral type. Not so in CLR—signed and unsigned versions have different names.

Note that because C++ has a richer set of basic types than the CLR, not all primitive C++ types can be directly mapped to CLR types. For example, `int`, `__int32`, and `long int` all map to the same runtime type `System::Int32`. The compiler uses a custom modifier to distinguish them in the metadata. However, other languages might not understand the meaning of the modifier, and as a result will be unable to distinguish the two as separate types. The same is true about `double` and `long double`. That said, keep in mind that although using both `int` and `long int` is valid in MC++ programs, it is not considered CLS compliant.

Here is an example of a class definition that is not CLS compliant:

```
#using <mscorlib.dll>
public __gc class MyClass
{
    void f( int );
    void f( long int );
};
```

Strictly speaking, using unsigned integer types is not CLS compliant either. Not all languages are required to recognize them. Some such as C# do, but others such as Visual Basic do not.

Boxing and Unboxing

Unlike gc classes, value types do not all have a common base class. You cannot convert a pointer to a value type to System::Object*. But what if you need to?

Imagine yourself implementing a class List[1] that supports the following simple functionality:

```
#using <mscorlib.dll>
public __gc class List
{
    Object* pTheObject_;
    List* pNext_;
public:
    void AddTail( Object* );
    Object* GetTail();
};
```

Naturally, the list operates with the most generic type available: System::Object. That means the list can actually contain objects of any gc type[2]—but not a value type. Value types cannot be passed to functions expecting arguments of type System::Object*.

What you need here is *boxing*—the process of converting a value type to a gc object. When a value is boxed, it is copied bitwise to a newly allocated gc object, the "box." This new object has a bigger footprint than the original value type; in addition to the value type itself, it also contains the virtual function table and other data.

To box a value type in MC++, use the keyword __box:

```
using namespace System;
int main()
{
    List *pList = new List;
    Int32 i = 10;
    pList->AddTail( __box(i) );
}
```

Now, because the boxed i is a gc object, AddTail can accept it as a parameter.

---

[1] When writing real code, don't implement your own list. The common language runtime already has lists called ArrayList and SortedList.

[2] You might ask a very valid question here—why not use generics (also known in C++ as templates)? Well, unfortunately generics are not supported in the common language runtime yet.

It is often necessary to extract the boxed value type from the "box." This process is called *unboxing*. When unboxing a pointer to System::Object, you need to know what you are unboxing *to*. For example, if you know the boxed object is of type V, convert it to V* this way:

```
V* pV = __try_cast<V*>(pObject);
```

Operator __try_cast is described in detail in Chapter 6. For now, you just need to understand that it works similarly to dynamic_cast, except that unsuccessful casts result in an exception.

The same is true here—if pObject does not point to a boxed V, this code will throw an exception of type InvalidCastException.

Unlike boxing, unboxing is a relatively cheap operation. It only shifts the pointer inside the boxed object but doesn't copy the object. Of course, you can do the copying yourself. Compare the previous example with this one:

```
V v = *__try_cast<V*>(pObject);
```

Boxing is an important concept of the .NET Framework. Some languages, for example C#, do not have a special keyword for boxing—they perform it implicitly. If you were using class List in C#, the boxing would be hidden:

```
public class TestList
{
    public static int Main()
    {
        List list = new List();
        list.AddTail( 10 );     // 10 is boxed implicitly
        return 0;
    }
}
```

Unlike in C#, boxing in MC++ is always explicit, which makes you think twice before using this expensive operation.

Boxed Types

The result of boxing is not a pointer to System::Object, although it might look like it is. In fact, boxing of a value type V yields a special type "boxed V," which is a gc class, and thus (indirectly) inherits from System::Object.

That's why there is an implicit conversion from a pointer to boxed value type to System::Object*. The conversion is valid, but it loses an important piece of information—the type of the boxed object. For every boxed type, the type of the embedded object is known at compile time; however, System::Object* can point to *any* boxed value type, and you'll never know to which until you try a dynamic cast or use reflection mechanisms to find that out.

The result of operation __box has type "boxed V"—but how to *declare* a variable of this type? It's quite straightforward: you use the keyword __box, followed by the type declaration. Here is an example of using the keyword __box in two different contexts—as a type specifier (left-hand side of the assignment) and an operation (right-hand side):

```
__box Int32* pbI = __box(5);
```

The boxed type carries the information of what is inside the "box." That's why the conversion from a pointer, to a boxed type to the pointer, to the value type being boxed does not require a cast. Here is an example:

```
#using <mscorlib.dll>
using namespace System;
int main()
{
    Int32 a = 10;
    __box Int32* pba = __box(a);
    Int32 *b = pba;     // Note: no cast, implicit unboxing
}
```

For comparison, recall the unboxing example from System::Object* earlier. Using boxed types not only helps you to avoid a cast, it also allows the compiler to generate more efficient code, bypassing dynamic checks inside the unbox operation. If the types are known at compile time, the unbox operation generated from the boxed type is guaranteed to be safe, and it can never throw an exception.

There is another benefit to using boxed types. You can access a member of a value type being boxed as if it were a member of a boxed type. The following example demonstrates this:

```
#using <mscorlib.dll>
using namespace System;
__value struct POINT
{
    UInt32 x;
    UInt32 y;
};
int main()
```

```
{
    POINT a = {100, 200};
    __box POINT* pbp = __box(a);
    pbp->x = 300;     // Note: implicit unboxing under the hood
    Console::WriteLine( a.x );
    Console::WriteLine( pbp->x );
}
```

What is going on behind the scenes when pbp->x = 300 is executed? You can think about this code as being equivalent to the following:

```
POINT* tmpPoint = pbp;     // implicit unbox
tmpPoint->x = 300;     // change the value inside the "box"
```

Of course, the compiler is able to optimize away the temporary pointer tmpPoint. And that's not all—because the compiler has all the information about the type and layout of the values involved, the code is compiled into very efficient pointer arithmetic.

Inheritance

Value types have an important restriction—they cannot be inherited from.[3] It is also invalid to inherit a value type from a gc class, but you can inherit it from one or more gc interfaces. In fact, deriving a value type from an interface is a very convenient way to extend its functionality.

Imagine that your task is to design a value type, such that an array of these value types could be sorted. You don't go about reinventing the wheel by implementing your own sorting procedure; instead, you want to use the functionality provided by the Array::Sort method.

Array::Sort can only sort arrays of objects that implement interface IComparable. That's easy—just inherit your class from IComparable and implement the CompareTo method:

```
#using <mscorlib.dll>
using namespace System;
__value struct V : public IComparable
{
    int data_;
    V(int i) { data_=i; }
```

---

[3]   In the common language runtime, a class that cannot be a base class is called a
      sealed class.

```
    int CompareTo( Object* o )
    {
        V v = *_try_cast<V*>(o);
        return v.data_ < data_ ? 1 : v.data_ == data_ ? 0 : -1;
    }
};
```

Now because the value type V implements interface IComparable, an array of Vs can be sorted using Array::Sort:

```
int main()
{
    V arr[] = { 4, 3, 0, 1, 2, 5 };
    Array::Sort(arr);

    for( int i=0; i<arr->Length; i++ )
    {
        Console::WriteLine( arr[i].data_ );
    }
}
```

Note that although value types do not inherit from anything, boxed value types do: they inherit from System::ValueType. You cannot call a method of System::ValueType on a value type unless you box it:

```
#using <mscorlib.dll>
using namespace System;
__value struct RECT
{
    UInt32 left;
    UInt32 right;
    UInt32 top;
    UInt32 bottom;
};
int main()
{
    RECT rc = {0,0,100,100};
    String *s1 = rc.ToString();      // error: value type must be 'boxed' before
                                     // method 'ToString' can be called
    String *s2 = __box(rc)->ToString(); // OK
}
```

Of course, you can call ToString if you implement it yourself:

```
#using <mscorlib.dll>
using namespace System;
__value struct RECT
{
    UInt32 left;
    UInt32 right;
    UInt32 top;
    UInt32 bottom;
    String* ToString() { return S"RECT"; }
};
int main()
{
    RECT rc = {0,0,100,100};
    Console::WriteLine (rc.ToString());      // OK!
}
```

Where Do Value Types Live?

Most commonly, value types exist on the stack as local parameters, function arguments, or return values. But can you create a value type on the C++ heap or declare it in the global scope?

You can. But there is one severe restriction: such value types cannot contain pointers to gc classes—or more accurately, any gc pointers. (More about gc pointers in Chapter 6.)

The garbage collector must keep track of all roots of managed objects. It can only do that if the pointers to these objects reside either on the GC heap or on the stack. If you were able to declare a global value type that contains a pointer to a managed object, the garbage collector would lose track of this object, resulting in what is known as a GC hole. That's why the compiler will not allow you to do the following:

```
#using <mscorlib.dll>
using namespace System;
__value class V
{
    String* pStr;
};
V g_V;       // error!
int main()
{}
```

Note that the program would compile if class V didn't have the member pStr of type String*.

What about value types on the C++ heap? The same restriction applies: no managed members. There is one more hitch, though: when creating a value type on the C++ heap, use the unmanaged version of operator new—__nogc new:

```
#using <mscorlib.dll>
using namespace System;
__value class V {};
int main()
{
    V *pV = __nogc new V;
    // danger - memory leak!
}
```

The requirement to use __nogc new is intended to help you remember that the value type is going to be allocated on the C++ heap, not the GC heap. That's why this code has a memory leak—the object will not be garbage-collected. You have to delete it yourself by doing delete pV.

Alternatives to Boxing

Boxing is not the only way of putting a value type on the GC heap. The other way to achieve it is to make the value type a member of a gc class:

```
#using <mscorlib.dll>
__value struct V
{
    int i;
};
__gc class BoxedV
{
    V v_;
public:
    BoxedV( V v ) : v_(v) {}
    V unbox() { return v_; }
};
int main()
{
    V v = {5};
    BoxedV * pbv = new BoxedV(v);
    V v2 = pbv->unbox();
}
```

As a savvy C++ programmer, you would probably note that code like this calls for a template. Indeed, it does. Unfortunately, the current version of the common language runtime does not support generic programming. If it did, no compiler support for boxing would be necessary. Just define boxed V as boxed<V> and you are ready to go!

The garbage collector can move gc objects at any time. Value types embedded within gc classes are copied from one location to another. In the unmanaged C++ world, you have the ability to control object copying by implementing your own copy constructor on a class. Not so in the .NET environment—the common language runtime does not have the concept of a copy constructor, which is why copying embedded value types cannot be intercepted by specifying a copy constructor.

When a C++ class is destroyed, its destructor is executed. CLR gets away from the deterministic destruction model (see Chapter 3), introducing the concept of finalization.

The truth is that mixing C++ and .NET object models poses a serious problem. Deterministic destruction and copy construction are not supported by the common language runtime, and Managed C++ does not support destructors and copy constructors on value types.

Summary

There are two types of managed types: gc classes and value types. The gc classes live on the GC heap and enjoy automatic garbage collection—but they are quite expensive. Value types represent a cheaper alternative.

As we have shown you in this chapter, value types can be converted to the gc class by means of boxing. Conversion back to a value type is called unboxing. You also learned that one way to extend the functionality of a value type is to derive it from an interface and implement it—that is, implement its methods.

One of the things that make value types different from gc classes is that gc classes can only be accessed through a pointer; such pointers are called gc pointers. In the next chapter, you will learn more about gc pointers.

CHAPTER 6

Pointers, References, and Conversions

POINTERS REPRESENT A SPECIAL data type in programming languages. Unlike other data types, pointers do not hold the data itself—instead they hold the address of the data.

Pointers provide an efficient method of memory allocation, storage, and utilization. However, pointers are easy to misuse. Every experienced programmer is familiar with such problems as memory access violation, dereferencing invalid pointers, memory leaks, and dangling pointers. That's why many modern programming languages such as Java or C# tend to neglect pointers. The problem of memory management is taken care of by the Virtual Machine (Java) or the common language runtime (C#).

Managed C++ does not have the luxury of being able to get away from pointers. Considering its enormous legacy—billions of lines of C++ code—pointers are still present in MC++. The good news is that pointers in MC++ are not as troublesome as they are in C and C++. Although you can still use pointers to create effective algorithms and data structures, you don't have to worry about freeing the memory—it is freed by the garbage collector when no longer needed.

You might wonder, "Does this mean all my existing C++ programs compiled with the MC++ compiler will never suffer from memory leaks?" The answer is no. Although you can mix your unmanaged data with managed data, only managed data benefits from automatic garbage collection.

In this chapter, you will learn about such concepts as gc pointers, interior pointers, gc references, and pinning pointers. We describe what they are and how to use them. We then talk about conversions between these pointers and introduce a new keyword, __try_cast.

Gc Pointers

As you know from Chapter 3, gc classes are allocated in the part of memory called the GC heap. The garbage collector tracks objects allocated on the GC heap—and only on the GC heap. Unmanaged objects cannot be directly allocated on the GC heap—they are created either on the stack, on the C++ heap, or globally.

The garbage collector is usually not controlled by the application—it wakes up seemingly unpredictably whenever it "decides" to perform garbage collection. This happens when the application attempts to allocate an object on the GC heap and not enough memory is available, or when the application terminates. Garbage collection can also be triggered by a request from an application.

You can think of the process of garbage collection as memory recycling. Garbage collection frees unreachable objects and moves objects that are still in use within the GC heap to make it more compact and less fragmented.

When an object is moved, what happens to the pointers pointing to it? Obviously, they have to be updated—otherwise they would become invalid.

Pointers that can point to the GC heap and are monitored by the garbage collector are called *gc pointers*. Note the word "can" in the previous sentence—the GC heap is not the only type of memory a gc pointer can point to. A gc pointer to the C++ heap, for example, is valid, but such a pointer never points to a gc object.

A gc pointer is specified by the keyword __gc in front of the * (star). The following declares a gc pointer to `int`:

```
int __gc* gp;
```

You don't always have to use the keyword __gc to declare a gc object. A pointer to a managed type—whether it is a gc class or a value type—is a gc pointer by default. For example, declaration of a gc pointer to the managed class `String` is as simple as this:

```
String* pStr;
```

Declaring a gc pointer `pStr` to an object of type `String` tells the garbage collector that `pStr` will point to the object of type `String` allocated on the GC heap and that it must be updated whenever the garbage collector moves that object.

Gc pointers are somewhat similar to volatile variables in C++, the value of which can change by something other than the program itself.

Because all C++ built-in types have equivalent managed types, you can almost always avoid typing __gc. For example, another way to declare gp, a gc pointer to `int` is as follows:

```
Int32* gp;
```

If you need a regular pointer, or *nogc pointer*, to `Int32`, specify the keyword __nogc. The following code declares a nogc pointer to `Int32`, which is the same thing as `int*`:

```
Int32 __nogc* gp;
```

Because all pointers to managed types are gc by default, you very rarely have to use the __gc keyword in your code—your code will look cleaner without it.

Why Aren't All Pointers Gc Pointers?

At this point, you might ask, "Why aren't *all* pointers gc pointers, and why can't the garbage collector keep track of every pointer in my application?" There are several reasons. The most obvious reason is having to maintain the compatibility with the existing C++ code. Unmanaged programs may use their own memory management techniques—whether it is manual creation or destruction of objects, or reference counting, or whatever else it happens to be. These programs must work in MC++ the way they did when they were compiled for native execution.

Another reason is that because C++ is a powerful and complex language, keeping track of all pointers might simply be impossible or very difficult. Take a look at the following, perfectly legal C++ code:

```
union U
{
    int *p;
    int i;
};
```

Because U::i shares the same memory slot with U::p, when i is changed, so is p. When p is updated by the garbage collector, i changes without the user knowing anything about it—which is an open invitation for bugs. Likewise, changing the value of i also affects p.

Gc pointers have certain semantic restrictions that prevent you from writing dangerous code. You are not allowed to change a gc pointer without the garbage collector's knowing. That's why in the preceding example declaring p as a gc pointer would be rejected by the compiler.

It is very important to understand that only gc pointers can point to the GC heap. MC++ is designed to make it extremely hard for you to break this rule accidentally. That's why the conversion from a nogc pointer to a gc pointer is not allowed.

An address of anything in the GC heap is a gc pointer. That's why the following example will result in a compile-time error (converting from a nogc to gc pointer):

```
#using <mscorlib.dll>
__gc struct G
```

```
{
    int data;
};
int main()
{
    G* pG = new G;
    int* p = &pG->data; // error! &pG->data is a gc pointer
}
```

To make this code compile, p must be declared a gc pointer:

```
int __gc* p = &pG->data;
```

Because a gc pointer may point anywhere, conversion the other way around—from a nogc pointer to a gc pointer—is valid:

```
#using <mscorlib.dll>
int main()
{
    int* heap = new int;
    int __gc* p = heap; // valid but leaks memory
}
```

But remember: an object pointed to by p will not be garbage-collected—and this is why this example has a memory leak.

Interior Gc Pointers

A pointer is called an *interior pointer* if it points to the interior of an object rather than to its head. For example, System::String* is *not* an interior pointer because it points to the whole object—String. On the other hand, Int32* *is* an interior pointer because Int32, being a value type, can only reside in the GC heap as a member of some gc class, such as G::data in the example in the previous section.

Interior pointers pose a serious challenge to garbage collection algorithms: the garbage collector must be able to mark an object as reachable without being told the start of the object.

The garbage collector used in .NET uses a garbage collection algorithm called *mark-and-compact*. It takes considerably more effort for the GC to "mark" the whole object given an interior pointer. For performance reasons, the GC only allows such pointers to be allocated on the runtime stack, therefore reducing the number of them considerably.

In particular, an interior gc pointer cannot reside in the GC heap, as demonstrated here:

```
#using <mscorlib.dll>
using namespace System;
__gc struct G
{
    Int32* pInt; // error!
};
```

Note that just because pInt is the first member of the class G doesn't mean it points to the whole object. As with all managed classes, class G inherits from System::Object and therefore has a table of virtual functions and the class Object inside itself. Also, members of gc classes do not have to be ordered in the same way they were declared in the class. The runtime can reorder them anyway it pleases.[1]

Because pInt is a gc pointer and a member of a gc class, the compiler gives the following error message:

```
'pInt' : cannot declare interior __gc pointer or reference as a member of 'G'
```

Because of the same restriction, you are not allowed to declare a gc pointer to an interior gc pointer:

```
Int32* __gc* pp; // error!
```

If this were valid, the only thing it could point to would be an interior gc pointer inside a gc class—something that could never exist, as you just have learned.

Note the use of the keyword __gc in the last declaration: Int32* __gc*. Although a pointer to a value type is by default a gc pointer, a pointer to a pointer to value type is not. Thus Int32** is identical to Int32 __gc* __nogc*, which is a valid construct. Similarly, Int32*** means Int32 __gc* __nogc* __nogc*, and it can go on like that. This syntax makes it a bit more difficult for you to come up with an ill-formed declaration—you will never get an invalid type without using __gc and __nogc specifiers.

On the other hand, a gc pointer to a gc pointer to a gc class is valid:

```
String** ppS; // OK
```

This declaration is equivalent to:

```
String __gc* __gc* ppS; // OK
```

---

[1]   Actually, you can change this by using the structlayout attribute on the class.

Note that interior gc pointers are not limited to value types. `String** ppS`, in the previous example, is an interior gc pointer as well. It can point to a variable of type `String*`, a member of a gc class. But be aware, `ppS` could also point to a variable of type `String*` allocated on the stack. However, the fact that it *might* point to inside a gc class makes it an interior pointer. As a result, it cannot be declared as a member of a gc class.

Having said that, it should not be surprising that the following declaration is ill-formed:

```
String** __gc* pppS; // error!
```

This is because the topmost gc pointer points to an interior gc pointer. Remove __gc and it will work.

Gc References

Roughly speaking, references are pointers that look and feel like objects. References are always initialized; the compiler will never let you declare an uninitialized reference. The problem of using a NULL reference does not exist because there is no such thing as a NULL reference.

Because references don't suffer from problems attributed to pointers, many C++ programmers favor them. For this reason, MC++ supports managed references. As in C++, you can often use references instead of pointers. In fact, in some cases you *have* to use references to get what you want (for example, when defining a managed operator on a gc class, as discussed in Chapter 10).

As far as the runtime is concerned, a MC++ reference is the same thing as a pointer. To distinguish a reference from a pointer, the MC++ compiler emits a special modifier into the metadata. The runtime ignores this modifier and doesn't see any difference between a managed reference and a managed pointer.

That's the nature of references—on the surface, they behave very much like objects, whereas internally they are implemented as pointers. A class passed by a reference is actually passed by a pointer—even though you can use "`.`" instead of "`->`" to access its members.

References that refer to an object in the GC heap are called *gc references*. As with gc pointers, gc references are declared with the keyword __gc. For instance, a gc reference to the runtime class `System::Object` is declared thus:

```
System::Object __gc& object;
```

Here, because `System::Object` is a managed type, no __gc specifier is required. That's why the following declaration is identical to the previous one:

```
System::Object& object;
```

Because references are in many ways safer than pointers, you can do yourself a favor by using gc references in place of pointers where possible. For example, even though operator new returns a pointer to the newly created object, you can still avoid using pointers when creating objects. Here is how:

```
MyObject& my_object = *new MyObject;
```

Gc references must obey the same rules as pointers. Most importantly, only a gc reference can refer to the GC heap. It is not possible to pass an object from the GC heap by a "normal," *nogc* reference, as is attempted in the following example:

```
#using <mscorlib.dll>
__gc struct G
{
    int data;
};
void PassByRef( int& );
int main()
{
    G* pG = new G;
    PassByRef( pG->data ); // error!
}
```

When compiled, this example produces the following error message:

```
An object from managed heap (member of a managed class) cannot be converted to
an unmanaged reference
```

Const Gc References

A good programming practice in C++ is to pass values by *const* references. This way the input parameter is guaranteed to never change its value. There are several advantages to const references. Imagine a class with a unary constructor. You can pass a value of a type expected by the constructor to a function expecting a const reference to the class. The compiler will create a temporary object and pass it to the function by reference.

This trick doesn't work with const gc references because all gc objects can only be created on the GC heap and never on the stack. However, temporaries generated by the compiler are stack-allocated. Here is an example that will show you the problem:

```
#using <mscorlib.dll>
__gc class ZipCode
{
    int zipCode_;
public:
    ZipCode( int zipCode ) : zipCode_(zipCode) {};
};
void PassByRef( const ZipCode& );
int main()
{
    PassByRef( 90210 ); // error
}
```

If you try to compile this code, the compiler will complain:

```
Cannot create a temporary managed object of type 'const ZipCode'
```

This issue is not a major obstacle, however. You just have to do a little more typing and create a temporary object yourself (on the GC heap, of course), as demonstrated here:

```
#using <mscorlib.dll>
__gc class ZipCode
{
    int zipCode_;
public:
    ZipCode( int zipCode ) : zipCode_(zipCode) {};
};
void PassByRef( const ZipCode& );
int main()
{
    ZipCode& beverly_hills = *new ZipCode( 90210 );
    PassByRef( beverly_hills );
}
```

Pinning Pointers

Managed C++ was designed to make reusing existing unmanaged code as easy as possible. Your ability to reuse existing C++ code would be seriously hampered if the data pointed to by gc pointers were completely inaccessible to unmanaged code.

Imagine reusing an existing C or C++ library of functions to work with satellite images. One of the functions, GetGeoCoordinates, converts screen coordinates of a given point into its geographical coordinates, latitude and longitude:

```
GetGeoCoordinates( int x, int y, double* lat, double* lon );
```

You want to use this function for your managed class GeoPoint:

```
#using <mscorlib.dll>
__gc class GeoPoint
{
    int x_;
    int y_;
    double lat_;
    double lon_;
public:
    void SetGeoCoordinates();
};
```

However, using the function directly is impossible:

```
void GeoPoint::SetGeoCoordinates()
{
    GetGeoCoordinates(x_, y_, &lat_, &lon_ ); // error!
}
```

The compiler will not allow you to convert gc pointers (&lat_ and &lon_) to nogc pointers, which are expected by GetGeoCoordinates.

Rewriting the existing code usually is not an option. That's the idea of code reuse—it must "just work" without having to be rewritten. The most straightforward solution would be to create auxiliary variables on the stack and use them as output parameters:

```
void GeoPoint::SetGeoCoordinates()
{
    double dLat = lat_;
    double dLon = lon_;
    GetGeoCoordinates(x_, y_, &dLat, &dLon ); // OK
    lat_ = dLat;
    lon_ = dLon;
}
```

As you see, not only is code like this inefficient (copying values back and forth), it also takes a lot of typing.

Managed C++ provides a solution for this problem, called *pinning*. Conversion from a gc pointer to a nogc pointer is not allowed because the object can move in the GC heap, making the nogc pointers invalid. To prevent an object from being moved, it has to be pinned.

To pin an object, create a pinning pointer to it. A pinning pointer is declared using the keyword __pin followed by *. Let's rewrite GeoPoint::SetGeoCoordinates using a pinning pointer:

```
void GeoPoint::SetGeoCoordinates()
{
    GeoPoint __pin* pPinned = this;
    GetGeoCoordinates(x_, y_, &pPinned->lat_, &pPinned->lon_ ); // OK
}
```

The garbage collector will not move the objects to which the pinning pointer is pointing.

Because a pinning pointer can point to the GC heap, it is also considered a gc pointer. But since the object it points to will not move during the garbage collection, conversion from a pinning pointer to a nogc pointer is allowed. That's why this example works: double __pin* to double* is a valid conversion.

Note that the compiler optimizer usually eliminates (optimizes away) temporary variables such as pPinned in the preceding code—just because they don't appear to do anything useful. But in this case, optimizing away pPinned would undermine the whole idea of pinning an object. To prevent the optimizer from eliminating pinning pointers, they are marked internally as volatile. Therefore, the real type of pPinned is double __pin* volatile. Now if you see "volatile" in error messages generated by the compiler, you'll know why it is there.

Pinning Pointers Are Dangerous!

An object remains pinned for as long as there is at least one pinning variable pointing to it (or to a part of it). As soon as the last pinning pointer ceases to exist (by going out of scope), the object is no longer considered pinned. So it is important to understand that if the pinning pointer is assigned to a nogc pointer, that nogc pointer must not be used after the pinning pointer has vanished.

Here is an example of very unsafe (though valid) code:

```
#using <mscorlib.dll>
__gc struct G
```

```
    {
        int data_;
    };
    int* GetInt( G* pG )
    {
        int __pin* pPin = &pG->data_;
        return pPin; // danger! danger!
    }
    int main()
    {
        G* pG = new G;
        int* pi = GetInt( pG );
        // using pi hereafter is unsafe
    }
```

In this example, pinning pointer pPin is being assigned to pi, the variable of type int*, a nogc pointer. But because pPin goes out of scope with the end of the function, pi ends up pointing to inside of the gc object, for which there are no pinning pointers! The object can move at any time, making pi invalid.

Bear in mind that the compiler will not warn you about pinning pointers going out of scope. You just have to remember that pinning can make it possible for you to end up with a nogc pointer pointing to the GC heap—an extremely dangerous situation you want to avoid.

Conversions

To support existing C++ programs, MC++ preserves all standard C++ conversion rules. All that is different is conversion to and from pointers and references to managed types, which is why we tackle the subject of conversions in this chapter.

C-Style Cast

A C-style cast is probably the most infamous of all casts. It is not easy to see by looking at a C-style cast whether it ends up being a static_cast, reinterpret_cast, or const_cast.

Because parentheses are used so extensively in C and C++, C-style casts are also very difficult to detect by looking at the code or using some search tool such as grep.

Managed C++ discourages use of the C-style cast. When used to convert a pointer to a base class into a pointer to a derived class, a C-style cast as shown in the following code will compile to __try_cast and result in a warning:

```
#using <mscorlib.dll>
using namespace System;
int main()
{
    Object* o = S"hello";
    String* s = (String*)o; // warning!
}
```

When compiled, this code will issue this warning message:

```
warning: C-style cast from 'System::Object __gc *' to 'System::String __gc *' is
deprecated
```

dynamic_cast

dynamic_cast results in a dynamic check performed by the runtime. This cast is
used commonly in managed code.

Use dynamic_cast when you need to convert a pointer to a base class into
a pointer to a derived class. If the cast is successful, the result is a pointer to the
derived class object. If the result is unsuccessful, dynamic_cast yields 0.

Here's an example of how you would use dynamic_cast:

```
#using <mscorlib.dll>
using namespace System;
int main()
{
    Object* o = S"hello";
    String* s = dynamic_cast<String*>(o);
}
```

__try_cast

Because exceptions are so widely used in managed code (see Chapter 14), MC++
introduces a new keyword, __try_cast, to denote another type of a dynamically
checked cast. The semantics of __try_cast are similar to that of dynamic_cast,
except that __try_cast throws an exception if it fails.

The following code will generate a runtime exception, System::InvalidCastException:

```
#using <mscorlib.dll>
using namespace System;
__gc class MyClass{};
int main()
{
    Object* o = new MyClass;
    try
    {
        String* s = __try_cast<String*>(o);
    }
    catch( InvalidCastException* )
    {
        Console::WriteLine( "Conversion failed" );
    }
}
```

static_cast, const_cast, and reinterpet_cast

The rest of the casts have their usual meaning. Still, there are few things you should know about using these casts:

- static_cast is used mostly to perform an unchecked cast from a pointer to a base class to a pointer to derived class.

- const_cast is used to cast away the const modifier on an object or a pointer.

- Since unchecked pointer casts can break the type safety of gc pointers, using reinterpret_cast between pointers should only be done when absolutely necessary.

Summary

In this chapter, you became acquainted with a fundamental concept of MC++—the gc pointer. You learned about two kinds of gc pointers—interior and pinning pointers. As you have seen, pinning pointers are helpful, but easy to misuse.

At the end of this chapter, we discussed what you should and should not do to convert managed pointers. Most of the old C++ techniques work, and in addition there is one more keyword, __try_cast, that comes very handy in managed environment.

In the next chapter, we take a look at another fundamental concept of MC++—managed arrays. Understanding gc pointers is essential for understanding managed arrays, because every managed array is, internally, a gc pointer to an object in the GC heap.

CHAPTER 7

Arrays

AN *ARRAY* IS A BASIC DATA STRUCTURE of any programming language. It is understood to be a collection of elements of the same type. A number (index) is used to access elements. Arrays have upper and lower bounds, and the elements are contiguous within those bounds.

In C++, the lower bound of an array is always zero, and the upper bound is determined either statically or dynamically. A static array is declared by writing the type of the array, followed by the array name and the upper bound in square brackets, like this:

```
int ArrayOfInts[10];
```

The compiler then allocates enough memory to hold 10 ints.

A dynamic array is allocated in the runtime by the operator new:

```
int GetNumber();
int main()
{
    int n = GetNumber();
    int *ArrayOfInts = new int[n];
    // process the array
    delete []ArrayOfInts;
}
```

Common language runtime has its own concept of arrays. In MC++, they are known as *managed arrays*. As you will see in this chapter, managed arrays are superior to regular C++ arrays, or unmanaged arrays, in many ways.

Declaring Managed Arrays

A managed array is declared with the element type followed by the keyword __gc in front of the upper bound in square brackets.

Managed arrays are always allocated dynamically on the GC heap, and like unmanaged arrays, managed arrays have a lower bound of zero.

The following example creates a managed array of 10 integers:

```
#using <mscorlib.dll>
int main()
{
    // Declare and allocate managed array of 10 integers
    int MyArray __gc[] = new int __gc[10];
}
```

Note that the __gc keyword is not necessary if the type of the element is managed. For example, if you use Int32 instead of int, it does not need __gc:

```
#using <mscorlib.dll>
using namespace System;
int main()
{
    // Declare and allocate managed array of 10 integers
    Int32 MyArray[] = new Int32[10];
}
```

If a managed array is not what you want, you can still create an unmanaged array of value types by specifying __nogc instead of __gc:

```
#using <mscorlib.dll>
__value struct V {};
int main()
{
    V arr __nogc[10];
}
```

Keep in mind, however, that the common language runtime does not directly support unmanaged arrays. This imposes constraints on the element types in such an array. Specifically, the array is not allowed to contain gc pointers. If the value type V from the preceding example had a member of type String*, for instance, the unmanaged array of V would be rejected by the compiler.

So, arrays of managed types are considered managed. But what about an array declared inside a managed class—should it be managed too? The answer is be explicit. When declaring an array inside a managed class, you *must* use either __gc or __nogc, as shown here:

```
#using <mscorlib.dll>
__gc class G
{
    int arrManaged __gc[];       // managed array
    int arrUnmanaged __nogc[5]; // unmanaged array
};
```

Managed Arrays As Safe Arrays

In C++, overstepping array bounds usually leads to unpredictable results—the program behaves wrongly or crashes. To make matters worse, C++ arrays allocated on the stack often represent a major security threat; exploiting their unsafe nature, a hacker can execute malicious code on your computer.

Not so with managed arrays—an attempt to access a nonexistent element causes the runtime exception IndexOutOfRange. Try this example:

```
#using <mscorlib.dll>
using namespace System;
int main()
{
    // Declare and allocate managed array of 10 integers
    int MyArray __gc[] = new int __gc[10];
    // Try to access 21st element
    Console::WriteLine( MyArray[20] );
}
```

When executed, this program throws this exception:

```
Exception occurred: System.IndexOutOfRangeException: An exception of type
System.IndexOutOfRange Exception was thrown.
   at main()
```

Arrays protected from the problem of overstepping bounds are known as *safe arrays*. A managed array is a safe array. As usually, safety doesn't come free—the safety check is performed every time an element of the array is being accessed, affecting the performance. However, considering the advantages (security and making your code less error prone), the performance penalty is not too steep a price.

Structure of a Managed Array

Let's look more closely at the inner structure of a managed array. Unlike an unmanaged array, which is just a chunk of memory, a managed array actually points to a certain object inside the GC heap,[1] which is why managed arrays can only be allocated dynamically. Once allocated, the managed array remains in memory for as long as it is referenced and is freed by the garbage collector, like any other managed object. You don't have to delete it yourself (indeed, you cannot).

Elements of managed arrays can be either value types or pointers to gc classes. This is best illustrated by the following example:

```
#using <mscorlib.dll>
__nogc class U {};
__value class V {};
__gc class G {};
int main()
{
    U ArrU[5];      // unmanaged array of nogc class U
    V ArrV[] = new V[5];    // managed array of value type V
    G* ArrG[] = new G*[5]; // managed array of pointers to G
    // each element of ArrG must be created individually
    for( int i=0; i<5; i++ )
    {
        ArrG[i] = new G;
    }
}
```

As shown in Figure 7-1, the unmanaged array ArrU is a contiguous set of objects. On the other hand, managed arrays ArrV and ArrG both point to a structure that starts with a field called an *array descriptor*. The descriptor holds information about the array, such as its size (upper and lower bounds) and rank (number of dimensions). The descriptor ArrV is followed by the elements ArrV[0] through ArrV[4]. For ArrG, the array of pointers to gc class G, the descriptor is followed by pointers to gc class G.

---

[1]   This fact is not evident from the declaration, however. If MC++ followed C++ rules precisely, a managed array of ints, for example, would be declared as follows:

```
int (*MyArray) __gc[];
```

Syntax like this would be debilitating. Designers of MC++ decided to sacrifice the correctness of the syntax for the sake of simplicity and hide the pointer. Make no mistake though—the pointer is hidden, but it is still there implicitly.

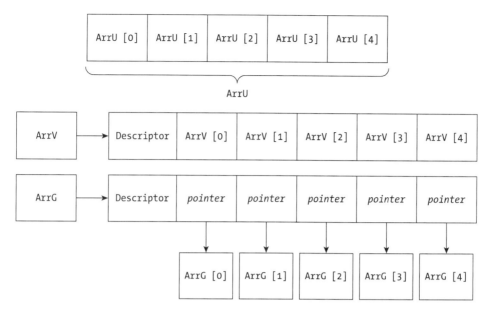

Figure 7-1. Internal structure of a managed array

When a managed array is created, its elements are initialized to zero. Each pointer in array ArrG becomes NULL, but no objects are allocated. For this reason, you have the additional task of initializing each element by dynamically creating objects of type G (see the preceding code example).

It is interesting that an array of pointers to gc objects does not really have to be homogeneous (that is, having all objects of the same type). Each "pointer to" element of ArrG points to an object of type G, but can also point to any object of type *derived* from G. Thus, because System::Object is the base class of any other gc class, an array of pointers to System::Object can, in fact, hold gc objects of any type.

Multidimensional Arrays

Arrays that use more than one index to distinguish the elements are called *multidimensional*. Think of a multidimensional array as an array of arrays where each subarray may have a different size. A multidimensional array is called *rectangular* if it is allocated in a contiguous chunk of memory with subarrays having the same size. An *m*n* table is an example of a rectangular array.

Managed arrays supported in the current version MC++ are all rectangular. As in regular C++, you can still declare nonrectangular arrays by hand—but usually this means more typing.

Managed multidimensional arrays are written with the type followed by the array name, which in turn is followed by one or more commas inside square brackets. The rank of the array is equal to the number of commas plus one.

The following example shows how to create and use a two-dimensional array, which is by far the most common type of multidimensional array:

```
#using <mscorlib.dll>
using namespace System;
int main()
{
    const int width = 10;
    const int height = 10;
    Double matrixA[,] = new Double[width,height];
    Double matrixB[,] = new Double[width,height];
    // ...
    Double matrixResult[,] = new Double[width,height];
    for( int i=0; i<width; i++ )
        for( int j=0; j<height; j++ )
        {
            matrixResult[i,j] = matrixA[i,j] + matrixB[i,j];
        }
}
```

You may be thinking, "Why use commas to separate indexes in managed multidimensional arrays? Why not use usual C++ notation with square brackets and write matrixA[i][j] instead of matrixA[i,j]?" Well, here is what makes multidimensional arrays different in managed and unmanaged cases: if you specify just one index, unmanaged matrixA[i] will still be an array—but this is not true in managed cases. Managed matrixA[i] is not an array—it is a syntactically invalid construct.

When using managed multidimensional arrays, remember to specify as many indexes as there are dimensions.

Class System::Array

As we mentioned earlier, a managed array is a pointer to a managed class. This class is called Array and it is defined in the common language runtime namespace System.

Managed arrays supported in MC++ are nothing more than a convenient wrapper around System::Array. Even if there were no direct support for managed arrays in MC++, you would still be able to use the common language runtime arrays, albeit in a more laborious and less efficient way. Here is how to create and use an array of five ints relying only on functionality provided by System::Array:

```
#using <mscorlib.dll>
using namespace System;
int main()
{
    Array *pArr = Array::CreateInstance (__typeof(Int32), 5);
    for( int i=0; i<5; i++ )
    {
        pArr->SetValue( __box(i*10), i );
    }
    for( int i=0; i<5; i++ )
    {
        Console::WriteLine( pArr->GetValue( i ) );
    }
}
```

As you can see, writing code like this is inconvenient, to say the least. You would be better off letting the compiler do its job—not only does it save time, but it also generates more efficient code. Having to box the value before placing it into the array (because Array::SetValue expects an object as the first parameter) is the most obvious inefficiency, but not the only one.

Compare the previous example with the following program that uses managed arrays to achieve the same effect:

```
#using <mscorlib.dll>
using namespace System;
int main()
{
    Int32 arr[] = new Int32[5];
    for( int i=0; i<5; i++ )
    {
        arr[i] = i*10;
    }
    for( int i=0; i<5; i++ )
    {
        Console::WriteLine( arr[i] );
    }
}
```

You can compare the MSIL generated from these two programs by viewing the output files with ildasm.exe and examining the differences.

Fortunately, managed arrays can take advantage of the functionality provided by System::Array without giving up the convenience of syntactic notation. Because managed arrays are instances of classes inherited from System::Array, every method or property of System::Array is available for managed arrays (properties are discussed in Chapter 9). In the example that follows, you will see how to use the method Sort and the property Length of the class Array.

```
#using <mscorlib.dll>
using namespace System;

__value class X : public IComparable
{
    int data_;
public:
    X(int i) { data_=i; }
    void Print() { Console::WriteLine( data_ ); }
    int CompareTo( Object* o )
    {
        X*pX = __try_cast<X*>(o);
        return pX->data_ < data_ ?
            1 : pX->data_ == data_ ?
            0 : -1;
    }
};
int main()
{
    // Fill up the array with random data
    X arr[] = { 4, 3, 5, 7, 0 };
    // Sort it
    Array::Sort(arr);
    for( int i = 0; i < arr->Length; i++ )
    {
        arr[i].Print();
    }
}
```

When executed, this program prints:

```
0
3
4
5
7
```

In this example, class X inherits from the interface IComparable and implements the method CompareTo. It is then used by the static method Array::Sort to compare the objects while sorting the array.

The program then prints out the contents of the array arr. It uses property Length to get the number of elements of the array.

Because managed arrays inherit from System::Array, there is an implicit conversion from the former to the latter. However, if you want to convert from System::Array to a managed array, an explicit cast is required:

```
#using <mscorlib.dll>
using namespace System;
int main()
{
    String *arrWords[] = {S"Hello,", S"World!"};
    Array* pArr = arrWords;    // no cast needed
    arrWords = __try_cast<String*[]>(pArr);    // need to cast
}
```

Jagged Arrays

Although sometimes inconvenient and less efficient than managed arrays, class System::Array can be used anywhere in place of managed arrays. In addition, there are things that can be done only using System::Array. One example is creating nonrectangular arrays, also known as *jagged arrays*. Unlike rectangular arrays, each subarray of a jagged array might have different length (hence the name "jagged").

To create a jagged array, first create an array of subarrays and then allocate each subarray individually:

```
#using <mscorlib.dll>
using namespace System;
int main()
{
    Array *pArr = Array::CreateInstance(__typeof(Int32[]), 5);
    for(int i=0; i<5; i++)
    {
        pArr->SetValue( Array::CreateInstance( __typeof(Int32), i*10 ), i );
    }
}
```

The class System::Array can be also used to create arrays with nonzero lower bounds:

```
#using <mscorlib.dll>
using namespace System;
int main()
{
    Int32 lo_bounds[] = {1900};
    Int32 lengths[] = {200};
    Array *pYears = Array::CreateInstance(__typeof(Int32), lengths, lo_bounds);
}
```

In this example, the lower bounds and lengths of each dimension (1900 and 200, respectively) are passed as an array to function Array::CreateInstance, which expects the type of the element and two arrays (lengths and bounds of each dimension) as parameters.

Functions Returning Arrays

In regular C++, a function can return a pointer to data or a pointer to an array, but not an array itself. In MC++, a function *can* return an array. Here is how:

```
#using <mscorlib.dll>
using namespace System;
String* GetTheStringArray() []
{
    return new String*[10];
}
int main()
{
    String* arr[] = GetTheStringArray();
}
```

Note that as is usual in C++, array brackets are written at the end of the type.

When a managed array is returned from a function, no copying is involved; only the pointer is being passed. This is, of course, because a managed array is a pointer. In fact, this makes returning a managed array very similar to returning a pointer to an array in regular C++, but the syntax is much cleaner.

Returning an array from a function is a good alternative to returning a pointer, a practice commonly used by C and C++ programmers. Not only is it more readable, but it is often more efficient because the length of the array is already embedded inside it, and thus no additional parameter specifying the length of the array is necessary.

Summary

In this chapter, we described an important concept of MC++: managed arrays. Managed arrays are superior to unmanaged arrays, in that they are safe, include information about their size and dimensions, and can be returned from functions.

In the next chapter, we look at enumerators—another concept carried over from C++ and enhanced in MC++.

CHAPTER 8

Enumerations

ENUMERATIONS (ALSO CALLED ENUMS) were introduced in C as a convenient alternative to macros. Instead of using the preprocessor to defining each constant separately, like this:

```
#define car        0
#define truck      1
#define minivan    2
```

A programmer could define constants, such as car, truck, and minivan, using the keyword enum:

```
enum Vehicle{ car, truck, minivan };
```

Unfortunately, enums in C do nothing more than beautify your code by getting rid of preprocessor declarations. A C enumerator has type int, so a function that expects an enum will also accept any other value of type int:

```
void ProcessVehicle( enum Vehicle );
#define    SUV    10    /* sport utility vehicle */
int main()
{
    ProcessVehicle( car );    // OK
    ProcessVehicle( SUV );    // Also OK!
}
```

This usually leads to very annoying problems—if ProcessVehicle was not designed to handle vehicles of type SUV, the code will still compile, but the problem will only be discovered later, when the program executes.

C++ addressed this issue by making enums type safe: every enum has its own type, different from int, and conversion from int to an enum requires explicit cast. A C++ compiler will generate an error if you try to pass SUV to ProcessVehicle because SUV is not considered a vehicle—the enum Vehicle does not define it as such.

In this chapter, you will learn how to use enums in MC++. You will see how MC++ enums differ from C++ enums and what additional functionality they provide.

Declaring Enums in MC++

Enumerators are an essential element of a language that targets the common language runtime. Enums in MC++ are called *managed enums*. Although regular C++ enums can still be used in any MC++ application, managed enums provide much richer functionality.

To distinguish managed enums from unmanaged enums, the former are defined with the keyword __value, as shown in this example:

```
__value enum Vehicle{ car, truck, minivan };
```

Managed Enums Are Value Types

As the appearance of the keyword __value in front of the enum definition suggests, managed enums are value types—that is, they primarily exist on the stack. Because of this, conversion from an enum to Object* is not valid. Only a boxed enum can be converted to Object*:

```
#using <mscorlib.dll>
using namespace System;
void PrintTree( Object* pTree )
{
    Console::WriteLine(S"The tree is: {0}", pTree);
}
__value enum Tree{ linden, birch, maple };
int main()
{
    Tree tree = maple;
    PrintTree( S"oak" );
    PrintTree( __box(tree) ); // note boxing
}
```

When executed, this program prints the following:

```
The tree is: oak
The tree is: maple
```

This simple example is worth looking at a little closer. When function PrintTree is called the first time, the argument S"oak" of type System::String* is converted to System::Object*—which is really nothing new. The second function call is a bit trickier: __box(tree), which represents a pointer to a special *boxed enum* type (very similar to a boxed value type, discussed in Chapter 5) is being converted to System::Object*. This is possible because a boxed enum is a gc class, as is System::String, and derives from System::Object.

But that's not all—the boxed enum bears the syntactic name of the enum. This is why the result of converting pTree to a string inside Console::WriteLine is "maple."

Most of the functionality related to a managed enum is provided by the BCL class System::Enum, which is the base class for all boxed enums. (Similar to value types, unboxed managed enums do not inherit from anything—only their boxed equivalents do.) Here is how you can enumerate all enums of a given type:

```
#using <mscorlib.dll>
using namespace System;
__value enum Tree{ linden, birch, maple };
int main()
{
    Array* theArray = Enum::GetValues(__typeof(Tree));
    for ( int i = 0; i < theArray->Length; i++ )
    {
        Console::WriteLine( theArray->GetValue(i) );
    }
}
```

In this example, we used the static method GetValues of class Enum. This method takes a pointer to class System::Type (the result of the __typeof operation) and returns a pointer to an instance of class System::Array. The program then walks through all the elements of the array and prints them out. The output of the program is:

```
linden
birch
maple
```

Note that even if the enum Tree were defined in a different assembly, code that iterates through all its elements would not need to be recompiled every time the enum definition changes. This is because the information about the enum is collected in the runtime, by a mechanism called reflection.

Underlying Type

Now let's consider that you need to design a database of the vehicles of employees working in your organization. Yielding to popular demand, you will now define SUV as a member of the enum Vehicle:

```
enum Vehicle{ car, truck, minivan, SUV=10 };
class VehicleRecord
{
    int     EmployeeID;     // owner of the vehicle
    Vehicle type;
public:
    // . . .
};
```

Memory is cheap, but not in your organization. You will discover that class VehicleRecord occupies at least 8 bytes (assuming int has 32 bits on your machine), even if you instructed your compiler to use minimal packing alignment for structures. This is because the data member type has the same size as int, although having a single byte would be enough to cover all existing vehicle types.

Of course, to get the smallest memory footprint, you can use bit fields:

```
enum Vehicle{ car, truck, minivan, SUV=10 };
class VehicleRecord
{
    int     EmployeeID;     // owner of the vehicle
    Vehicle type : 8;     // type is an 8-bit value
public:
    // . . .
};
```

Unfortunately, bit fields can't be used in arrays: an array of ten enums would also take up as much space as if it were an array of ints.

Managed enums provide a solution by allowing you to specify the *underlying type*:

```
#using<mscorlib.dll>
using namespace System;
__value enum Vehicle : Byte { car, truck, minivan, SUV=10 };
int main()
{
    Vehicle v = car;
}
```

Here the enum Vehicle is defined with an underlying type Byte. A variable of type Vehicle takes up as much memory as Byte. No more than 256 vehicle types can be defined.

Of course, an enum still has its own type, different from the underlying type. Conversion from the enum to the underlying type is valid, whereas the opposite is not:

```
#using<mscorlib.dll>
using namespace System;
__value enum Vehicle : Byte{ car, truck, minivan, SUV=1 };
int main()
{
    Byte b = car;     // OK - conversion from Vehicle to Byte
    Vehicle v = b;    // error! unable to convert from Byte to Vehicle
}
```

As you can see, ability to specify an underlying type for managed enums comes as a natural extension to C++, where enums can have only one underlying type—int.

Weak Enum Names

Try to compile the following code:

```
enum Jewelry { necklace, brooch, pin, ring, earring };
enum Phone { busy, ring, disconnect };
```

When processing the enum Phone, the compiler will complain: ring has already been defined in the same scope—as a member of the enum Jewelry. The symbol ring has become ambiguous.

A typical C programmer might solve this problem, known as *scope pollution*, by adding a cryptic prefix to each constant inside the enum:

```
enum Jewelry { jwNecklace, jwBrooch, jwPin, jwRing, jwEarring };
enum Phone { phBusy, phRing, phDisconnect };
```

Another possible solution is to use C++'s namespaces and classes. Defining each enum inside a separate namespace or class can eliminate the problem:

```
namespace Jewelry
{
    enum Jewelry { necklace, brooch, pin, ring, earring };
}
```

```
namespace Phone
{
    enum Phone { busy, ring, disconnect };
}
```

There are two ways to access an enum defined inside a namespace. The most obvious is to provide the explicitly qualified name:

```
void main()
{
    Phone::Phone p = Phone::ring;
}
```

The alternative is to use `using namespace`, which brings all the symbols from the specified namespace into the current scope—and therefore runs the risk of introducing other name collisions.

The good news about managed enums is that they are not subject to the scope pollution problem. The following code compiles:

```
#using <mscorlib.dll>
__value enum Jewelry { necklace, brooch, pin, ring, earring };
__value enum Phone { busy, ring, disconnect };
```

This works because MC++ solves scope pollution by using *weak enum names*. Weak enums can coexist with each other in the same scope, and can even coexist with other "strong" symbols:

```
int main()
{
    Jewelry jewelry = necklace;     // necklace is unambiguous
    int ring = 1;                // "strong" name
    // ring is ambiguous, explicit qualification required:
    Phone phone = Phone::ring;
    ring = Jewelry::ring;        // ring becomes 3
    int necklace = 0;           // defining "strong" necklace
    Jewelry jewelry2 = Jewelry::necklace;    // Jewelry::necklace is now weak!
}
```

In this example, three symbols with name `ring` coexist in the scope of the function `main`. Names of the enums are weak—therefore, to disambiguate them, an explicit qualification is needed.

Similarly, when the new symbol int `necklace` is defined, `Jewelry::necklace` becomes weak and needs a qualifier thereafter—this is because "strong" int `necklace` dominates weak `Jewelry::necklace`.

Visibility of Managed versus Unmanaged Enums

Managed enums follow the same visibility rules as other type definitions in MC++ (see Chapter 3). If you want to make your enum visible outside of the assembly, declare it public:

```
#using <mscorlib.dll>
public __value enum Color {red, green, blue};
```

Enums can be defined inside a class definition. Here is an example:

```
#using<mscorlib.dll>
__gc class Semaphore
{
    __value enum State {Signaled=1, Nonsignaled=0};
    State state_;
public:
    void Lock();
    void Unlock();
};
```

Remember that in MC++ you can use both managed and unmanaged enums—but if you define an enum inside a managed class, make the enum managed as well.

Another thing to keep in mind about unmanaged enums is that they are not visible outside the assembly. Even using the public keyword in front of the enum definition will not help—it is rejected by the compiler. The runtime does not understand unmanaged enums.

So, when to use managed enums and when to use unmanaged enums? The answer is rather straightforward: use managed enums whenever you want to take advantage of the "bonus" functionality they provide. However, if you are working with code written in regular C++, you can still use unmanaged enums. Everything will work as usual, but you will not get any of the extra functionality, and the unmanaged enums will not be accessible to the rest of the .NET world.

Summary

In this chapter, we have talked about a very special kind of value type: managed enums. As you have seen, the major benefits of managed enums over regular C++ are their ability to specify an underlying type and getting away from the problem of scope pollution by introducing the concept of weak enum names.

In the next chapter, we take up another concept of MC++ that has its roots in regular C++ as well as other languages—properties. You will see how to use managed properties, what you can and cannot do with them, and what benefits they provide.

CHAPTER 9
Properties

YOU HAVE HEARD ABOUT data encapsulation. Roughly speaking, what it means is that all data members should be hidden behind public interfaces. Quite often you might find yourself writing code like this:

```
class Student
{
    int age_;
    // . . .
public:
    // . . .
    int GetAge() { return age_; }
    void SetAge(int age) { age_=age; }
};
```

And then you might use class Student in the following manner:

```
int CompareByAge(Student* student1, Student* student2 )
{
    return student1->GetAge() - student2->GetAge();
}
```

What's wrong with this code? The data encapsulation principle is obeyed—but at the price of code readability.

And this is exactly when *properties* are useful. A convenient syntactic notation long enjoyed by Visual Basic programmers, properties have actually been around in Visual C++ for quite some time supported by __declspec(property). However, the __declspec(property) syntax wasn't very popular with C++ programmers.

Fortunately, properties have made their way into the .NET family of languages, including MC++. This chapter shows how to use scalar and indexed properties, explains what you can and cannot do with properties, and demonstrates how properties work.

Managed Properties: First Steps

Properties supported in MC++ are called *managed properties*. A property is declared using the __property keyword followed by a property method declaration. Note that the name of property methods must start with the prefix get_ or set_. The method with the get_ prefix is called a *getter* and the method with the set_ prefix is called a *setter*. The name of the getter must be the same as the name of the setter except for the prefix. Here is how you would rewrite the preceding example using managed properties:

```
#using<mscorlib.dll>
 __gc class Student
{
    int age_;
    // . . .
public:
    // . . .
    __property int get_Age() { return age_; }
    __property void set_Age(int age) { age_=age; }
};
```

Using properties is now just as simple as this:

```
int CompareByAge(Student* student1, Student* student2)
{
    return student1->Age - student2->Age;
}
```

As you can see, a property can be used like a data member. In this example, the compiler replaces Age with a call to the appropriate method, which in this context is get_Age.

Note the keyword __gc in front of the class declaration. Managed properties can only be declared in managed classes—that is, either gc classes or value types.

Scalar and Indexed Properties

The common language runtime supports two types of properties: *scalar* and *indexed*. The MC++ compiler also supports both of them.

A scalar property is defined by a getter that does not take any parameters and a setter that takes exactly one parameter. A property is indexed if the getter takes one or more parameters and the setter takes more than one parameter.

To illustrate managed properties, let's consider the following scenario. Imagine that you need to design a database of students. Given a student's name or ID, this simple database should be able to return the student's address. Here is how you can do it:

```
#using <mscorlib.dll>
using namespace System;
__gc class Student
{
    String* name_;
    String* address_;
    /* ... */
public:
    __property String* get_Address() { return address_; }
    __property void set_Address( String* address )
    { address_ = address; }
    /* ... */
};
__gc class Database
{
    Student* students_[];
    int MapNameToId( String* name );
public:
    __property String* get_Address( int id )
    {
        return students_[id]->Address;
    }
    __property String* get_Address( String* name )
    {
        int id = MapNameToId( name );
        return students_[id]->Address;
    }
protected:
    __property void set_Address( int id, String *address )
    {
        students_[id]->Address = address;
    }
    __property void set_Address( String* name, String *address )
    {
        int id = MapNameToId( name );
        students_[id]->Address = address;
    }
};
Database* OpenDatabase();
```

Access to a student's address(es) is now achieved as follows:

```
int main()
{
    Database* pDatabase = OpenDatabase();

    String* address1 = pDatabase->Address["John"];
    String* address2 = pDatabase->Address[89640];
}
```

In the preceding sample, method Student::get_Address takes no arguments and returns a String*. This is an example of a scalar property. In contrast, Database::get_Address takes an argument, an index. That's why this kind of property is called indexed.

Implementing Property Access Methods

As you may have noticed, there are actually two get_Address methods defined in the class Database. One of them takes a student ID (int) as a parameter, whereas the other one takes String*, which demonstrates that property methods can be overloaded.

Overall, getters and setters are just regular functions. Not only can they be overloaded, they can also be declared virtual, pure virtual, or static. Property methods don't have to have the same access level. As in the example in the preceding section, Database::get_Address is public but Database::set_Address is protected. Furthermore, a property does not have to have both a getter and a setter; having either one is enough to define a property.

If property methods are declared as static, no object is needed to access the property. This is similar to how you would access a static data member, as demonstrated here:

```
#using<mscorlib.dll>
using namespace System;
void main()
{
    // Print current directory
    Console::WriteLine( Environment::CurrentDirectory );
}
```

This example uses the BCL class Environment, with a property called CurrentDirectory. Note that because the property is static, no instance of the class Environment is required. The same result could be achieved by calling the getter get_CurrentDirectory, which is a static member function:

```
void PrintDir()
{
    // Print current directory
    Console::WriteLine( Environment::get_CurrentDirectory() );
}
```

If you are concerned about performance overhead associated with a function call when using a property—don't worry. Property methods can be inlined, the same way as regular C++ member functions.

Parameters of Property Access Methods

Let's go back to our class Student example presented earlier and look closer at the getter and the setter. As you can see, get_Age takes no arguments and returns an int (one could argue that unsigned char, for instance, would be more appropriate, but let's ignore that for now).

The setter, set_Age, is a method that takes int as an argument. Note that the type of the setter parameter is the same as the return type of the getter—int. The MC++ compiler requires these two types to be identical. That understood, we could now say that the property Age has type int.

When it comes to indexed properties, keep in mind that to assign a value to the property you must pass it in the *last* argument of the setter. Let's look at the class Database in the example in the section "Scalar and Indexed Properties" earlier. What if you mistakenly defined the set_Address methods with the wrong order of parameters? For example:

```
#using <mscorlib.dll>
using namespace System;
  __gc class Database
{
    // . . .
protected:
    __property void set_Address( String *address, int id )
    {
        students_[id]->Address = address;
    }
    __property void set_Address( String *address, String* name )
    {
        int id = MapNameToId( name );
        students_[id]->Address = address;
    }
};
```

In case of the first set_Address, you will get an error because the type of the setter's last argument (int) doesn't match the getter's return type (String*).

The second case is far more dangerous: the code will compile but produce wrong results. We will get back to this issue in the next section. For now, just remember that the last argument of the setter is used for passing a value to the property.

A well-designed property behaves exactly as if it were a public data member. Consider an example of using our class Student, defined earlier in this chapter:

```
void ResetAges(Student* student1, Student* student2)
{
    return student1->Age = student2->Age = 0;
}
```

This would certainly work if Age were a public data member of class Student. However, this code gives an error:

```
'Student::set_Age' : cannot convert parameter 1 from 'void' to 'int'
```

The problem lies in the return type of Student::set_Age, which is void. When properties are expanded into function calls, the compiler comes up with this:

```
void ResetAges(Student* student1, Student* student2)
{
    return student1->set_Age( student2->set_Age(0) );
}
```

This code doesn't work because student2->set_Age(0) returns void and there is no conversion from void to int.

The solution? Define your setter as a method returning the property type or a reference to the property type:

```
__property int set_Age(int age) { age_= age; return age_; }
```

Bear in mind, however, that this approach has certain performance implications—returning a variable doesn't come free. In some cases, the compiler can "optimize away" such overhead, but this is not always possible.

How Properties Work

When you define a property by declaring a getter or a setter, the MC++ compiler "pretends" a data member is defined. This data member is called a *pseudo* member because it doesn't actually exist. The compiler replaces the pseudo member in your code by a call to the appropriate method which, depending on the context, is either the getter or the setter:

```
#using <mscorlib.dll>
__gc class MyArray
{
    // ...
public:
    // ...
    __property int get_Length();
    __property void set_Length(int);
};

void IncrementLength( MyArray* pArray )
{
    int nLen = pArray->Length; // calls pArray->get_Length();
    pArray->Length = nLen + 1; // calls pArray->set_Length(nLen + 1);
}
```

Remember, we warned you in the last section that the value of the property must be passed in the last argument of the setter. Now it's time to shed some light on this situation. Here is how the compiler generates the function call for the setter: given an indexed property `Address`, the compiler will convert the expression

```
pDB->Address[S"John Smith"] = S"Seattle";
```

into

```
pDB->set_Address(S"John Smith", S"Seattle");
```

passing the value from the right side of the assignment in a last argument of the setter. That's why if this last argument expects anything else other than the new value of the property, you will not get the result you want.

What if you want to increment a property using `operator++`? You can do that as follows:

```
void IncrementLength2( MyArray* pArray )
{
    ++pArray->Length;
    // compiler generates:
    // pArray->set_Length( pArray->get_Length() + 1);
    pArray->Length++;
    // compiler generates:
    // int tmp; tmp = pArray->get_Length(),
    //     pArray->set_Length( tmp + 1), tmp;
}
```

As in unmanaged C++, the post-increment operator is less efficient than the pre-increment operator—it requires a temporary variable to hold the value of the property before the increment. Hence this advice: where you can, consider using a pre-increment operator instead of a post-increment operator.

What You Cannot Do with Properties

As we said earlier, a good property behaves like a data member. Is there anything you can do with a data member but not with a property? Unfortunately, yes. Let's recall the earlier example with class `Student`. Consider the following:

```
#using <mscorlib.dll>
__gc class Student
{
    int age_;
    // ...
public:
    // ...
    __property int get_Age() { return age_; }
    __property void set_Age(int age) { age_=age; }
    void Birthday();
};
void IncrementAge( int* pAge )
{
    (*pAge)++;
}
void Student::Birthday()
```

```
{
    IncrementAge( &Age ); // error!
}
```

With what you now know about properties, it should come as no surprise that this code won't work. Still wondering why? Look at the call to IncrementAge—the function expects a parameter of type int*, but the property, Age, is provided instead. What can the compiler do? The pseudo member Age can be replaced with either get_Age or set_Age, neither of which would yield the desired result. That's why *taking address of a property is illegal*—and results in a compile-time error.

There is also one restriction to overloading property methods. Examine the following code:

```
#using <mscorlib.dll>
using namespace System;
__gc class Product
{
    // . . .
};
__gc class Inventory
{
    // . . .
public:
    // . . .
    __property int get_ItemsSold(int ProductID);
    __property void set_ItemsSold(int ProductID, int value);
    __property int get_ItemsSold() __gc[];*/ // error!
};
void SellProduct( Inventory* pInventory, int ProductID )
{
    pInventory->ItemsSold[ProductID]++;
}
```

As you can see, the method get_ItemsSold is overloaded: the first function takes one argument (int), and the other one takes no arguments but returns a managed array. Now we have an ambiguity problem in the function SellProduct: how do you convert the property ItemsSold into a getter/setter function call? It is impossible to determine from the context whether either of the methods int get_ItemsSold(int) or int get_ItemsSold()__gc [] should be called. So, what we want you to take away from this is *an array property declaration shall not overload an indexed property*.

Summary

As this chapter has shown, managed properties are easy to use because the syntax for defining them is much simpler than that of regular C++ properties. Being syntactic sugar for function calls, properties behave like data members, making code that uses them cleaner and easier to understand.

In the next chapter, we will dive into another advanced topic of MC++—operators. Like properties, operators provide a more natural way of coding by hiding function calls "under the hood." You will see how to define and use operators and user-defined conversions for value types as well as gc classes.

CHAPTER 10

Operators

ONE OF THE MANY FEATURES of C++ is its ability to extend itself by means of operators. There are two kind of operators that can be defined by the user: *infix
operators* and *conversion operators* (also called *user-defined conversions*, or
UDC). This chapter will review how to define and use operators in C++ and then
show how things work in the managed world.

Back to C++

Defining infix operators, such as +, -, *, /, and others, provides an intuitive interface to the users of your class, which lets them program in the language of the
problem domain. For example, when dealing with matrixes, it is natural to use
the mathematical symbols + and – rather than the functions add and sub:

```
class Matrix
{
    // ...
public:
    Matrix(unsigned int width, unsigned int height);
    Matrix operator+(const Matrix& c) const;
    Matrix operator-(const Matrix& c) const;

Matrix operator+(double d) const;
    Matrix operator-(double d) const;
};
int main()
{
    Matrix a(5,6);
    Matrix b(5,6);
    // ...
    Matrix c = a + b;  // calls operator+(const Matrix&)
    Matrix d = c + 10; // calls operator+(double)
}
```

Operators also provide uniformity with the built-in types, which means a class with the operators looks and feels like a built-in type. This is why `Matrix d = c + 10` works. (Note: there is a problem with this code, which will be discussed a little later in the section "Infix Managed Operators.")

Because you redefine the existing meaning of an operator, this process is also known as *operator overloading.*

Overloaded operators are sometimes more than just syntactic sugar for function calls. They can also provide semantic integrity for your class. For instance, classes that have member pointers to objects frequently need a specialized assignment operator in order to copy the objects being pointed to.

Conversion operators extend the functionality of your class in a different way—they allow your class to be converted to another type. For example, imagine that you are implementing an image-processing program for weather forecasts. The input to this program is satellite images of the temperature of the Earth's surface.

To keep the size of the images small, you decide to store the temperature in a 16-bit integer instead of using a floating-point type. Class Temperature would be defined thus:

```
class Temperature
{
    short int temp_;
    static const int nFactor_ = 100;
public:
    Temperature(double temp) : temp_((short int)(temp *  nFactor_)) {}
    operator double() { return (double)temp_ / (double)nFactor_; }
};
void main()
{
    Temperature Seattle(42.5);
    Temperature Madrid(71.25);
    double AverageTemp = (Madrid + Seattle)/2;
}
```

Class `Temperature` stores 42.5 (the temperature in Seattle) as integer value 4250. User-defined conversion to type `double` divides the value by 100, getting back the original temperature 42.5.

When the compiler concludes that no standard conversions can take place, it looks for user-defined conversions. If there is one, the compiler executes it. In our example, when the compiler encounters the expression `Madrid + Seattle`, it finds a user-defined conversion from class `Temperature` to `double` and executes it.

Infix Managed Operators

What is a managed operator? The operators described earlier were declared inside unmanaged classes. Simply put, we'll call them unmanaged operators. Accordingly, *managed* operators are those declared inside managed classes.

Some languages, such as C++ and C#, have the ability to define operators. Others, such as Java and Visual Basic, do not. Similarly, although the common language runtime allows operator overloading, not all .NET languages are able to take advantage of it. Managed C++ is one of those that can—but with certain restrictions, as you will see in this chapter.

The syntax for defining managed operators is different from that of unmanaged operators. First, managed operators do not use the keyword `operator`. Operators in the common language runtime were designed so that if a language is not able to make use of them "the easy way" (for instance, using infix notation), it can do it "the hard way," that is, by using the underlying function name.

All operators are written using specially-called static member functions whose names start with op_. For instance, the operator + is implemented by function `op_Addition,` and so on (you can find the complete list in Table 10-1). If a language, such as VB, cannot use operator + via infix notation (that is, a+b), it can still do it by calling `op_Addition` explicitly: `MyClass.op_Addition(a,b)`.

Table 10-1. Common Language Runtime Operator Names

BINARY OPERATORS		UNARY OPERATORS	
op_Addition	+	op_Increment	++
op_Assign	=	op_Decrement	−
op_BitwiseAnd	&	op_Negation	-
op_BitwiseOr	|	op_UnaryNegation	-
op_Division	/	op_UnaryPlus	+
op_Equality	==		
op_ExclusiveOr	^		
op_GreaterThan	>		
op_GreaterThanOrEqual	>=		
op_Inequality	!=		
op_LeftShift	<<		
op_LessThan	<		
op_LessThanOrEqual	<=		
op_LogicalAnd	&&		
op_LogicalOr	||		
op_Modulus	%		
op_Multiply	*		
op_RightShift	>>		
op_Subtraction	-		

In fact, this isn't much different from how unmanaged operators work. From the C++ compiler point of view, an operator is a normal function—yes, with a weird name, but still just a function.

If so, why not stick with tried-and-true operator syntax and leave the job of generating op_ methods to the compiler? Because these methods are static and the unmanaged operators are not. What's wrong with the operators not being static? For the answer, let's return to the earlier example featuring class Matrix. We told you it has a problem, remember? Try to rewrite

```
Matrix d = c + 10;
```

as

```
Matrix d = 10 + c;
```

This will result in a compile-time error, which, of course, violates the principle of commutativity for matrixes—something you want to maintain in order for your class to look and feel like a built-in type (and like a real matrix). For this code to compile, there must be an addition operator that can take an int or double as the left-hand argument.

Obviously, the straightforward solution is to define such an operator. Because you cannot add an operator to type double, a global operator is your usual choice. Since it has to have access to nonpublic methods of the class, it also has to be declared friend inside the class. That's not very elegant, is it? Besides, global functions do not exist in the .NET Framework, so the C++ language was extended to allow definition of operators in terms of static member functions.

Well, enough theory. If you can't wait to define your first managed operator, here is an example of a value class Matrix, which uses managed operators for addition and subtraction:

```
#using <mscorlib.dll>
using namespace System;
__value class Matrix
{
    // . . .
public:
    Matrix(UInt32 width, UInt32 height);
    static Matrix op_Addition(Matrix a, Matrix b);
    static Matrix op_Subtraction(Matrix a, Matrix b);

    static Matrix op_Addition(double a, Matrix b);
    static Matrix op_Subtraction(double a, Matrix b);
    static Matrix op_Addition(Matrix a, double b);
    static Matrix op_Subtraction(Matrix a, double b);

    static bool op_Equality(Matrix l, Matrix r);
};
void main()
{
    Matrix a(10,15);
    Matrix b(10,15);
    // . . .
    Matrix c = (a - b) + 10;
    Matrix d = 10 + (a - b);
```

```
        if( c == d )
        {
            Console::WriteLine(S"All right");
        }
    }
```

In this example, class `Matrix` defines two arithmetical operators, `op_Addition` and `op_Subtraction`, and a logical operator, `op_Equality`. When the compiler encounters addition or subtraction operators applied to objects of class `Matrix`, it translates them into corresponding function calls. Thus, `(a - b) + 10` gets translated into `Matrix::op_Addition(Matrix::op_Subtraction(a, b), 10)` and `c == d` into `Matrix::op_Equality(c, d)`.

Increment and Decrement Operators

Regular C++ allows you to implement post- and pre-increment operators (that is, x++ and ++x) differently. This is very rarely useful, and the syntax is difficult to remember. (Do you still remember which one is written with a dummy `int` argument?) So, in most cases one operator is implemented in terms of the other: post-increment calls pre-increment and returns the value of the object before the increment. Decrement operators work similarly.

Things are different in MC++. There is only one managed operator for each operation—op_Increment and op_Decrement. The implementation of an operator must return the new (that is, changed) object. The compiler will do the rest.

Here is how you could implement an increment operator for class `Month`, which can only hold values from 1 to 12. (The decrement operator is written using op_Decrement and is analogous.)

```
#using <mscorlib.dll>
__value class Month
{
    int value_;
public:
    Month(int month) : value_(month) {};
    static Month op_Increment(Month month)
    {
        month.value_ = month.value_ == 12 ? 1 : month.value_+1;
        return month;
    }
};
int main()
```

```
{
    Month m(12);
    ++m;  // the compiler generates: m = Month::op_Increment(m);
    m++;  // the compiler generates:
    // Month tmp=m, m = Month::op_Increment(m), tmp;
}
```

Note that the post-increment operator (m++) is translated into a comma expression, the result of which is the object before changing. This is what makes post-increment operators less efficient than pre-increment operators. In fact, this is no different from regular C++, except that there the inefficiency is more evident, because you create the temporary object yourself when implementing the post-increment operator.

If you are careless, post-increment operators can be worse than just inefficient—they can lead to results different from what you would expect in expressions like m=m++ or AddMonths(m++, m). Such expressions are ambiguous and you should avoid them.

The conclusion: once you have implemented one op_ . . . method, both post- and pre-increment (decrement) operators become available—but you should call the former only when you really need its specific behavior and prefer the latter in all other cases.

User-Defined Conversions

A conversion is called *explicit* if it requires a type cast. This raises the programmer's awareness about the dangerous nature of the conversion. For example, the conversion from double to int is explicit because it can lose precision:

```
double dSpeed = 45.5;
int nSpeed = (int)dSpeed;
```

Conversely, an *implicit* conversion doesn't need a cast:

```
double dSpeed = 45; // conversion from int do double
```

It is natural to think of an implicit conversion as a conversion that doesn't lose any information, such as the conversion from int to double.

Only one kind of conversion operator can be defined in a C++ class: operator double of class Temperature will always be called when you convert Temperature to double—whether you cast it or not.

Not so in Managed C++. You are given the freedom to define either an implicit or explicit conversion, or both. To keep the legacy of C++, in the absence of an explicit conversion, an implicit conversion can also be invoked by a cast.

Conversion operators are written using static methods op_Implicit and op_Explicit; the former is used for implicit conversion, whereas the latter is used for explicit conversions.

Now let's go back to the example with class Temperature shown earlier. We will rewrite class Temperature, making it a value type:

```
#using <mscorlib.dll>
using namespace System;
__value class Temperature
{
    short int temp_;
    static const int nFactor_ = 100;
public:
    Temperature(double temp) { temp_ = (short int)(temp *  nFactor_); }
    static double op_Implicit(Temperature t)
        { return (double)t.temp_ / (double)nFactor_; }
    static int op_Explicit(Temperature t) { return (int)(t.temp_ / nFactor_); }
};

void main()
{
    Temperature Seattle(42.5);
    Temperature Madrid(71.25);

    double dAverageTemp = (Madrid + Seattle)/2;          // implicit conversion
    int iAverageTemp = ((int)Madrid + (int)Seattle)/2; // explicit conversion

    Console::WriteLine(dAverageTemp);
    Console::WriteLine(iAverageTemp);
}
```

In this example, class Temperature defines an implicit conversion to double and an explicit conversion to int. When executed, the program prints:

```
56.875
56
```

Watch Out for Ambiguities

As usual, along with the new functionality come different ways to misuse it. For example, imagine that, being overly defensive, you decide to define both conversions (to int and to double) as explicit:

```
#using <mscorlib.dll>
using namespace System;
__value class Temperature
{
    short int temp_;
    static const int nFactor_ = 100;
public:
    Temperature(double temp) { temp_ = (short int)(temp * nFactor_); }
    static double op_Explicit(Temperature t)
        { return (double)t.temp_ / (double)nFactor_; }
    static int op_Explicit(Temperature t)
        { return (int)(t.temp_ / nFactor_); }
};
```

This might not be a bad idea—having to explicitly cast an object to the desired type can improve code readability and make it less error-prone. But look closer at these two functions: these overloaded functions differ only by the return type!

Although this is not valid in C++, Managed C++ has to allow this as a special case. In fact, this is no different than defining different conversion operators on the same C++ class, which is, of course, perfectly valid.

So, what is the problem? In languages that do not support user-defined conversions, a programmer must call the op_Explicit method explicitly to achieve the desired effect. However, such a function call would be ambiguous:

```
Temperature::op_Explicit(Seattle); // error: convert to int or to double?
```

In some cases, even the MC++ compiler will not be able to find the right function. Consider:

```
char cMadrid = (char)Madrid;
```

This code would give an ambiguity error: "Ambiguous user-defined conversion." Should Madrid be converted first to double and then char or to int and then to char?

Defining both explicit and implicit conversion to the same type is another example of a poor design. Consider this:

```
#using <mscorlib.dll>
__value class Temperature
{
    short int temp_;
    static const int nFactor_ = 100;
public:
    Temperature(double temp) { temp_ = (short int)(temp *  nFactor_); }
    static double op_Explicit(Temperature t) { return t.temp_ / nFactor_; }
    static double op_Implicit(Temperature t) { return t.temp_ / nFactor_; }
};
void main()
{
    Temperature Seattle(42.5);
    double dSeattle = (double)Seattle; // error! op_Implicit or op_Explicit ?
}
```

It is unclear whether the compiler should call op_Explicit or op_Implicit to convert the object Seattle to double. Furthermore, because the cast invokes an implicit conversion in the absence of the explicit one, the code will silently change its meaning if, during future maintenance, function op_Explicit ceases to exist.

As these examples show, the compiler never tries to second-guess a programmer's intentions. Instead, it asks you to specify exactly what you want. By making it difficult to abuse a feature, the compiler helps you write code that is easier to understand and less prone to errors.

Convert-To versus Convert-From Operators

Now, once again, let's go back to the earlier example with class Temperature. How many user-defined conversions are there? One?

Actually, there are two: the constructor Temperature::Temperature(double) is also a user-defined conversion! But unlike the other conversion operator (operator double) that defines a conversion *to* some other type, the constructor defines a conversion *from* a type.

Managed C++ does not support convert-from operators—it has unary constructors[1] for these purposes. This means you still can define a convert-from

---

[1]   Constructors that take a single argument.

operator, but to use it in MC++, you have to call it by its given name because it isn't called implicitly. Here is how:

```
#using <mscorlib.dll>
public __value class Temperature
{
    short int temp_;
    static const int nFactor_ = 100;
public:
    static Temperature op_Implicit (double temp)
    { Temperature theTemp; theTemp.temp_ = temp * nFactor_; return theTemp; }
};
```

Now using the class Temperature in a C# program is as simple as this:

```
using System;
public class UsingTemperature
{
    public static int Main(String[] args)
    {
        Temperature t = 50;
        return 0;
    }
}
```

Note that if the convert-from operator were defined as op_Explicit, you would have to cast the value explicitly in the C# program this way:

```
Temperature t = (Temperature)50;
```

Value Types versus Gc Classes

So far in this chapter, we have only defined operators on value types, not gc classes. Does this mean managed operators are limited to value types? Not quite. Let's try to define managed operators on the gc class Matrix and see what happens:

```
#using <mscorlib.dll>
using namespace System;
__gc class Matrix
```

```
{
    // . . .
public:
    Matrix(UInt32 width, UInt32 height);
    static Matrix* op_Addition(Matrix* a, Matrix* b);
    static Matrix* op_Subtraction(Matrix* a, Matrix* b);
    // . . .
};
```

Now when it comes to calling the operator, you might expect the following to work:

```
int main()
{
    Matrix* pA = new Matrix(10,15);
    Matrix* pB = new Matrix(10,15);
    Matrix* pSum = pA + pB;      // oops!
}
```

But it doesn't! The compiler gives a compile-time error: "unable to perform pointer arithmetic on managed type `Matrix __gc*`."

This is not a bug in the compiler. Indeed, the operator + is applied to the *pointers*, not objects! And you want to add two objects, not pointers. Therefore, the error is completely legitimate.

Perhaps you might want to try this:

```
Matrix* pSum = *pA + *pB;
```

However, when compiled, this code will produce errors:

```
error C2664: 'Matrix::op_Addition' : cannot convert parameter 1 from 'Matrix' to
'Matrix __gc *'
No user-defined-conversion operator available that can perform this conversion,
or the operator cannot be called
```

There are at least two problems with this code. First, as the error message suggests, the function `op_Addition` expects pointers, not objects. That's the way you defined it because gc classes cannot be passed by value. Second, even if it worked, the result of the addition of two objects must be an object, not a pointer, as defined by `op_Addition`.

The truth is, if you define an operator on a gc class using pointers, there is no way to call it other than through a explicit function call (that is,

`Matrix* pSum = Matrix::op_Addition(pA,pB);).` However, other languages can still use it. If you make class `Matrix` public, it can be used from C# with no problem.

What about Gc References?

Fortunately, references offer a solution. Because the runtime does not make a difference between gc references and gc pointers (more about this in Chapter 6), you can take advantage of the "object" semantics without having to pass the gc object by value—which you cannot do.

Here is how to define the operators using references:

```
#using <mscorlib.dll>
using namespace System;
__gc class Matrix
{
    // . . .
public:
    Matrix(UInt32 width, UInt32 height);
    static Matrix& op_Addition(Matrix& a, Matrix& b);
    static Matrix& op_Subtraction(Matrix& a, Matrix& b);
    // . . .
};
```

Using the operator is pretty straightforward:

```
int main()
{
    Matrix* pA = new Matrix(10,15);
    Matrix* pB = new Matrix(10,15);
    Matrix* pSum = &(*pA + *pB);
}
```

Note the & in the last statement. Because the sum of two matrixes is a matrix, you have to take the address of the result to assign it to pSym, a pointer. Of course, you can define `op_Addition` as a function that returns `Matrix*` instead of `Matrix&`, which would make taking the address of the result unnecessary. However, this would be a rather shortsighted solution—try to sum three matrixes in one statement and you'll see why:

```
*pA + *pB + *pC; // error, cannot add Matrix* to Matrix
```

Yes, the & is a bit cumbersome, and you can avoid it if you don't mix pointers with references. Just use references everywhere you can and you'll see how nice and easy it becomes:

```
void main()
{
    Matrix& a = *new Matrix(10,15);
    Matrix& b = *new Matrix(10,15);
    Matrix& sum = a + b; // wow!
}
```

The lesson is when defining an operator on a gc class, use references, not pointers. References allow the operator to be used in MC++ programs as well as in all other languages.

Summary

The concept of user-defined operators is represented quite differently in C++ and in the CLR. In MC++, the language was extended to allow definitions of operators in terms of static member functions—as they work in CLR. As you have seen, this works very well for value types, but for gc classes you have to remember to use gc references as parameters of the operator.

A user-defined conversion is another useful type of an operator. You can define explicit and implicit conversions. Sometimes this may lead to ambiguities, and we've discussed how to avoid them.

In the next chapter, we will discuss another way of extending the functionality of your class—by means of attributes.

CHAPTER 11

Attributes

DECLARATIVE PROGRAMMING IS A WAY of describing algorithms at a higher level than simple program statements involving low-level constructs such as loops and jumps. In this programming paradigm, what is needed in a computation is specified via declarative statements, and the details of how it is achieved are left to the compiler.

Previous versions of the Visual C++ compiler worked in conjunction with the Microsoft Interface Definition Language (MIDL) compiler to develop COM applications. MIDL describes COM types using attributes. An *attribute* is a declarative annotation attached in an *attribute block* (a declaration in a pair of square brackets) to a syntactic element such as a class, function, and parameter. An attribute consists of an attribute name and an optional list of arguments. Multiple attributes within an attribute block are separated by commas.

Here is an example of a COM interface that has attributes:

```
// IPublisher interface with one method
[object, uuid(F1D97BEC-6614-4e11-8C90-8E0D8AAB666B)]
interface IPublisher: IUnknown
{
    [id(0x01)]HRESULT GetLatestBook([in] BSTR author, [out,retval] BSTR *title);
};
```

The attributes `object` and `uuid` are applied to the interface, the attribute `id` is applied to the method, and the attributes `in`, `out`, and `retval` are applied to the function parameters. These attributes are predefined keywords in MIDL.

Attributes in Visual C++ .NET extend the C++ language (using DLLs called *attribute providers*) by injecting code at compile time. They are used to simplify native application development with COM and managed application development with the .NET Framework.

In this chapter, attributes in the context of COM programming are not discussed. Only the attributes in the managed contexts (also known as *custom attributes*) are described. We use attributes and custom attributes interchangeably in this book.

Custom Attributes

In MC++, custom attributes are the declarative annotations added to syntactic elements such as a class, data member, return type, parameter, or member function. Custom attributes have the same syntax used for IDL attributes. The attribute block of a custom attribute consists of a constructor call followed by an optional list of field/property names that are assigned values. When a custom attribute is applied to a syntactic element, the metadata for that syntactic element is *extended* with the information in that attribute.

There are two types of attributes—predefined and user-defined. Some of the predefined attributes are `System::AttributeUsageAttribute` (used to define user-defined custom attributes), `System::Runtime::InteropServices::DllImportAttribute` (used to call native C functions), `System::CLSCompliantAttribute` (ensures that the CLS-compliancy rules are followed), and `System::Runtime::InteropServices::StructLayoutAttribute` (describes the layout of a managed class). In an attribute block, the use of the suffix `Attribute` of an attribute name is optional. You can refer to an attribute without the suffix (for instance, `DllImport`). As their qualified names indicate, predefined attributes are defined under the `System` namespace directly or in a nested namespace.

User-defined attributes are managed classes (gc classes and value classes) that inherit from `System::Attribute`. To define a gc class as a custom attribute, you can use the BCL class `System::Attribute` as the base class and/or you can apply the attribute `System::AttributeUsageAttribute` to the gc class. In the absence of explicit declaration of the `System::Attribute` class as the base class, the MC++ compiler inserts it as a base class when `System::AttributeUsageAttribute` is applied on the class. The primary difference between defining an attribute using `System::Attribute` and `System::AttributeUsageAttribute` is that the latter allows you to choose the targets on which the attribute can be applied, whereas the former has the default of all syntactic elements as targets. We will show the list of all targets later in this chapter.

Defining a Custom Attribute with System::Attribute

The following example shows a user-defined attribute that inherits from `System::Attribute`:

```
#using<mscorlib.dll>
using namespace System;
using namespace System::Runtime::InteropServices;
```

```
public __gc struct MyAttribute : Attribute {
   String* str;
   MyAttribute(String* name) : str(name){}
};
[MyAttribute(S"My Custom String")]
public __gc struct AManagedClass {
};
```

In this code, the class `MyAttribute` is a user-defined custom attribute. This attribute can be applied to any syntactic entity related to a managed type (gc class, value type, or an interface). In this example, the custom attribute is applied to the gc class `AManagedClass`.[1]

The following listing shows partial metadata for the two classes in the code sample:

```
.class public auto ansi MyAttribute extends [mscorlib]System.Attribute {
   // text stripped
} // end of class MyAttribute

.class public auto ansi AManagedClass  extends [mscorlib]System.Object {
  // text stripped
.custom instance void MyAttribute::.ctor(string) =
         ( 01 00 10 4D 79 20 43 75 73 74 6F 6D 20 53 74 72   // ... My
Custom Str
                                69 6E 67 00 00 )             // ing..
  // text stripped
} // end of class AManagedClass
```

Notice the custom attribute in the metadata for the class `AManagedClass`, which shows the encoding for the string `My Custom String`. You can apply the attribute `MyCustomAttribute` to any syntactic element that can be a target. The enumerator `System::AttributeTargets` specifies all possible targets. We will show the list of targets in the next section.

Defining an Attribute with AttributeUsageAttribute

You have seen how to create and use an attribute that inherits from `System::Attribute`. You can also define an attribute using the predefined

---

[1] If the attribute has a default constructor and you want to use that constructor, you can specify the attribute name in the attribute block without the parentheses. For example, if `MyAttr` attribute has a default constructor, and if it can be applied on gc classes, you can use it on a gc class as `[MyAttr] __gc struct S{};`

attribute called `AttributeUsageAttribute` in the
`System::Runtime::InteropServices` namespace.

The `AttributeUsageAttribute` class inherits from `System::Attribute` and is
a sealed value type. It has a constructor that takes one parameter that indicates
what the attribute targets are. `AttributeUsage` has three properties that can be
initialized by passing arguments when `AttributeUsage` is applied to a user-
defined class:

- `ValidOn`: This positional parameter specifies the targets of the custom
  attribute such as class and method. The default is all targets.

- `AllowMultiple`: This named parameter indicates whether a specified custom attribute can be applied multiple times on a given target. The default
  is false.

- `Inherited`: This named parameter specifies whether a particular custom
  attribute can be inherited by derived classes and overriding methods. The
  default is false.

In this section, you will learn to declare a simple attribute that can only be
applied to a gc class. Suppose that you need documentation tracking during
a software project implemented in MC++. Typically, during the early phase
of a software development cycle, it is common to have classes that need to be
implemented and documented. Custom attributes can be used to track the status
of the implementation and documentation.

```
// filename: DocAttribute.cpp
#using<mscorlib.dll>
using namespace System;
// Define custom attribute
[AttributeUsage(AttributeTargets::Class)]
public __gc class  DocumentationAttr {
public:
    DocumentationAttr(String *str) : m_DocStr(str){}
    __property String *get_DocStr() {
            return m_DocStr;
    }
private:
    String *m_DocStr;
};
```

Here, the predefined custom attribute `AttributeUsageAttribute` is applied to
the gc class `DocumentationAttr` to define a user-defined custom attribute. The
custom attribute class `DocumentationAttr` is defined to target gc classes only. This

is similar to any predefined custom attribute (for example,
`System::ObsoleteAttribute`) that can be applied to gc classes.
`AttributeUsageAttribute` extends the metadata for the gc class
`DocumentationAttr`, which can be seen by looking at the metadata generated.

You can compile this sample code into an assembly DLL that can be
imported by applications that use the attribute.

The enumerator `System::AttributeTargets` defines the possible targets for
a custom attribute. The enumeration values defined are:

- `All`: Attribute can be applied to any syntactic element.

- `Assembly`: Attribute can be applied to an assembly. This target has a special
  syntax; the attribute name in an attribute block should have the prefix
  `assembly:` (for instance, if `MyAttr` is a custom attribute with a constructor
  taking an `int`, the assembly attribute can be specified as
  `[assembly:MyAttr(12)];`).

- `Class`: Attribute can be applied to a gc class.

- `Constructor`: Attribute can be applied to a constructor.

- `Delegate`: Attribute can be applied to a delegate (delegates are discussed in
  Chapter 12).

- `Enum`: Attribute can be applied to an enumeration.

- `Event`: Attribute can be applied to an event (events are discussed in
  Chapter 13).

- `Field`: Attribute can be applied to a data member.

- `Interface`: Attribute can be applied to a gc interface.

- `Method`: Attribute can be applied to a member function.

- `Module`: Attribute can be applied to a netmodule. Similar to the `Assembly`
  target, this attribute has a special syntax. The attribute name in an attribute block should have the prefix `module:`. (Refer to Appendix C for
  a discussion on assemblies and netmodules.)

- `Parameter`: Attribute can be applied to a parameter.

- `Property`: Attribute can be applied to a property.

- `ReturnValue`: Attribute can be applied to a return value. Similar to the `Assembly` attribute, this attribute has a special syntax. The attribute name in an attribute block should have the prefix `returnvalue:`.

- `Struct`: Attribute can be applied to a value class.

These targets can be combined with the bit-wise `OR` operation (`|`) to form an argument to the constructor `AttributeUsageAttribute` so that an attribute can be applied to more than one target.

So far, you have seen how to define a custom attribute. The following example shows how to use the user-defined custom attribute defined previously.[2]

```
#using <mscorlib.dll>
#using "DocAttribute.dll" // from the previous sample
using namespace System;
// Attach custom attribute to a class
[DocumentationAttr("to be implemented")]
public __gc
class AClass  {
      // . . .
};
// Attach custom attribute to another class
[DocumentationAttr("to be documented")]
public __gc
class BClass  {
   public:
      void Func(){}
};
```

In this code, DocumentationAttr is applied to two gc classes, AClass and BClass. So, the metadata for these two gc classes is extended with the custom attribute DocumentationAttr.

At this point, you know how to define a user-defined custom attribute and how to use it on its targets. The following code shows how to retrieve the custom attribute information applied on a syntactic element. You can merge this code with the previous code sample to generate an executable assembly.

```
// Print the the contents of the custom attribute 'MyCustomAttr'
void PrintDocumentationAttrContents(Type* pT) {
   // Access custom attributes for an Object via CLR Reflection
   Object* pObjs __gc[] = Attribute::GetCustomAttributes(pT);
```

---

[2]   The example is split into two code snippets, the first of which is shown here. You need to keep them together in one file to compile and execute.

```
        for(int i=0; i < pObjs->Length; i++) {
            if(pObjs[i]->GetType()->Equals(__typeof(DocumentationAttr))) {
                Console::Write(pT->ToString());
                Console::Write(S" is  ");
                Console::WriteLine(static_cast<DocumentationAttr*>(pObjs[i])->DocStr);
            }
        }
}
int main() {
    Type* pT = __typeof(AClass);
    PrintDocumentationAttrContents(pT);
    pT = __typeof(BClass);
    PrintDocumentationAttrContents(pT);
}
```

The class System::Type represents a type in the .NET Framework. It is the primary class used in all reflection operations on types. (More on this class can be found in Appendix C.) The custom attributes on a gc class can be observed using reflection via the method Attribute::GetCustomAttributes, which returns all custom attributes defined on the type as a gc array of Object* pointers. Searching the gc array for DocumentationAttr returns the custom attribute instance of DocumentationAttr attached to the gc class. Note that the keyword __typeof takes the name of a type as the argument and returns a managed object of type System::Type*. Refer to the documentation on the System::Attribute class to see how the overloaded functions Attribute::GetCustomAttributes can be used to retrieve information about attributes.

The output of the program is

```
AClass is  to be implemented
BClass is  to be documented
```

Defining an Inheritable Attribute with Multiple Targets

Here is an example that uses all three parameters. We extend the previous code sample so that it can be applied to methods, too.[3]

```
#using<mscorlib.dll>
#include <assert.h>
```

---

[3] We split the code sample into three parts, the first of which appears here. To compile the code sample, you need to keep all three parts together in one file.

```
using namespace System;
using namespace System::Reflection;

// Define custom attribute
[AttributeUsage(AttributeTargets::Class|AttributeTargets::Method, AllowMultiple =
true, Inherited = true)]
public __gc class  DocumentationAttr {
public:
      DocumentationAttr(String *str) : m_DocStr(str){}
      __property String *get_DocStr() {
                return m_DocStr;
      }
private:
      String *m_DocStr;
};
```

In this code, the user-defined custom attribute `DocumentationAttr` is defined
with the `AttributeUsage` attribute specifying different targets. The targets now
include member functions along with gc classes. This attribute can be inherited
and applied multiple times on the same target.

The parameters in an attribute block that have a name followed by a value
are called *named parameters*. In an attribute block, you can initialize named
parameters by using their names after the attribute constructor. In the preceding
example, the parameters `AllowMultiple` and `Inherited` are named parameters.
The remaining parameters in an attribute block are called *positional parameters*.
In the previous code sample, `ValidOn` is a positional parameter that takes the
value `AttributeTargets::Class|AttributeTargets::Method`. Note that the named
parameters `AllowMultiple` and `Inherited` are public properties of
`AttributeUsageAttribute`. An important point to know is that the named parameters of an attribute must be serializable.

The valid types for parameters (both positional and named) to an attribute
are integral types, `float`, `double`, `wchar_t`, `char*`, `wchar_t*`, `System::String*`,
`System::Type*`, `enum`, and a one-dimensional array of any of these types. All attribute parameters should have public accessibility.

The MC++ compiler allows a simplified syntax to define a custom attribute.
The attribute block in the previous code sample can be replaced with:

```
[attribute(Class|Method, AllowMultiple = true, Inherited = true)]
```

The attribute `AttributeUsage` is replaced by the identifier `attribute`, and the
enumerators don't need to have qualifications.

The following code shows how to apply the user-defined attribute to
multiple targets:

```
// Attach custom attribute to a class
[DocumentationAttr("to be documented")]
public __gc
class AClass {
  public:
    [DocumentationAttr("to be implemented")]
    [DocumentationAttr("to be documented")]
    virtual void VirtualFunc() {
        // ...
    }
};

// Inheritable custom attributes get attached
public __gc
class BClass : public AClass {
  public:
    void VirtualFunc() {
        // ...
    }
};
```

In this code, the user-defined custom attribute DocumentationAttr is applied to the gc class AClass and its member function VirtualFunc, which is a virtual function. Note that the attribute is applied two times on this function. The gc class BClass inherits from AClass and overrides the method VirtualFunc. The custom attribute on the member function VirtualFunc in BClass is inherited from the overridden function in the base class AClass.

The following code inspects the custom attributes and prints each message in the CustomStr property:

```
//Print the the contents of the custom attribute 'DocumentationAttr'
void PrintCustomAttrContents(Object* pT) {

    Object *pObjs __gc[] = 0;
    MemberInfo *mem;

    Type *typ = dynamic_cast<Type *>(pT);
    if (typ != 0) {
        // argument's type is Type *
        pObjs = Attribute::GetCustomAttributes(static_cast<Type *>(pT));
    }
```

```
        else {
            mem  = dynamic_cast<MemberInfo *>(pT);
            if (mem != 0) {
                // argument's type is MemberInfo *
                pObjs = Attribute::GetCustomAttributes(static_cast<MemberInfo *>(pT));
            }
            else {
                assert (!"Unknown parameter passed");
            }
        }

        //Access custom attributes for an Object via Reflection
        if (pObjs != 0) {
            for(int i=0; i < pObjs->Length; i++) {
                if(pObjs[i]->GetType()->Equals(__typeof(DocumentationAttr))) {
                    if (typ != 0) {
                        Console::Write(S"Class  '");
                    }
                    else {
                        Console::Write(S"   Member function '");
                    }
                    Console::Write(pT->ToString());
                    Console::Write(S"' is  ");
                    Console::WriteLine(static_cast<DocumentationAttr*>
                                        (pObjs[i])->DocStr);
                }
            }
        }
}

int main() {
    Type* pT = __typeof(AClass);
    PrintCustomAttrContents(pT);

    MemberInfo *m __gc[]  = __typeof(AClass)->GetMember("VirtualFunc");
    PrintCustomAttrContents(m[0]);

    pT = __typeof(BClass);
    PrintCustomAttrContents(pT);

    m = __typeof(BClass)->GetMember("VirtualFunc");
    PrintCustomAttrContents(m[0]);
}
```

The function `PrintCustomAttrContents` extracts the custom attributes on the parameter `Type*` passed by the `main` function. This list is searched for the attribute `DocumentationAttr` and the strings from the property `DocStr` are printed.

The output of the preceding program is:

```
Class  'AClass' is  to be documented
    Member function 'Void VirtualFunc()' is  to be documented
    Member function 'Void VirtualFunc()' is  to be implemented
Class  'BClass' is  to be documented
    Member function 'Void VirtualFunc()' is  to be documented
    Member function 'Void VirtualFunc()' is  to be implemented
```

A Few Commonly Used Attributes

In this section, we will discuss a few commonly used attributes. The attributes commonly used in data marshaling are `InAttribute` and the `OutAttribute`. `CLSCompliantAttribute` is used to specify that a program element such as a type or method is CLS compliant. `StructLayoutAttribute` is used to explicitly specify how the layout of a value type or a gc class should be done.

InAttribute and OutAttribute

`InAttribute` and `OutAttribute` are commonly used to specify how data should be marshaled between a native and a managed component in the Platform Invoke Service (discussed in Chapter 16) and in method invocations between COM and .NET components (discussed in Chapter 19). These attributes can be applied to function parameters when calling functions from native DLLs. The syntax is the same as in the example for IDL attributes at the beginning of this chapter. The `In` attribute indicates that data should be marshaled from a calling function to a called function. The `Out` parameter indicates that the data should be marshaled from a called function to a calling function. The data marshaling service considers these attributes as hints for how to marshal the data corresponding to the parameters that have these attributes applied.

The following code sample shows how to use the `In` attribute in a call to a function in a native DLL using the attribute `DllImport`. Assume that the parameter to the function is of type `Val` (that is, a value type):

```
#using <mscorlib.dll>
using namespace System;
using namespace System::Runtime::InteropServices;
```

```
[DllImport("sample")]
extern "C" int SampleFunc( [in] Val VInstance );
```

In this code, the attribute `DllImport` is used to declare a function in a managed component. The function is implemented in a native DLL called `sample.dll`. With the help of the declaration, a managed function can call the native function `SampleFunc` by passing an integer as an argument. The attribute `In` is applied on the parameter `VInstance`, indicating that data should be marshaled from the managed side to the native side. (`DllImport` is discussed in more detail in Chapter 17.)

CLSCompliantAttribute

The attribute `CLSCompliantAttribute` is used to indicate that an assembly, a module, or a type is compliant with the common language specification. By applying this attribute to one of these targets, it is guaranteed that any .NET-targeted language can consume it. The current version of the MC++ compiler simply keeps the attribute in the metadata and does not enforce any CLS compliance rules on the target.

StructLayoutAttribute

The attribute `StructLayoutAttribute` in the `System::Runtime::InteropServices` namespace allows you to control the physical layout of the data members of a value type or a gc class. The CLR typically controls layout of gc classes and value types. You can use the `StructLayoutAttribute` attribute to specify a layout that is different from the default layout provided by the CLR.

The enumeration `LayoutKind` in the `System::Runtime::InteropServices` namespace defines three enumerators to be used to specify the layouts:

- `Auto`: Layout is controlled by the CLR.

- `Sequential`: Data members are laid out in sequential order as specified in the definition of a gc class or a value type.

- `Explicit`: The position of each data member is explicitly specified using the `FieldOffsetAttribute`.

The default layout for value types is `Sequential`.

Summary

In this chapter, we introduced custom attributes and showed how to define and use custom attributes through the BCL class System::Attribute and also through the attribute System::AttributeUsageAttribute. You have seen how to define attributes that are inheritable and can be applied to multiple targets.

In the next chapter, we will discuss delegates and show how attributes can be used on them.

Delegates

FUNCTIONS PROVIDED BY A CALLER and invoked by the called function are known as *callback functions.* Callback functions are used when a function is expected to call different functions (with the same parameter types and return types) based on its arguments. A specific example that uses a callback function is the C runtime function qsort (from the stdlib.h SDK header file), which sorts arrays of arbitrary types. qsort takes a callback function that compares two elements as an argument and invokes that function during sorting.

Traditionally, callback functions are implemented using function pointers. When a callback is required from a function that takes a function pointer as a parameter, a caller passes the address of a function whose signature (parameters and return type) matches that of the function pointer parameter.

Delegates are similar to C++ function pointers, but they offer richer functionality (you will see examples later in this chapter). You can think of delegates as a managed equivalent of callback functions.

In this chapter, we discuss function pointers and show how to use a delegate to implement the same functionality. We explain what multicast delegates are and show how to implement them. You will learn how to use delegates to call native functions. Finally, we describe how to invoke delegates asynchronously.

A Look Back at Function Pointers

Let's look at a sample that uses qsort to implement the sorting of strings. Since the qsort function is used to sort elements of any type, it requires the comparison function to be provided by the caller. Every time qsort needs to compare two elements, it calls this user-supplied routine—in other words, it calls back the caller.

```
// sorting strings using qsort
#include <stdlib.h>
#include <string.h>
#include <stdio.h>
int compare( const void *param1, const void *param2 )
{
   /* Compare param1 and param2 */
   return _stricmp( * ( char** ) param1, * ( char** ) param2 );
}
```

```
int main() {
    char* strArray[4] = {"Horse", "Elephant", "Donkey", "Camel"};
    /* _CRTIMP void    __cdecl qsort(void *,
                                     size_t,
                                     size_t,
                                     int (__cdecl *)(const void *, const void *));
    The last parameter is a function pointer
    */
    qsort( (void *)strArray, (size_t)4, sizeof( char * ), compare );
    /* print sorted array: */
    for( int i = 0; i < 4; ++i )
        printf( "%s\n", strArray[i] );
}
```

The last parameter of qsort is a function pointer that takes two parameters of type void* and returns an int. A callback function used as an argument for this parameter compares the two arguments passed by qsort and returns –1, 0, or 1 depending on whether the first argument is less than, equal to, or greater than the second argument.

In this sample, the function _stricmp from the string.h header file is used as a callback function. It compares two strings. When sorting the strArray array, the qsort function calls _stricmp. The output of the program is as follows:

```
Camel
Donkey
Elephant
Horse
```

As this example shows, function pointers are a useful feature for implementing callbacks. It is also possible to use static and nonstatic member functions as function pointer parameters to implement callbacks.

However, there are a few drawbacks to using function pointers to implement callbacks.

- When nonstatic member functions are used as callback functions, you can only pass the methods (whose signatures match that of the function pointer parameter) of a class and its subclasses as arguments. It is not possible to use a method of another unrelated class as an argument even though its signature matches the function pointer.

- You cannot use the same function pointer to use both static and nonstatic methods of a class as callback functions.

- Only one callback can happen at a time with a function pointer. If callbacks to different functions are needed, you must find a way to gather a list of all of those functions and iterate through the list in the callee to make callbacks.

- You cannot use function pointers to enforce constraints, such as the methods of a particular class (and not those of other classes, including subclasses) can only be used as function pointers.

Delegates

Delegates are a feature supported by the .NET Framework. All .NET-targeted languages implement delegates. Delegates provide simple solutions to the drawbacks attributed to function pointers.

A *delegate* is a gc class that can hold pointers to the member functions, including properties (static or nonstatic) of managed classes whose signatures match the delegate's signature. It provides methods to add and remove functions that are used as callback methods (let's call these methods *delegated methods*). This delegate class inherits from the BCL class `System::MulticastDelegate`, which inherits from `System::Delegate`.

Here is a declaration of a function pointer and a corresponding declaration of a delegate:

```
typedef void (*CoolFunc)(int flowLevel); // function pointer
public __delegate  void CoolFunc (int flowLevel); // delegate
```

As you can see, the definition of a delegate is similar to a function prototype declaration with the additional keywords `public` (or `private`) and `__delegate`. That's all you have to do to declare this delegate. The compiler automatically translates this declaration into a gc class that inherits from `System::MulticastDelegate`. The name of the gc class is the same as that of the delegate (`CoolFunc` in this case). The keyword `public` (or `private`) indicates that the delegate is public (or private) to the assembly in which it is defined.

You can also declare delegates as members of managed classes. Here's an example:

```
__value struct V {
    __delegate void ValueDelegate(int I);
};
```

To use a member method of a managed class as a delegated method, you create an instance of the delegate. A delegate constructor takes two arguments: a pointer to an instance of the class containing the member function if it is non-static (0 if the function is static) and the address of the member function. To make a callback, you can call the Invoke method on the delegate object.

Note that you can use attributes on the delegate itself, and on the return type and parameters of the delegate. Recall from Chapter 11 that one of the targets to apply an attribute is `Delegate`.

A Delegate for a Single Function Callback

Suppose that you are writing a program that automates the flow of air in an air conditioner. You can envision the function `AirFlowController` as a part of an API provided by a weather center to be used by different clients. Assume that this function controls the airflow in the air conditioner based on the current weather conditions.

The following code shows how a delegate can be used to implement the air conditioner example. For simplicity, we implement the `AirFlowController` method along with the client code. We also assume that the implementation of `AirFlowController` is used to test the functionality of the clients by assuming random weather conditions.

```
// air cooling program
#include <time.h>
#include <stdlib.h>
#using <mscorlib.dll>
using namespace System;

// delegate declaration
__delegate  void ControlAirFlow(int flowLevel);

__gc class AirConditioner {
  public:
    void TurnOff() { Console::WriteLine(S"AirConditioner::TurnOff"); }
    void BlowColdAir(int flowLevel) {
        if (flowLevel == 0) { TurnOff(); }
        else {
            Console::Write(S"AirConditioner::BlowColdAir at level ");
            Console::WriteLine(flowLevel);
        }
    }
};
```

```
void AirFlowController(ControlAirFlow* pCoolD) {
    enum Temperature {normal = 0, warm, hot};
    // generate random weather conditions
    srand( (unsigned)time( NULL ) );
    Temperature currentCondition = (Temperature) (rand()%3);

    switch (currentCondition) {
     case normal:  Console::WriteLine(S"Normal weather, air control not needed");
                    break;
     case warm:    Console::WriteLine(S"Warm weather");
                    break;
     case hot:     Console::WriteLine(S"Hot weather");
                    break;
    }
    pCoolD->Invoke(currentCondition);
}
int main() {
    // create an instance of AirConditioner
    AirConditioner *cooler = new AirConditioner ();
    // create a single delegate with a member function
    ControlAirFlow *pCoolD = new ControlAirFlow(cooler,
                                        & AirConditioner::BlowColdAir);
    // call the function that invokes the delegate
    AirFlowController (pCoolD);
}
```

In this sample, we have a definition of a `ControlAirFlow` delegate. The `AirConditioner` class implements the `BlowColdAir` method, whose signature matches that of the delegate.

The `AirFlowController` method implements the functionality of the corresponding method from the section on function pointers. The differences between the managed and native routines are that the managed version of the method takes just one parameter, a pointer to the delegate `ControlAirFlow`, and the callback in the managed version is simply a call to the `Invoke` method on the delegate. Unlike function pointers, where the name of the function pointer must be used to make a callback, all delegates use the same method, `Invoke`.

The `main` method maps to the corresponding `main` method from the function pointer sample. To attach a member function to the delegate as a callback function (delegated function), a delegate must be created. In this sample, a delegate is created by using an object of `AirConditioner` and the address of the `BlowColdAir` method. This delegate object is passed to the `AirFlowController` method.

The delegated function is invoked (as a callback) by calling the `Invoke` function on the delegate object pointed to by the `pCoolD` variable in the

AirFlowController method. If the value of the currentCondition were Normal, the output would be as follows:

```
Normal weather, air control not needed
AirConditioner::TurnOff
```

In this sample, the access specifier for the delegate is not given. The default value for the access specifier is private. This delegate becomes private to the assembly resulting from the code. To make the delegate accessible to the importing modules, the access specifier public must be used on the delegate.

Earlier in this section, we mentioned that static member functions could be used as delegated functions. Suppose that the BlowColdAir method is a static method in the AirConditioner class.

```
__gc class AirConditioner {
  public:
    static void TurnOff() { Console::WriteLine(S"AirConditioner::TurnOff"); }
    static void BlowColdAir(int flowLevel) {
        if (flowLevel == 0) { TurnOff(); }
        else {
            Console::Write(S"AirConditioner::BlowColdAir at level ");
            Console::WriteLine(flowLevel);
        }
    }
};
```

In the main function, this static method can be used to create a delegate, as follows:

```
ControlAirFlow *pCoolD = new ControlAirFlow(0, &AirConditioner::BlowColdAir);
```

Notice that the first argument to the constructor is 0, which indicates that the method that follows is a static member function. The rest of the code remains the same, including the code relating to how the delegate is invoked.

You can create delegates using the member functions or properties of a value class provided the value class implements a gc interface with those member functions or properties. The signatures of delegated functions and the declared delegate must match. You are not allowed to overload delegates. The reason for this is that even though the declaration of a delegate may resemble a function prototype, internally it is a gc class. Delegates can have any managed type as a return type. For static functions, the first parameter to the delegate constructor is 0.

Enforcing Constraints

We mentioned earlier that function pointers cannot be used to enforce safety constraints, such as the members of a particular class can only be used as arguments to a function with a function pointer parameter. In this section we show how delegates can be used to enforce such a constraint.

You already know that all delegates inherit from System::MulticastDelegate, which inherits from System::Delegate. The public property Target of the System::Delegate class returns the object that is used to create a delegate.

Suppose that in the sample in the previous section we want to enforce the constraint that the AirFlowController function should allow the members of the AirConditioner function only as the delegated functions for the delegate CoolFunc. We can rewrite the AirFlowController function as follows:

```
void AirFlowController(ControlAirFlow* pCoolD) {
    if (!pCoolD->Target->GetType()->Equals(__typeof(AirConditioner))) {
      Console::WriteLine(S"Invalid argument");
      return;
    }
    enum Temperature {normal = 0, warm, hot};
    // generate random weather conditions
    srand( (unsigned)time( NULL ) );
    Temperature currentCondition = (Temperature) (rand()%3);

    switch (currentCondition) {
     case normal:  Console::WriteLine(S"Normal weather, air control not needed");
                   break;
     case warm:    Console::WriteLine(S"Warm weather");
                   break;
     case hot:     Console::WriteLine(S"Hot weather");
    }
    pCoolD->Invoke(currentCondition);
}
```

In this function, we have a check at the beginning to see if the target object used to create the delegate is an instance of the AirConditioner class. When you replace the AirTrafficController function in the sample from the previous section with the preceding function, you won't be able to use a member function of any other class as a delegated function in the AirTrafficController function.

Refer to the BCL documentation on System::Delegate and System::MulticastDelegate classes for more details on their members.

Note that you can also use attributes to enforce any constraints. The following code shows how to apply an attribute on a delegate:

```
// Define a custom attribute
[AttributeUsage(AttributeTargets::Delegate)]
public __gc class  MyAttr {
public:
    MyAttr(Type *str) : m_Type(str){}
    __property Type *get_LegalType() {
            return m_Type;
    }
private:
    Type *m_Type;
};
// apply the attribute on the delegate
[MyAttr(__typeof(AirConditioner))]
public __delegate  void ControlAirFlow(int flowLevel);
```

You can use the code in the preceding sample to see how to apply attributes on delegates. Notice the target Delegate in the attribute block of the attribute class MyAttr. Attributes are discussed in detail in Chapter 11.

Implementation Details

When parsing a delegate declaration, the MC++ compiler generates[1] a gc class that inherits from System::MulticastDelegate. The following code shows the mapping of the delegate declaration from the previous section.

```
__delegate __gc
    class ControlAirFlow : public System::MulticastDelegate
{
public:
    ControlAirFlow(System::Object *, System::IntPtr );
    virtual void Invoke(int flowLevel);
    virtual System::IAsyncResult *BeginInvoke(int flowLevel,
                                              System::AsyncCallback *,
                                              System::Object *);
    virtual void EndInvoke(System::IAsyncResult *);
};
```

[1] You can see this by using the /Fx compiler option. The compiler generates a file with .mrg added to the name of the file being compiled (for example, if a filename is sample.cpp, the generated filename will be sample.mrg.cpp).

Any delegate class generated by the compiler inherits from System::MulticastDelegate. As shown in the preceding code, the constructor of the delegate ControlAirFlow takes two parameters. The first parameter (the target of the delegate) represents the object whose member function is the delegated function. This parameter's value is 0 if the member function happens to be static. The second parameter represents the address of the delegated function.

The Invoke method is used to call the delegated function *synchronously*— that is, the caller waits for the completion of the invocation as in a single threaded application. The sample shown in the previous sections use the Invoke method. When a call to Invoke is made, the program control goes to the BlowColdAir method and the execution of the AirFlowController function is suspended. The execution continues in the AirFlowController function after the control returns from the BlowColdAir method.

The functions BeginInvoke and EndInvoke are used to begin and end the execution of a delegated function *asynchronously*—that is, the caller can continue execution after calling BeginInvoke and then wait for the invocation to be completed before calling EndInvoke. Asynchronous invocation is discussed at the end of this chapter.

A Multicast Delegate

So far, you have seen an example of a simple delegate where only one function is used as a delegated function. Some applications require more than one method to be invoked as callback functions. Multicast delegates are used for this purpose. A *multicast delegate* is a delegate that allows more than one delegated function to be attached a delegate and calls each one of them when the Invoke method on the delegate is called.

The following sample shows how to use a multicast delegate. The declaration of the delegate is the same for both simple and multicast delegates. In this sample, we assume that there are two air control devices: a ceiling fan and an air conditioner. Both devices are to be connected to the weather center and control the airflow.

```
// airflow control program
#using <mscorlib.dll>
using namespace System;
#include <time.h>
#include <stdlib.h>

// delegate declaration
__delegate  void ControlAirFlow(int flowLevel);
```

```
__gc class CeilingFan {
  public:
    void TurnOff() { Console::WriteLine(S"CeilingFan::TurnOff"); }
    void Rotate(int speedLevel) {
        if (speedLevel == 0) { TurnOff(); }
        else {
            Console::Write(S"CeilingFan::Rotate at speed level ");
            Console::WriteLine(speedLevel);
        }
    }
};

__gc class AirConditioner {
  public:
    void TurnOff() { Console::WriteLine(S"AirConditioner::TurnOff"); }
    void BlowColdAir(int flowLevel) {
        if (flowLevel == 0) { TurnOff(); }
        else {
            Console::Write(S"AirConditioner::BlowColdAir at level ");
            Console::WriteLine(flowLevel);
        }
    }
};

void AirFlowController (ControlAirFlow* pCoolD) {
    enum Temperature {normal = 0, warm, hot};
    // generate random weather conditions
    srand( (unsigned)time( NULL ) );
    Temperature currentCondition = (Temperature) (rand()%3);

    switch (currentCondition) {
      case normal:  Console::WriteLine(S"Normal weather, air control not needed");
                        break;
      case warm:    Console::WriteLine(S"Warm weather");
                        break;
      case hot:     Console::WriteLine(S"Hot weather");
                        break;
    }
    pCoolD->Invoke(currentCondition);
}
```

```
int main() {
    // create an instance of AirConditioner
    AirConditioner *cooler = new AirConditioner();
    // create a single delegate with a member function
    ControlAirFlow *pCoolD = new ControlAirFlow(cooler,
                                        &AirConditioner::BlowColdAir);

    // create an instance of CeilingFan
    CeilingFan *fan = new CeilingFan();
    // create a single delegate with a  member function
    ControlAirFlow *pFanD = new ControlAirFlow(fan, &CeilingFan::Rotate);

    // combine the two delegates to create a multicast delegate
    pFanD += pCoolD;

    // call the function that invokes the delegate
    AirFlowController (pFanD);
}
```

In this sample, the delegate `ControlAirFlow` represents delegated functions that return void and take an int as a parameter. The code in this sample is the same as in the previous example except for the addition of the new gc class `CeilingFan` and a code change in the main function. The `CeilingFan` class has two methods, `Rotate` and `TurnOff`.

Multiple functions can be delegated through the same delegate using the member operator +=. The compiler maps this operator to the `Combine` method of `System::Delegate`. The return value of `Combine` is a multicast delegate. This method can be directly used instead of calling the += operator. In this sample, the pFanD variable becomes a multicast delegate with two delegated functions after the call to the += operator. The invocation of Invoke on a multicast delegate results in calls to all delegated functions of that delegate.

To remove a delegated function from a multicast delegate, the operator -= can be used. The compiler maps this operator to the `Remove` method of `System::Delegate`. The first parameter of this function is the source delegate and the second parameter is the delegate (representing delegated functions) that is being removed. This method can be directly used instead of the -= operator. If the value of the variable currentCondition is 2, the output of the preceding program is as follows:

```
Hot weather
CeilingFan::Rotate at speed level 2
AirConditioner::BlowColdAir at level 2
```

Delegates for Native Functions

You have seen how a member of a managed class can be used as a delegated function. A delegate can also represent pointer to a C++ member function (a nogc pointer—that is, a pointer into the C++ heap) provided that the function is implemented in a native DLL and a managed wrapper is used as a proxy via the DllImport custom attribute to invoke the unmanaged function. Consider the following example:

```
#using <mscorlib.dll>
using namespace System;

// DllImport is defined in System::Runtime::InteropServices
using namespace System::Runtime::InteropServices;

// wrapper class for the strlen function
__gc struct StringRoutines {
    [DllImport("msvcr70")]
        static int strlen( const char* );
};

// delegate declaration
__delegate int MyStrLen(const char *pText);

int main() {
    // create delegate
    MyStrLen *p = new MyStrLen(0, &StringRoutines::strlen);

    // invoke the delegated function
    int len = p->Invoke("Hello");

    Console::Write(S"Length of the string \"Hello\" is ");
    Console::WriteLine(len);
}
```

In this sample, a managed wrapper class called StringRoutines is created to wrap the strlen function from msvcr70.dll. The DllImport custom attribute is defined in the System::Runtime::InteropServices namespace. This attribute is used to import exported functions from native DLLs. An instance of the delegate is created by passing the address of the member function of the wrapper class as the argument to the delegate constructor. When the delegate is invoked, the `strlen` function of `msvcr70.dll` is executed. The output of the preceding program is as follows:

```
Length of the string "Hello" is 5
```

Asynchronous Invocation of a Delegate

In multithreaded applications, it is sometimes useful to be able to make a call to a function and continue execution without waiting on the called function to return. The caller and the callee can continue to execute simultaneously. The execution of the caller can be suspended and resumed upon the return from the called function. This method of calling functions is called an *asynchronous invocation*.

To support asynchronous invocations on delegates, the `BeginInvoke` and `EndInvoke` methods are used. As shown earlier, the syntax for these two methods is as follows:

```
virtual System::IAsyncResult *BeginInvoke(int flowLevel,
                                          System::AsyncCallback *,
                                          System::Object *);
virtual void EndInvoke(System::IAsyncResult *);
```

In the `BeginInvoke` method, all parameters should match the parameters of the delegate, except for the last two parameters. The return type of this method is `System::IAsyncResult*`. The `AsyncCallback` parameter is a delegate that represents a callback method in the component that calls `BeginInvoke`. The `IAsyncResult` interface is used to represent the status of the asynchronous operation.

In our air conditioner program, if we want to implement asynchronous calling semantics, the only function that needs to change is `AirFlowController`, which makes invocations on the delegate.

```
// air cooling program
void AirFlowController(ControlAirFlow* pCoolD) {
    IAsyncResult* asr;
    enum Temperature {normal = 0, warm, hot};
    // generate random weather conditions
    srand( (unsigned)time( NULL ) );
    Temperature currentCondition = (Temperature) (rand()%3);
```

```
      switch (currentCondition) {
        case normal:  Console::WriteLine(S"Normal weather, air control not needed");
                      break;
        case warm:    Console::WriteLine(S"Warm weather");
                      break;
        case hot:     Console::WriteLine(S"Hot weather");
                      break;
      }
      asr = pCoolD->BeginInvoke(currentCondition, 0, 0);
      // do something
      Console::WriteLine(S"waiting");
      asr->AsyncWaitHandle->WaitOne();
      Console::WriteLine(S"waiting over");
      pCoolD->EndInvoke(asr);
    }
```

In this sample, a simple use of `BeginInvoke` is shown. The last two arguments are set to 0, which indicates that the delegated function need not invoke any delegates after its execution. A call to `BeginInvoke` returns an object of `AsyncResult` that implements the `IAsyncResult` interface. `AsyncResult` has a property called `AsyncWaitHandle`. The `WaitOne` method suspends the current thread until the handle corresponding to `AsyncWaitHandle` is released. After the waiting is over, a call to the `EndInvoke` function concludes the asynchronous invocation and continues the execution in the main thread. You can use this code to replace the `AirFlowController` method in the air conditioner program when asynchronous invocation semantics are needed. If the value of the variable `currentCondition` is 0, the output is as follows:

```
Normal weather, air control not needed
waiting
AirConditioner::TurnOff
waiting over
```

Refer to the .NET documentation to find details on `AsyncWaitHandle`, `IAsyncResult`, and `AsyncCallback`.

Summary

In this chapter, we briefly discussed function pointers and showed how delegates offer richer functionality. You learned how to enforce certain constraints on delegated functions using delegates. We showed the implementation details of delegates and explained how to use multicast delegates. You saw how to invoke native functions using delegates and how to invoke a delegate asynchronously.

In the next chapter, we explain events and show how to use delegates to implement them.

CHAPTER 13

Events

AN *EVENT* IS A MESSAGE SENT by an object to another object that wants to receive the message from the sender. The object sending the message is called an *event source*. The object receiving the message is called an *event receiver*. Programming based on events has become popular with graphical user interface (GUI) applications where user actions such as a mouse click are the events passed back to the application.

The event model supported by the .NET Framework is called a *publish-subscribe* model. In the publish-subscribe event model, a publisher (a server process that can send messages to a list of objects that are interested in receiving the message from the sender) publishes the events and a subscriber (a client object that wants to receive messages from a publisher) registers with the publisher for a particular event. When an action happens that makes a publisher act upon an event (in other words, when an event is raised), all subscribers to that event are notified. If an event notification is no longer needed, a subscriber can unregister with the publisher for that event. As an example of publish-subscribe mode, you can think of a daily news service as a publisher and customers who register with the news service as subscribers. An event in this case is the delivery of news to the customer. The news event is raised when the news reports are gathered, consolidated, and prepared for delivery; all subscribers are notified by the delivery of the news to them.

In the .NET Framework, delegates handle the communication between an event source and an event receiver. A delegate is a gc class that inherits from `System::MulticastDelegate`. It can hold references to the member functions of other managed classes whose signatures match that of the delegate declaration. Refer to Chapter 12 for a detailed discussion on delegates.

The Visual C++ .NET compiler supports *unified events*—the same programming model is used for native C++ events, COM events, and managed events. In this chapter, we focus on event programming for managed classes. We first discuss events as data members, followed by events as member functions. You will see how to define user-defined event accessor methods. We also explain static and virtual events, and how to use them.

Events As Data Members

In any managed class, events can be declared as data members. As mentioned earlier, events are implemented using delegates. The declaration of a data event uses the keyword __event followed by a pointer to a delegate.

Assuming a delegate with the name FlashNewsDelegate, you can declare an event as a data member as follows:

```
#using <mscorlib.dll>
using namespace System;
public __delegate void FlashNewsDelegate(String* news);
public __gc class CyberNews {
   public:
       __event FlashNewsDelegate *flashNews;
};
```

In this code, we use the delegate FlashNewsDelegate to declare the event flashNews.

There are two ways of registering and unregistering with a data event. In this section, we discuss the first of the two ways. The first way is to use the += and -= operators. The second way is to use the methods Add and Remove of the System::Delegate class. We look at the second way in the next section.

To register and unregister with a data event, you can use the operators += and -= respectively. To raise a data event, call a method whose name matches the event name and whose signature (parameters and return type) matches that of the delegate used to declare the event. The keyword __raise can be used before the function call to signify the event raising, although it is optional. An event can only be raised by a member of the class containing the event.

The following example shows how to declare and use an event. Suppose that the application is a news service that provides news to its customers. Customers register with the news service and receive news when a news event happens. They can unregister when they do not wish to receive news.

```
#using <mscorlib.dll>
using namespace System;
// declare the delegate
public __delegate void FlashNewsDelegate(String* news);

[event_source(managed)] // optional
public __gc class CyberNews {
   public:
       // declare event
       __event FlashNewsDelegate *flashNews;
```

```
            // Fire the event
            void NewsHappened(String* news) {
                __raise flashNews(news); // use of __raise is optional
            }
    };
    [event_receiver(managed)] // optional
    __gc class Customer {
        public:
            // event handler
                void ReadNews(String* news){
                Console::WriteLine(news);
            }
            // register with the event
            void SubscribeToNews(CyberNews* publisher) {
                publisher->flashNews += new FlashNewsDelegate(this,
                                                        &Customer::ReadNews);
            }
            // unregister with the event
            void UnsubscribeToNews(CyberNews* publisher) {
                publisher->flashNews -= new FlashNewsDelegate(this,
                                                        &Customer::ReadNews);
            }
    };
    int main() {
        CyberNews* pSource =  new CyberNews();
        Customer* pCustomer = new Customer();
        // register with the event
        pCustomer->SubscribeToNews(pSource);
        // Fire the event
        pSource->NewsHappened(S"Great News");
        // unregister with the event
        pCustomer->UnsubscribeToNews(pSource);
        // Fire the event
        pSource->NewsHappened(S"More Great News");
    }
```

In this sample code, an event, flashNews, is declared in the gc class
CyberNews. This event is implemented using the delegate FlashNewsDelegate,
which takes a System::String object as a parameter and has a void return type.
The attribute event_source is optional when events are declared in managed
classes (gc classes and value types).

The operators += and -= are used to register and unregister the event receiver Customer. These binary operators take the event as the first parameter and a delegate object as the second parameter. As seen in the previous chapter, the constructor of a delegate takes the delegated object as the first parameter and the address of the delegated function of the delegated object as the second parameter. In the previous example, the member function SubscribeToNews uses the += operator on the event CyberNews::flashNews to register the delegate object FlashNewsDelegate, which takes the Customer object as the first argument and the address of ReadNews as the second parameter. The member function UnsubscribeToNews uses the -= operator on the same event to unregister the member function ReadNews of Customer.

When the event flashNews is raised on the CyberNews object (via the gc pointer pSource), the event notifies the registered object Customer by invoking the handler function ReadNews on it. After the Customer object is unregistered, raising the event flashNews does not have any effect, because there are no registered objects.

The output of the preceding program is:

```
Great News
```

Implementation Details: Events As Data Members

You have seen how the MC++ compiler injects code while parsing delegates in the previous chapter. In this section, we look at the code that is generated when the compiler compiles the event example from the previous section.

You can use the compiler option /Fx to see the injected code for events. The following listing shows the injected code for the class CyberNews:

```
[event_source(managed)] // optional
public __gc class CyberNews {
    public:
    // declare event
    __event FlashNewsDelegate *flashNews;
    // Fire the event
    void NewsHappened(String* news) {
        __raise flashNews(news); // use of __raise is optional
    }
    void add_flashNews(::FlashNewsDelegate* eh) {
        flashNews = static_cast<::FlashNewsDelegate*>
                                (System::Delegate::Combine(flashNews, eh));
    }
```

```
    void remove_flashNews(::FlashNewsDelegate* eh) {
        flashNews = static_cast<::FlashNewsDelegate*>
                                   (System::Delegate::Remove(flashNews, eh));
    }
    void raise_flashNews(System::String* i1) {
        if (flashNews != 0) {
            flashNews->Invoke(i1);
        }
    }
    CyberNews() {
        flashNews = 0;
    }
};
```

As you can see, there are new methods introduced to the class:
add_flashNews, remove_flashNews, raise_flashNews. The Combine, Remove, and
Invoke methods of the System::Delegate class are called respectively for
these methods.

When compiling the invocations on the operators += and -= in the code sample, the compiler translates them to the add_flashNews and remove_flashNews
methods of the delegate flashNews, respectively. You can replace the calls to these
operators with the calls to the methods add_flashNews and remove_flashNews,
respectively. Use the following methods to replace the methods of the Customer
class in the example:

```
    // register with the event
    void SubscribeToNews(CyberNews* publisher) {
      publisher->add_flashNews(new FlashNewsDelegate(this,
                                                &Customer::ReadNews));
    }
    // unregister with the event
    void UnsubscribeToNews(CyberNews* publisher) {
      publisher->remove_flashNews(
                        new FlashNewsDelegate(this, &Customer::ReadNews));
    }
```

Apart from using the /Fx compiler option, you can also inspect the code
with ILDasm (ildasm.exe) to see the injected code (in MSIL).

Events As Member Functions

Events can also be declared as member functions of managed classes. To declare a member function as an event, the keyword __event is applied to the function declaration. The member function event must not have a body. The MC++ compiler automatically generates code for it. Here is how member function events are handled in the MC++ compiler: When parsing an event member function, the compiler generates a delegate class with the prefix __Delegate_ attached to the event name. This generated delegate is private to the class containing the event. The compiler-injected code can be viewed by using the /Fx compiler option.

Member function events cannot use the operators += and -= to register and unregister subscriber objects. Instead, the intrinsic functions __hook and __unhook are used (code for an intrinsic function is generated as inline code, so there is no function call/return overhead). The following code sample is a reimplementation of the previous example. The gc classes representing the event source and the event receiver are implemented in different files. The event receiver is compiled into an assembly DLL that is imported in the receiver file.

```
// EventSource.cpp
// Compile with /clr /LD
#using <mscorlib.dll>
using namespace System;
[event_source(managed)] // optional
public __gc class CyberNews {
    public:
        __event void FlashNews(String* news);

    // Fire the event
    void NewsHappened(String* news) {
        __raise FlashNews(news); // use of __raise is optional
    }
};

// EventReceiver.cpp
// Compile with /clr
#using <mscorlib.dll>
using namespace System;
#using "event_source.dll"
[event_receiver(managed)] // optional
__gc class Customer {
    public:
        void ReadNews(String* news){
            Console::WriteLine(news);
    }
```

```
    void SubscribeToNews(CyberNews* publisher) {
        __hook(&CyberNews::FlashNews, publisher, &Customer::ReadNews);
    }
    void UnsubscribeToNews(CyberNews* publisher) {
        __unhook(&CyberNews::FlashNews, publisher, &Customer::ReadNews);
    }
};
int main() {
    CyberNews* pSource = new CyberNews();
    Customer* pCustomer = new Customer();
    pCustomer->SubscribeToNews(pSource);
    pSource->NewsHappened(S"Great News");
    pCustomer->UnsubscribeToNews(pSource);
}
```

Here, the gc class CyberNews is the event source and the gc class Customer is the event receiver. The member function FlashNews of CyberNews is an event due to the use of __event keyword. The function call to FlashNews in the NewsHappened function shows the invocation of the event. The keyword __raise is optional.

The member function ReadNews of the gc class Customer is the event handler. To register with the event source, the event receiver uses the __hook intrinsic function. To unregister with the event source, the event receiver uses the __unhook intrinsic function. In the main function, the ReadNews member function of Customer is registered with the FlashNews event of CyberNews by the call to the SubscribeToNews member function. When the event is raised in the NewsHappened function, the function ReadNews is invoked via the FlashNews event. After unsubscribing to the event, raising the event has no effect on the function ReadNews. The output of the program is:

```
Great News
```

Implementation Details: Events As Member Functions

Similar to how data member events work, the MC++ compiler injects code while compiling member function events. The injected code corresponding to the event source class from the previous section is shown here:

```
[event_source(managed)] // optional
public __gc class CyberNews {
  public:
    __event void FlashNews(String* news);
    // Fire the event
```

```
void NewsHappened(String* news) {
FlashNews(news);
}
__delegate __gc class __Delegate_FlashNews :
                                public System::MulticastDelegate    {
  public:
      __Delegate_FlashNews(System::Object *, System::IntPtr );
      virtual void Invoke(System::String __gc * news);
      virtual System::IAsyncResult *BeginInvoke(
        System::String __gc * news, System::AsyncCallback *, System::Object *);
      virtual void EndInvoke(System::IAsyncResult *);
};
__Delegate_FlashNews* FlashNews;
void add_FlashNews(CyberNews::__Delegate_FlashNews* eh) {
    FlashNews = static_cast<CyberNews::__Delegate_FlashNews*>
                        (System::Delegate::Combine(FlashNews, eh));
}
void remove_FlashNews(CyberNews::__Delegate_FlashNews* eh) {
    FlashNews = static_cast<CyberNews::__Delegate_FlashNews*>
                        (System::Delegate::Remove(FlashNews, eh));
}
void raise_FlashNews(System::String* i1) {
    if (FlashNews != 0) {
        FlashNews->Invoke(i1);
    }
}
}
CyberNews() {
    FlashNews = 0;
}
};
```

The class __Delegate_FlashNews is a nested, private class inside the
CyberNews class. It has Invoke, BeginInvoke, and EndInvoke as member functions
along with the constructor. As mentioned in the previous chapter, the
functions BeginInvoke and EndInvoke are used in asynchronous programming
contexts. The function Invoke calls the delegated functions.

For the event member function FlashNews, the compiler generates the member functions for the classes CyberNews, add_FlashNews, remove_FlashNews, and
raise_FlashNews along with a constructor that initializes the event to 0. In the
presence of a user-defined constructor, the code to initialize the event is injected
at the beginning of the constructor. The add_FlashNews and remove_FlashNews
functions correspond to the += and -= operators, respectively, for data events. The

MC++ compiler injects the calls to add_FlashNews and remove_FlashNews members of CyberNews corresponding to the __hook and __unhook intrinsic functions. The compiler-generated code for the event receiver class is shown here:

```
[event_receiver(managed)] // optional
__gc class Customer {
   public:
      void ReadNews(String* news){
            Console::WriteLine(news);
      }
      void SubscribeToNews(CyberNews* publisher) {
            __hook(&CyberNews::FlashNews, publisher, &Customer::ReadNews)
            (publisher)->add_FlashNews(
                new CyberNews::__Delegate_FlashNews(this, &Customer::ReadNews));
      }
      void UnsubscribeToNews(CyberNews* publisher) {
            __unhook(&CyberNews::FlashNews, publisher, &Customer::ReadNews)
            (publisher)->remove_FlashNews(
                new CyberNews::__Delegate_FlashNews(this, &Customer::ReadNews));
      }
};
```

User-Defined Event Accessor Methods

You have seen how the compiler injects code when compiling event data members in a managed class. The event accessor methods that the compiler automatically generates are the add_, remove_, and raise_ prefixed to the event name. The MC++ compiler allows users to define these event accessor methods.

In the following listing, we reimplement the event source class CyberNews from the first section, "Events As Data Members."

```
#using <mscorlib.dll>
using namespace System;
// declare the delegate
public __delegate void FlashNewsDelegate(String* news);
[event_source(managed)] // optional
public __gc class CyberNews {
   public:
     FlashNewsDelegate *newsDelegate;
     // Fire the event
```

```
    void NewsHappened(String* news) {
        if (newsDelegate != 0) {
            newsDelegate(news);
        }
    }
    __event void add_flashNews(::FlashNewsDelegate* eh) {
        newsDelegate = static_cast<::FlashNewsDelegate*>
                            (System::Delegate::Combine(newsDelegate, eh));
    }
    __event void remove_flashNews(::FlashNewsDelegate* eh) {
        newsDelegate = static_cast<::FlashNewsDelegate*>
                            (System::Delegate::Remove(newsDelegate, eh));
    }
    __event void raise_flashNews(System::String* i1) {
        if (newsDelegate != 0) {
            newsDelegate->Invoke(i1);
        }
    }
    CyberNews() {
        newsDelegate = 0;
    }
};
```

While implementing events with user-defined event accessors, you need to define a delegate and one or more of the accessor methods. The delegate name suffix for the user-defined event accessors must be different from the user-defined delegate. The keyword __event must be added to all user-defined event accessor methods.

In an event receiver, you can call these methods directly to register, unregister, and fire the events.

Virtual Events

The MC++ compiler allows virtual events with the keyword virtual added to the event declaration. The semantics of virtual events are similar to those of virtual functions. To illustrate the use of virtual events, let's extend our example scenario. Imagine that the company providing the cyber news to the customers is to be expanded to provide an extended service along with the existing service to the customers. The application is modified to provide this extended functionality.

Assume that the customers are now required to ask for an event object before subscribing.

The application spans two files: an event source file and an event receiver file. The gc class `CyberNewsMarketing` with a static member function that returns an event object is added to the event source file:

```
// EventSource.cpp
// compile with /clr /LD
#using <mscorlib.dll>
using namespace System;
public __delegate void FlashNewsDelegate(String* news);

[event_source(managed)] // optional
public __gc class CyberNews {
    public:
        virtual __event FlashNewsDelegate *flashNews;
        // Fire the event
        virtual void NewsHappened(String* news) {
          flashNews(news);
        }
};
[event_source(managed)] // optional
public __gc class BigCyberNews : public CyberNews {
public:
    virtual __event FlashNewsDelegate *flashNews;
    String* GatherDetailedNews(String* news) {
        // gather detailed news
        return String::Concat(S"Details: ", news);
    }
    // Fire the event
    void NewsHappened(String* news) {
        news = GatherDetailedNews(news);
        flashNews(news);
    }
};
public __gc struct CyberNewsMarketing {
    static CyberNews *GetNewsService() {
        return new BigCyberNews();
    }
};
```

The event flashNews is declared to be virtual. So, a subclass of CyberNews can define its own flashNews accessor functions. In the preceding code, the method NewsHappened is redefined to call GatherDetailedNews function before invoking the event. In the following code, you will see how the virtual event is invoked.

```
// EventReceiver.cpp
// Compile with /clr
#using <mscorlib.dll>
using namespace System;
#using "EventSource.dll"
[event_receiver(managed)] // optional
__gc class Customer {
    public:
        void ReadNews(String* news){
          Console::WriteLine(news);
        }
        void SubscribeToNews(CyberNews* publisher) {
            publisher->flashNews += new FlashNewsDelegate(this,
                                                &Customer::ReadNews);
        }
        void UnsubscribeToNews(CyberNews* publisher) {
            publisher->flashNews -= new FlashNewsDelegate(this,
                                                &Customer::ReadNews);
        }
};
int main() {
    CyberNews* pSource =  CyberNewsMarketing::GetNewsService();
    Customer* pCustomer = new Customer();
    pCustomer->SubscribeToNews(pSource);
    pSource->NewsHappened(S"Great News");
    pCustomer->UnsubscribeToNews(pSource);
}
```

Here, the event receiver is modified to call the GetNewsService function before subscribing to the event. The GetNewsService function can return a different event source each time it is called, but the customer need not change. The output of the preceding program is:

```
Details: Great News
```

Static Events

Events can be declared static. A static event is defined with the keyword `static` attached to the event declaration. Applications can access static events either via the `this` pointer or with a qualified name. The usage of static events is similar to that of the static members of classes. As an example, the first code sample of this chapter can be modified to use static events as follows:

```
#using <mscorlib.dll>
using namespace System;
// declare the delegate
public __delegate void FlashNewsDelegate(String* news);

[event_source(managed)] // optional
public __gc class CyberNews {
   public:
      // declare event
      static __event FlashNewsDelegate *flashNews;
      // Fire the event
      static void NewsHappened(String* news) {
        __raise flashNews(news); // use of __raise is optional
      }
};
[event_receiver(managed)] // optional
__gc class Customer {
   public:
      // event handler
      void ReadNews(String* news){
        Console::WriteLine(news);
      }
      // register with the event
      void SubscribeToNews(CyberNews* publisher) {
        CyberNews::flashNews += new FlashNewsDelegate(this,
                                                &Customer::ReadNews);
      }
      // unregister with the event
      void UnsubscribeToNews(CyberNews* publisher) {
        CyberNews::flashNews -= new FlashNewsDelegate(this,
                                                &Customer::ReadNews);
      }
};
```

```
int main() {
    CyberNews* pSource =  new CyberNews();
    Customer* pCustomer = new Customer();
    // register with the event
    pCustomer->SubscribeToNews(pSource);
    // Fire the event
    CyberNews::NewsHappened(S"Great News");
    // unregister with the event
    pCustomer->UnsubscribeToNews(pSource);
    // Fire the event
    CyberNews::NewsHappened(S"More Great News");
}
```

In this example, the nonstatic event flashNews from the original code sample is modified to be a static event in the gc class CyberNews. The nonstatic member method NewsHappened is modified to be a static method.

The member methods of the gc classes Customer, SubscribeToNews, and UnsubscribeToNews are modified to call the static event flashNews via the fully qualified name CyberNews::flashNews.

Calling the static member function NewsHappened via the fully qualified name CyberNews::NewsHappened raises the event. The output of the previous program is same as that of the original sample:

```
Great News
```

Attributes on Events

In Chapter 11, you have seen that one of the targets of an attribute is Event. Attributes can be added to events, event accessor methods, and event data members. In the following code, we show how to add attributes to events:

```
#using <mscorlib.dll>
using namespace System;

[ attribute(All, AllowMultiple=true) ]
public __gc struct MyAttribute {
    String* str;
    MyAttribute(String* name) : str(name){}
};

// declare the delegate
public __delegate void FlashNewsDelegate(String* news);
```

```
[event_source(managed)] // optional
public __gc class CyberNews {
    public:
        // declare event
        [event:MyAttribute("On Event"),
         method:MyAttribute("On Event Method"),
         field:MyAttribute("On Event Field")]
        __event FlashNewsDelegate *flashNews;

        // Fire the event
        void NewsHappened(String* news) {
            __raise flashNews(news); // use of __raise is optional
        }
};
```

In this code sample, the attribute MyAttribute is kept on the event, event methods, and the event field for the event flashNews. The custom attribute can be seen as part of the output of ILDasm on the assembly DLL generated for this code.

Summary

In this chapter, we introduced events. We showed how events are defined using delegates. You have seen the code that the compiler automatically generates for events that are data members as well as for events that are member functions. We explained how to define user-defined accessor functions for events, how to use virtual and static events, and how to attach custom attributes to events.

In the next chapter, we move on to exceptions, an integrated feature in the .NET Framework.

CHAPTER 14

Exceptions

USER ERRORS AND UNANTICIPATED situations sometimes cause applications to terminate abnormally. A robust application anticipates as many program conditions as
possible and handles them in such a way as to let the program either continue to
run or shut down in a controlled fashion.

You can find different error-handling techniques in software development.
The most commonly used technique is based on checking return values of
function calls. Most C programmers are familiar with code like this:

```
if( (stream  = fopen( "data", "r" )) == NULL ) {
    printf( "The file 'data' was not opened\n" );
}
else {
    printf( "The file 'data' was opened\n" );
}
```

Many software products, including operating systems, were written using
this method of error handling. As it turns out, this technique has a number
of drawbacks:

- Error codes are easy to ignore. Some software developers tend to forget to
  check a return value of the function, and others ignore them, sometimes
  not knowing if a function returns an error code.

- Code that checks return values for every function call is often weighed
  down by a myriad of if statements, which makes it difficult to maintain,
  read, and test. As a result, such code is prone to errors.

- Not all functions can return error codes. For example, to report an error in
  a constructor, you have to resort to a different error-handling method.

- Error codes are inconsistent. Some functions return int and others return
  HRESULT. Some functions return –1 to indicate an error while others return 0.

- Error codes do not carry enough information about the error. To get additional information about the nature of the error, a programmer must call
  another function (recall GetLastError from WinAPI) or test a global variable
  (such as errno in UNIX/C).

- When return values from functions are used as error codes and if you expect the function to return a value other than an error code, you are limited to passing parameters by reference.

- Last but not the least, returning an error code and checking it in the caller is often inefficient. There is no way to check just for error codes that are returned due to failures.

Exception handling is a technique that was developed to address the weaknesses of the return-code error-handling method. Exceptions are a feature in the C++ language. They are also an integral part of the .NET Framework.

In this chapter, you will see how exceptions are used in MC++. You will also learn how managed and unmanaged exceptions work together.

Unmanaged Exceptions

There are two types of unmanaged exceptions: *operating system–based* exceptions and *programming language–based* exceptions.

Operating system–based exceptions can occur at both the system and application levels. An example of an operating system–based exception is a division by zero or a memory access violation.

Programming languages often have their own mechanisms for handling exceptions. One of the main advantages of programming language–based exceptions is their portability. Exceptions in C++ are defined by the language standard and are expected to produce the same results on different platforms, just like any other feature of the language.

Structured Exceptions

Operating system–based exceptions on the Windows platform are called *structured* exceptions. Structured exceptions use the __try, __except, and __finally statements. Here is an example:

```
// Compile without /clr
#include <stdio.h>
#include <excpt.h>
int main() {
    __try{
        printf("in first try \n");
        int i = 1;
        int j = 0;
```

```
        i = i/j; // raises exception
    }
    __except( printf("in filter \n"), EXCEPTION_EXECUTE_HANDLER ) {
        printf("in except \n");
    }
    __try {
        printf("in second try \n");
        return 1;
    }
    __finally {
        printf("in finally \n"); // this is executed before exiting
    }
}
```

The output of this program is as follows:

```
in first try
in filter
in except
in second try
in finally
```

Before we explain what's going on in the program, we need to define a few key concepts. The block of code after __try is called a *guarded section*. The block of code after __except is called a *handler section*. The block of code after __finally is called a *termination handler*. Finally, the parenthesized expression after __except is called a *filter expression*.

When an exception (in this example, it is caused by division by zero) occurs in the guarded section, the filter expression is evaluated.[1] There are three possible values that can be returned by the filter expression, and these values are defined in the SDK header file excpt.h.

```
#define EXCEPTION_EXECUTE_HANDLER        1
#define EXCEPTION_CONTINUE_SEARCH        0
#define EXCEPTION_CONTINUE_EXECUTION    -1
```

The following list shows how each value is interpreted:

- EXCEPTION_CONTINUE_EXECUTION indicates that the execution can continue at the point of exception.

---

[1] In the absence of a filter, the application terminates.

- `EXCEPTION_CONTINUE_SEARCH` indicates that the execution can continue the search for another exception handler.

- `EXCEPTION_EXECUTE_HANDLER` indicates that the execution can continue in the current handler. In the preceding example, `EXCEPTION_EXECUTE_HANDLER` is used as the filter expression's value, and that's why the handler code is executed.[2]

Unlike the filter expression, the termination handler is always executed before the control flow leaves the matching __try section. That's why the program prints "in finally" before returning 1.

An important point to note about structured exceptions is that they are asynchronous. A structured exception can be raised separately from the normal program execution path. For example, a hardware exception can be raised and handled at any point in a program (divide by zero in the previous sample). You can find more details on structured exceptions in the Visual C++ online documentation. In the next section we discuss C++ exceptions that are synchronous.

C++ Exceptions

There is an important difference between structured and C++ exceptions. Unlike structured exceptions, C++ exceptions are *typed*, which means that the exception raised by a guarded section (the block of code after try) can be of any C++ type.

C++ exceptions use try, catch, and throw statements. Similar to structured exceptions, C++ exceptions have guarded, filter (the type declaration within parentheses after catch), and handler (the block of code after catch) sections. The filter expression evaluates to a C++ type. Unlike structured exceptions, C++ exceptions can only be raised programmatically using a throw statement.

```
// Compile with /GX and without /clr
#include <stdio.h>
int main() {
  try {
    printf("throwing: \"I am an exception\"\n");
    throw "I am an exception";
  }
  catch (const char* str) {
    printf("caught: \"%s\"\n", str);
  }
```

---

[2] This filter expression uses a comma. The return value of the whole filter expression is the value of the expression next to the last comma, `EXCEPTION_EXECUTE_HANDLER`.

```
  catch (int i) {
    printf("caught: %d\n", i);
  }
}
```

The output of the preceding program is as follows:

```
throwing: "I am an exception"
caught: "I am an exception"
```

When an exception is raised, it is handled as follows:

- The compiler searches for the closest matching `catch` handler in the same function as the throw. If the exception raised matches the filter expression, the corresponding handler is executed.

- If there is no `catch` handler that matches the exception raised, the compiler looks for a handler in the enclosing scope on the call stack. This lookup continues until a matching handler is found or the outermost scope is reached without a match, in which case the program generates an unhandled exception, which terminates the program.

- If a handler is found in another function, the compiler returns to the throw site and it begins executing termination handlers, if present, in all functions leading back to the function that will handle the throw.

- The matching `catch` handler is then executed. If stack unwinding semantics are needed (enforced with the `/EHsc` compiler option), all the local data of the `try` blocks enclosing the exception is destroyed.

You can find more information on C++ exception handling in the online documentation for Visual C++ .NET.

Managed Exceptions

A C++ exception that has a managed type is called a *managed* exception. The syntax for throwing and catching managed exceptions is similar to that of the C++ exceptions.

The BCL defines a gc class called `System::Exception` that inherits from `System::Object` and provides functionality for managed exceptions. While it is not necessary for managed exceptions to inherit from the class

System::Exception, it is usually a good practice to do so to leverage its functionality. The BCL defines several classes derived from System::Exception. Among them, the gc class System::ApplicationException can be used to define generic exceptions generated by applications.

In the following sample, the gc class MyException inherits from System::ApplicationException. The last WriteLine statement prints the value of the property StackTrace (inherited from System::Exception) that contains the stack trace at the point when the exception was raised.

```
#using <mscorlib.dll>
using namespace System;
public __gc class MyException : public ApplicationException {
    int num_;
    public:
        MyException(int i) : num_(i) {}
        int GetNum() {
            return num_;
        }
};
int main() {
    try {
        Console::WriteLine(S"Throwing a managed object of MyException");
        throw new MyException(10);
    }
    catch (MyException* pE) {
        Console::WriteLine(S"Caught a managed object of MyException");
        Console::Write(S"MyException object is created with ");
        Console::WriteLine(pE->GetNum());
        Console::WriteLine(pE->StackTrace);
    }
}
```

In this sample, an instance of MyException is created in a try block and thrown. The runtime inspects the catch handlers to find a handler whose filter contains a type that matches the type of the thrown object. There is only one catch handler in this example and it has a filter with the same type, MyException*. The output of the preceding example is as follows:

```
Throwing a managed object of MyException
Caught a managed object of MyException
MyException object is created with 10
    at main()
```

Along with `System::ApplicationException`, another significant subclass of `System::Exception` is `System::SystemException`.

The gc class `System::SystemException` is used by the CLR to raise exceptions from the runtime that are not thrown directly by the application. These exceptions signal erroneous conditions that do not cause the application to terminate and can be handled by the application if needed. User-defined exceptions should not inherit from this class.

The gc class `System::ApplicationException` is related to the applications that run under the .NET Framework. Users' programs typically derive from this class to write their own exceptions. Similar to `System::SystemException`, `System::ApplicationException` does not add any new functionality to `System::Exception`.

The properties defined in the `System::Exception` class are as follows:

- `InnerException`: It is possible to wrap a raised exception with another exception in a handler block and pass the wrapper exception to the next handler. The wrapped exception is called an `InnerException`. When a handler catches the wrapper exception, the inner exception can be retrieved. This way, a chain of exceptions raised starting from the first exception can be passed to the outermost exception handler.

- `HelpLink`: In order to provide extensive information about an exception, a URL link can be added to the exception constructor. The `HelpLink` property can be used to retrieve the link.

- `HResult`: Each exception thrown by the runtime is mapped to a unique `HRESULT` that can be used while interoperating with a COM component.

- `Message`: The runtime provides a text message that helps the user understand the nature of an exception. Developers can pass a text string to the exception constructor. If there is no user-defined text message available, the runtime provides a default message.

- `Source`: This property is the name of the application or object that caused the exception.

- `StackTrace`: This property contains the call stack information when an exception is raised.

- `TargetSite`: This property can be used to retrieve the method information of the function (using Reflection) that threw the exception when the call stack is available but the function is not available. In the absence of a call stack, this property returns null.

Some of the interesting public member functions of System::Exception are as follows:

- Equals: Finds out if two objects are same

- GetType: Returns the System::Type* instance of the exception object

- ToString: Returns the fully qualified class name, the Message text if available, and the stack trace text

Refer to the .NET documentation for an extensive description of the System::Exception class and its subclasses.

The __finally clause can be used for managed exceptions. The __finally block is executed whether or not a catch handler for an exception is executed.

Here is an example:

```
#using <mscorlib.dll>
using namespace System;
public __gc class MyException : public ApplicationException {
    int count_;
    public:
            MyException(int i) : count_(i) {}
            int GetCount() {
                return count_;
            }
};
int main() {
    try {
        Console::WriteLine(S"Throwing a managed object of MyException");
        throw new MyException(10);
    }
    catch (MyException* pE) {
        Console::WriteLine(S"Caught a managed object of MyException");
        Console::Write(S"MyException object is created with ");
        Console::WriteLine(pE->GetCount());
        Console::WriteLine(pE->ToString());
    }
    __finally {
        Console::WriteLine(S"in __finally block");
    }
}
```

In this sample, the code inside the catch block is executed when the exception is thrown in the try block. The code inside the __finally block is executed next. The output of the preceding program is as follows:

```
Throwing a managed object of MyException
Caught a managed object of MyException
MyException object is created with 10
MyException: Error in the application
   at main()
in __finally block
```

Throwing and Catching Value Types

In MC++, only boxed value types can be thrown or caught. This is because the type of a managed exception must be a gc pointer. Boxing creates a copy of the value type in the GC heap and returns a managed pointer to it (the boxing of value types is explained in detail in Chapter 5). The following example shows how to use value types in try and catch statements:

```
#using <mscorlib.dll>
using namespace System;
public __value class V {
    public:
        void Func() {
            Console::WriteLine(S"V::Func()");
        }
};
int main() {
    try {
        V v;
        Console::WriteLine(S"throwing a value type object of V");
        throw __box(v); // boxed v is thrown
    }
    catch (__box V *pBoxedV) {
        Console::WriteLine(S"caught a value type object of V");
        pBoxedV->Func();
        V *pV = pBoxedV;  //  implicit unboxing
        pV->Func();
    }
    __finally {
        Console::WriteLine(S"in __finally block");
    }
}
```

In this sample, the local object v inside the try block is boxed before throwing. The filter of the catch handler has the type of the boxed V. This value can be unboxed and used inside the catch handler.

The output of the preceding program is as follows:

```
throwing a value type object of V
caught a value type object of V
V::Func()
V::Func()
in __finally block
```

Mixing Managed and Unmanaged Exceptions

Managed exceptions can handle both synchronous and asynchronous exceptions. In managed code, unmanaged exceptions are wrapped with the BCL type System::Runtime::InteropServices::SEHException, which inherits from System::Runtime::InteropServices::ExternalException, which in turn inherits from System::SystemException. While looking up a matching catch handler, the CLR considers a filter type of SEHException as a match. Otherwise, when a C++ catch filter is encountered, the CLR unwraps the originally wrapped C++ type and passes it to the filter.

Note that catch (Object *) and catch (...) are so-called catch-all handlers—they can catch any exception. If both of these catch clauses are present at the same scope, the closest catch to the __try block is chosen first.

Consider the following example:

```
// Compile with /EHsc /clr
#using <mscorlib.dll>
using namespace System;
class E {
    public:
        void Func() {
            Console::WriteLine(S"E::Func()");
        }
};
int main() {
    try {
        Console::WriteLine(S"throwing an unmanaged object of E");
        throw new E();
    }
```

```
    catch (E* pE) {
        Console::WriteLine(S"caught an unmanaged object of E");
        pE->Func();
    }
    __finally {
        Console::WriteLine(S"in __finally block");
    }
}
```

The output of the preceding program is as follows:

```
throwing an unmanaged object of E
caught an unmanaged object of E
E::Func()
in __finally block
```

In this sample, a pointer to an instance of the unmanaged type E is thrown inside the try block. Internally, it is wrapped with the managed type SEHException. The try block has a C++ catch handler. While looking up the matching catch handler, the wrapped object is unwrapped before it is compared with the filter of the catch handler. This wrapping and unwrapping of the unmanaged object with SEHException is transparent to the user.

The gc class ExternalException in the System::Runtime::InteropServices namespace is the base exception for all COM interoperability exceptions and structured exceptions. This class adds the following functionality to System::SystemException:

- The new property called ErrorCode: This property returns the error code of the exception raised. It can be an HRESULT or a Win32 error.

- The new instance method called CanResume: This Boolean method returns the three possible filter expression values for structured exceptions. The current implementation of this method always returns false. This is because the current implementation of the CLR does not support resumable exceptions.

The following sample shows both unmanaged and managed exceptions being thrown and caught in the same program.

```
// compile with /EHsc /clr
#using <mscorlib.dll>
using namespace System;
public __gc class ExManaged : public ApplicationException {
```

```
public:
  void Func() {
    Console::WriteLine(S"ExManaged::Func()");
  }
};
class ExUnmanaged {
public:
  void Func() {
    Console::WriteLine(S"ExUnmanaged::Func()");
  }
};
int main() {
    try {
      try {
        Console::WriteLine(S"throwing a managed object of ExManaged");
        throw new ExManaged();
      }
      catch (ExManaged* pExManaged) {
        Console::WriteLine(S"caught a managed object of ExManaged");
        pExManaged->Func();
        Console::WriteLine(S"throwing an unmanaged object of ExUnmanaged");
        throw new ExUnmanaged();
      }
    }
    catch (ExUnmanaged* pExUnmanaged) {
        Console::WriteLine(S"caught an unmanaged object of ExUnmanaged");
        pExUnmanaged->Func();
    }
    __finally {
      Console::WriteLine(S"in __finally block");
    }
}
```

In this example, a managed type ExManaged and an unmanaged type ExUnmanaged are defined. An object of the type ExManaged is thrown in the inner try block. The catch handler for the type ExManaged has the matching filter for the exception. Inside the handler block there is another exception raised by throwing an object of ExUnmanaged. The handler for the outer try block catches this exception. The outer handler is executed, followed by the __finally block execution.

The expected output for the preceding program is as follows:

```
throwing a managed object of ExManaged
caught a managed object of ExManaged
```

```
ExManaged::Func()
throwing an unmanaged object of ExUnmanaged
caught an unmanaged object of ExUnmanaged
ExUnmanaged::Func()
in __finally block
```

Design Guidelines

In software development, error handling should be a fundamental design issue, not an afterthought. Discussing all the issues involved in using exceptions to design reliable error-handling mechanisms is beyond the scope of this book. However, we will look at two major issues with exception handling: performance and exception safety.

As many C++ developers have come to realize, exception handling comes at a cost. To throw and catch an exception is more expensive than, say, to call a function. Even if no exception is thrown, there is still a runtime overhead caused by the presence of the `try-catch` statements.

The CLR implements exception handling in such a way that if no exception is thrown, the runtime overhead is very small. However, you still have to use exceptions to handle only the exceptional cases. Thus, throwing an exception merely to pass a value from one function to another should be avoided.

Exception safety is another major topic that usually comes up when exceptions are mentioned. Basically, the code is considered exception-safe if it works correctly in the presence of exceptions. Such code is often difficult to write in C++—unexpected exceptions can interfere with the regular flow of control and cause various problems ranging from memory leaks to objects with inconsistent state. However, writing exception-safe code in MC++ is easier than in native C++ because all managed objects are garbage collected.

Summary

In this chapter, we introduced managed exceptions and showed how structured exceptions and native C++ exceptions are handled in MC++. The CLR was designed with exception handling as the fundamental error-handling technique in mind. The overhead is minimal when no exceptions are thrown. That's why exception handling is a design choice for handling exceptional cases in developing software that targets the .NET Framework.

Part Two

Interoperability

CHAPTER 15

Transition from Native to Managed Code

APPLICATION DEVELOPMENT USING MC++ falls into two main categories:

- New applications written with only managed components. The managed components can be written in other .NET-targeted languages such as Visual C# .NET and Visual Basic .NET.

- New applications are written or existing applications are modified where some components are managed and some components are native. The native components can be either COM components or native C++ components that do not involve COM.

Because of the large amount of native C++ code written over the years, it is reasonable to assume that many applications will be developed according to the scenarios of the second category, at least in the initial phases of application development for the .NET platform.

MC++ takes advantage of the functionality provided by the .NET Framework (such as using TlbImp, which is discussed in Chapter 17, to expose a COM server to a .NET component or using TlbExp, which is discussed in Chapter 18, to expose a .NET assembly to a COM client) to interoperate with existing COM components. The .NET Framework also facilitates interoperability with native software components that include COM components.

When you develop applications that involve both managed and native components, the choice of exposing native components as managed or managed components as native depends on the application's behavior and requirements. If too many function calls are between managed and native components, consider rewriting the native component as a managed component. On the other hand, if a native component's performance is optimized for a platform such as x86, and if only a few function calls are between managed and native components, it is useful to keep the native component and provide a wrapper that acts as an intermediary between the native and managed components.

In this chapter, we discuss the most basic techniques of interoperability between managed and native code and how to port native code to managed. More advanced topics, such as interoperability with COM, Platform Invocation service, and managed wrappers, are discussed in later chapters.

Managed and Unmanaged Code in the Same Source or Executable File

One of the advantages of MC++ is its capability to mix managed and unmanaged code in the same executable or source file. An existing C++ program can be compiled to generate managed code by using the /clr compiler option (Appendix A discusses the /clr compiler option in detail). The program will continue to compile and run,[1] and you can make incremental changes to add new managed functionality or modify the existing code.

There are two ways to indicate which parts of your program are managed and which parts are unmanaged. The first method is to use #pragma unmanaged and #pragma managed, as in the following example:

```
#using <mscorlib.dll>
using namespace System;
#include <stdio.h>
void ManagedFunction() {
      printf("Hello from ManagedFunction\n");
}
#pragma unmanaged
void UnManagedFunction() {
      printf("Hello from UnManagedFunction\n");
      ManagedFunction();
}
#pragma managed
int main() {
      UnManagedFunction();
}
```

The unmanaged pragma specifies that the compiler should generate native code, and the managed pragma indicates that managed code should be generated. In this example, native code is generated for the UnManagedFunction function and managed code is generated for the remaining parts of the program. This example demonstrates the transition from managed function (main) to unmanaged (UnManagedFunction) and then back to managed (ManagedFunction).

Note that metadata will be generated for both native and managed functions when the /clr compiler option is used.

Another method for specifying which code is managed and which code is to be compiled to native is to place managed and unmanaged functions in separate source files and compile them, respectively, with and without the /clr option and link object files together in one executable:

---

[1]   You need the CLR to be installed on the machine to execute any code compiled with the /clr compiler option.

```
cl unmanaged.cpp /c /MT
cl managed.cpp /clr /c
link unmanaged.obj managed.obj /out:result.exe
```

The /c compiler option tells the compiler to compile the source file into an object file but to not link it. The /MT[2] compiler option causes the compiler to use a multithreaded version of the C runtime, which is the default in managed mode. If this is not what you want, you will have to instruct the linker to ignore symbols from the single-threaded runtime by specifying /nodefaultlib:libc.lib in the linker command line. Note that MC++ applications are typically multithreaded because Finalize methods run in a separate thread.

The resulting executable will be called result.exe, as specified in the linker option /out.

Making Your C++ Class Managed

Your classes do not automatically become managed when you compile your code with the /clr option. There are several reasons why this is the case. First, because the C++ object model is quite different from that of the common language runtime (CLR), not every unmanaged class can become managed. For example, templates and multiple inheritance cannot be expressed in the CLR (although you can still use multiple inheritance for interfaces).

Second, some managed classes can only be created on the GC heap (these classes are called *gc classes*) while others can be created on the stack and, with some restrictions, on the C++ or global heap (these classes are called *value types*). If your managed class is being created both on the stack and on the heap, you cannot make it a gc class or a value type without limiting its functionality.

Assuming your class meets all the requirements, you can make it managed by adding the __gc or __value keyword in front of its definition.

Should your class be a value type (discussed in Chapter 5) or a gc class (discussed in Chapter 3)? It depends on how the class is used and you have to make a judgment call. If the class is used to represent short-lived objects that mainly exist on the stack and are passed by value, and it does not use inheritance, your choice is a value type. An example of a typical value type would be a complex number (with real and imaginary parts). If your class represents objects with a longer lifetime and a bigger footprint that are *never* created on the stack, your choice would most likely be a gc class. Finally, if your class does not meet either of these criteria, you will have to resort to less straightforward methods, such as embedding it into a managed class, as described in the next section.

---

[2] Other compiler options such as /MTd and /MD{d} are also available.

Embedding: Object or Pointer?

Suppose your class cannot be made managed by adding __gc or __value—for example, if it uses multiple inheritance or templates.

How do you expose the functionality of a class by means of another class? Usually, there are two choices: inherit from the class whose functionality you want to expose or embed it as a member. In our case, inheritance is not an option. You cannot inherit a managed class from an unmanaged class and vice versa.

So, we are left with just one option: embedding. Actually, there are still two alternatives—you can embed an object or a pointer to it. As it turns out, embedding an object is rarely a good idea. It doesn't work in all but very simple cases, and in these simple cases you would be better off making your class managed directly by applying __gc or __value.

When you embed an object in a managed class, all its data members will be placed inside this managed class, which means inside the GC heap. Imagine that a member function of the unmanaged class does something unsafe, from the GC point of view, with these data members, such as copying blocks of memory using memcpy. If garbage collection occurs during the execution of this function, the program will be in a corrupted state.

The compiler will help diagnose these unsafe situations. In MC++, addresses of all members of the embedded class, including the imaginary this pointer, are considered gc pointers. That's why the following example will result in a compile-time error:

```
#using <mscorlib.dll>
class Widget {
    char* name;
public:
    // . . .
    const char* GetName() const {
        return name;
    }
};
__gc class Managed_Widget {
    Widget widget;
public:
    const char* GetName() {
        return widget.GetName();  // error !
    }
};
```

When you try to compile the preceding sample, the compiler will complain:

```
error C2662: 'Widget::GetName' : cannot convert 'this' pointer from
              'Widget' to 'const Widget &'
An object from the gc heap (member of a managed class) cannot be
converted to a non-gc reference
```

The workaround is rather simple. Embed a pointer to `Widget` inside `Managed_Widget` and control its lifetime manually by creating the object in the constructor and destroying it in the destructor of `Managed_Widget`. Here's how:

```cpp
// Compile with /clr /EHsc /c
#using <mscorlib.dll>
#include <string>
class Widget {
      std::string name;
public:
      const std::string& GetName() const {
          return name;
      }
};
__gc class Managed_Widget {
      Widget *pWidget;
public:
      Managed_Widget() {
          pWidget = new Widget;
      }
      const std::string& GetName() {
          return pWidget->GetName();
      }
      ~Managed_Widget() {
          delete pWidget;
      }
};
```

Your object will be eventually deleted when the runtime performs garbage collection on `Managed_Widget`, but you don't have control over exactly when this happens. The destructor of `Managed_Widget` is transformed by the compiler into a `Finalize` method (discussed in Chapter 3), which is called by the garbage collector when the object becomes unreachable. When the constructor of the `Managed_Widget` class is executed, an object of the `Widget` class is created on the C++ heap. This object is destroyed by the `delete` operator when the destructor of the `Managed_Widget` class is executed.

All `Finalize` methods are executed in a separate thread. The CLR may call the `Finalize` methods after the program execution has finished. Make sure that the destructor of `Widget` does not do anything that may corrupt the program, such as accessing a resource that has been already disposed of.

Sometimes it may be necessary to embed a value type in a native C++ class. You can do this, but the value type must meet a few requirements:

- It cannot contain managed members or gc pointers.

- It cannot contain any private data members.

- It must have a sequential or explicit layout (specified using `System::Runtime::InteropServices::StructLayoutAttribute`, which is discussed in Chapter 11). A *sequential* layout indicates that when laying out the memory for this type, the runtime should order them sequentially as they appear in the definition of the value type. An *explicit* layout indicates that when laying out the memory for this type, the runtime should follow the layout exactly as specified in the definition of the value type.

The following sample shows how to embed a simple value type in a native C++ class:

```
#using <mscorlib.dll>
using namespace System::Runtime::InteropServices;
[StructLayoutAttribute(Sequential)]
__value struct Point {
  int x;
  int y;
};
class NativeGraphics {
  Point pArray __nogc [2]; // okay
  Point p; // okay
};
```

When you embed value types in native C++ classes, the current MC++ compiler requires the use of `StructLayoutAttribute` on value types. You can also embed nogc arrays of value types in native C++ classes, as shown in the example.

Using a Pinning Pointer

Embedding a pointer to an unmanaged class into a managed class works in most cases, but not always. Not all unmanaged classes can be created on the C++ heap—it might be not desirable, or it may even be impossible—if the programmer who designed that class declared a private operator new to prevent objects of this class from being created on the heap. Besides, using a pointer is usually less efficient: you have to dereference it to get back to the object pointed to.

Embedding an object is an appealing idea and you don't have to throw it out yet. As you saw earlier, the main problem with embedding an object is that the program might become corrupt when the execution of a member function and the garbage collector happens at the same time.

All you have to do is make sure that if the garbage collector is activated, it will not affect the unmanaged object. This means you have to pin it. *Pinning* (which is discussed in Chapter 6) is a way of informing the garbage collector not to move a managed object during a garbage collection cycle. Here's how:

```
// Compile with /clr /EHsc /c
#using <mscorlib.dll>
#include <string>
class Widget {
      int length_;
public:
      int GetLength() const {
         return length_;
      }
};
__gc class Managed_Widget {
      Widget widget_;
public:
      __property int get_Length() {
            Widget __pin* pWidget = &widget_; // pinning the object
            return pWidget->GetLength(); // now we can call the member-function
      }
};
```

In this sample, the assignment of the address of the widget_ field to a pinned pointer results in pinning the whole object. The garbage collector will not be able to move the whole object, even if you pin a part of it.

Note that you could also pin the whole managed object:

```
int get_Length() {
        Managed_Widget __pin *pManagedWidget = this;
        return pManagedWidget->widget_.GetLength();
}
```

This will give the same result.

Note that the effect of pinning lasts until the pinning pointer goes out of scope or is set to 0. At that point, the garbage collector is free to move that managed object. In the preceding sample, it happens after the Get Length function is executed.

Using the vcclr.h File

The vcclr.h file is an SDK header file that provides utility classes and functions that can be used in MC++ applications. In this section, we discuss how to embed a gc pointer to a managed object in an unmanaged class. We also show how to use the utility function PtrToStringChars.

Embedding an unmanaged class inside a managed class exposes it to the managed world. But what if you need it to work the other way around—if you want to integrate a managed class into an unmanaged context?

The major obstacle here is that the garbage collector cannot track objects pointed to by member pointers of unmanaged types. Therefore, the following would not compile:

```
#using <mscorlib.dll>
struct Gadget {
    System::String *name_; // error!
};
```

The .NET Framework provides a solution that is based on the runtime class System::Runtime::InteropServices::GCHandle. This class allows you to register the root of a managed object in nonstack memory. You can take advantage of this class by using the MC++ class gcroot defined in the header file vcclr.h. The implementation of the gcroot class uses GCHandle. Here's how you can use it:

```
#using <mscorlib.dll>
#include <vcclr.h>
struct Gadget {
    gcroot<System::String*> name_; // it works!
};
```

Now you can access this object as if it were a regular data member:

```
int main() {
      Gadget* pGadget = new Gadget;
      pGadget->name_ = S"MyNewGadget";
}
```

Speaking of the vcclr.h file, it is worth noting that it contains another utility useful for interoperability: the PtrToStringChars function. This function comes in handy if you need to access the "raw" string buffer of the String object. You can achieve the same result by copying the String object into an unmanaged buffer character-wise but, of course, this would be less efficient.

The PtrToStringChars function returns a gc pointer to System::Char. Because Char is a 16-bit Unicode symbol, its unmanaged equivalent is wchar_t, not char. Here's an example:

```
#using <mscorlib.dll>
using namespace System;
#include <stdio.h>
#include <vcclr.h>

int main() {
      String *s = S"Hello!\n";
      wchar_t __pin* pRawString = PtrToStringChars(s);
      wprintf( pRawString );
}
```

Note that the compiler *requires* you to pin the pointer before passing it to wprintf. This is how you ensure that the object doesn't move during the execution of wprintf.

It's All About Performance

Performance is an important issue to consider when you mix managed and unmanaged code. Just because the compiler makes mixing managed and unmanaged code very easy does not mean that your code will be efficient.

Calling between managed and unmanaged contexts adds overhead to the function calls. Managed and unmanaged functions have different calling semantics—this is what makes the transition expensive. A few additional instructions are executed to allow the passing of data between the managed and unmanaged sides.

Let's create a sample program that sorts an array of 100 elements. To squeeze the maximum performance out of the compiler, we use the /O2 compiler option in all of the samples that follow. To make it consume a measurable amount of time, we run the sorting procedure 100,000 times.

Here's the program:

```
#include <stdio.h>
#include <time.h>
#include <stdlib.h>

int compare( const void* px, const void* py ) {
      int x = *(int*)px;
      int y = *(int*)py;
      return x < y ? -1 : x > y ?  1 : 0;
}
int main() {
      clock_t t = clock();
      const int size = 100;
      int arr[size];
      for( int iter=0; iter<100000; iter++ ) {
            for( int i=0; i<size; i++ ) {
                  arr[i] = size - i;
            }
            qsort( (void *)arr, size, sizeof(int), compare );
      }
      printf("elapsed time: %2.2f sec\n", (clock()-t)/(double)CLOCKS_PER_SEC);
}
```

The program was compiled in the unmanaged mode (that is, without using the /clr compiler option). When executed on a test computer, it showed an elapsed time of 1.55 seconds.

When the same program was compiled with the /clr option and executed, the elapsed time jumped to 3.20 seconds. What happened? Is the CLR that inefficient?

No, it isn't. The problem is in the transition between managed and unmanaged code that occurs inside the unmanaged C runtime function qsort when it calls the managed callback function compare. To get around this problem, you can make the compare function unmanaged by wrapping it between #pragma unmanaged and #pragma managed:

```
#pragma unmanaged
int compare( const void* px, const void* py ) {
// . . .
}
#pragma managed
```

This technique eliminates the major performance bottleneck: qsort no longer has to call a managed function.

Compile the program with the /clr option and execute it. You will see that this little trick boosts the performance dramatically—the elapsed time gets down to 1.63 seconds. That's good enough, but you can do even better.

Remove the pragmas, add #using <mscorlib.dll> to the program, make the array managed, and use the CLR System::Array::Sort function to sort it:

```
#include <stdio.h>
#include <time.h>
#using <mscorlib.dll>

int main() {
        clock_t t = clock();

        const int size = 100;
        int arr __gc[] = new int __gc[size];

        for( int iter=0; iter<100000; iter++ ) {
                for( int i=0; i<size; i++ ) {
                        arr[i] = size - i;
                }
                System::Array::Sort( arr );
        }

         printf("elapsed time: %2.2f sec\n", (clock()-t)/(double)CLOCKS_PER_SEC);
}
```

Now compile and execute the program. The result might surprise you. The program becomes faster than its unmanaged equivalent, running in just 1.53 seconds.[3]

This example illustrates how performance is affected based on the choices you make when mixing managed and native code. A general guideline is to keep managed and unmanaged code apart and concentrate calls from managed to unmanaged code in just a few places.

---

[3]   These numbers are just guidelines. It should be noted that the performance of a sorting
    algorithm depends on the type of algorithm used and the type of input.

Final Remarks: Common Pitfalls

When you apply the information in this chapter to real-world transition tasks, you have to watch out for some common pitfalls.

Incompatible Compiler Options

When you first compile your application with the /clr option, you might see some errors saying /clr is not compatible with some other compiler options. For example:

```
Command line error D2016 : '/clr' and '/YX' command-line options are incompatible
```

You can avoid most of these kinds of errors by changing your project to use alternative options. For a detailed list of the various compiler options and their compatibility with /clr, refer to the documentation for Visual C++ .NET.

Working with C Code

Consider the following perfectly valid C program:

```
#include <stdio.h>
void PrintNumber();
int main() {
      PrintNumber(2001); // watch out!
}
void PrintNumber(int number) {
      printf( "number=%d\n", number );
}
```

Unlike C++, C allows incomplete function declarations, such as void PrintNumber(). The compiler cannot generate the correct code to call such a function in /clr mode without seeing the full declaration (or definition) of that function. This is because the MSIL requires specifying the full function signature in the function call. The compiler assumes void PrintNumber() means void PrintNumber(void) and it gives you an error if you try to pass a parameter to this function.

What is the solution? In some cases you don't have to cope with this issue at all—just compile your C file without the /clr option. You cannot use any managed classes in C anyway. You can link the modules compiled without the /clr compiler option with the modules that are compiled with the /clr compiler option.

If this does not work for you—for instance, if it causes an unacceptable performance hit (caused by calls to unmanaged functions defined in the C file)—you will have to come up with a better solution, such as changing the C code to make all function declarations match their definitions.

Avoiding Ambiguities

When working with MC++, you might get into the habit of including a using namespace System statement in all your source files. When you do this, you bring all symbols defined in the System namespace into the current scope. However, this practice can backfire: there is a chance that some of the symbols defined in the System namespace are already defined elsewhere in the same scope.

Here's the simplest example of this problem:

```
#using <mscorlib.dll>
using namespace System;
#include <windows.h>
```

Symbols from the System namespace conflict with some symbols defined in windows.h and the code does not compile.

There is no better solution to this problem than being careful where you include using namespace System. Try to concentrate your managed code in files that do not include windows.h.

If this is not feasible, do not specify using namespace System. Use fully qualified names for symbols from System, as follows: System::String instead of String, System::Console::WriteLine instead of Console::WriteLine, and so on. In some cases you may need to use #undef surgically for some of the symbols in the windows.h header file.

The Operator new with Placement Argument

When you have successfully compiled your program with the /clr compiler option, you may want to try to create a few managed objects, such as instances of the System::Object class:

```
System::Object* pObject = new Object();
```

If you are compiling an MFC application, you will see an error like this:

```
error C3828: 'System::Object': placement arguments not allowed while
              creating instances of managed classes
```

What does this error mean? The problem is in the operator new. MFC applications redefine it in Debug mode in the following way:

```
void* AFX_CDECL operator new(size_t nSize, LPCSTR lpszFileName, int nLine);
#define DEBUG_NEW new(THIS_FILE, __LINE__)
#define new DEBUG_NEW
```

The tailored operator new with placement argument is used for memory tracking and detection of memory leaks in MFC applications.

MC++ does not allow placement arguments for the operator new, because the user does not have control over where the managed object is placed. Managed objects can only exist in the GC heap.

The way out is to temporarily undefine the macro, as follows:

```
#undef new
      // create managed objects . . .
      System::Object* pObject = new Object();
#define new DEBUG_NEW
      // continue with MFC-defined operator new
```

Summary

In this chapter, we introduced the idea of mixing managed and native code using #pragma managed and #pragma unmanaged. We discussed the issues to consider when you need to convert a native C++ class into a managed class. We showed how to pin a pointer when a pointer to a managed object is passed to a native C++ function. You saw how to embed a pointer to a managed object in a native C++ class. Finally, we discussed the issues involved with compiling C code, using system header files, and compiling MFC applications.

In the next chapter, we discuss the Platform Invoke (PInvoke) service, which is used to call an exported function from a native C++ DLL.

CHAPTER 16

Platform Invoke Service

THE PLATFORM INVOKE (PINVOKE) SERVICE is one of the services provided in the .NET Framework to interoperate with native software components. It makes it possible for managed code to call functions defined in an unmanaged DLL.

The PInvoke service is responsible for the following actions:

- Locating the unmanaged DLL and loading it into memory

- Marshaling (translating from one representation into another) the arguments between managed and unmanaged contexts when their representations are different between the two contexts (for instance, an ANSI character on one side and a Unicode character on the other)

- Making the call into the unmanaged function

- Returning the results by marshaling, if the return value representation is different between the two contexts, back to the managed code

PInvoke supports calls to the exported global methods and nonstatic member functions in an unmanaged DLL.

In this chapter, we discuss how to make PInvoke calls using the `DllImport` custom attribute. We show how delegates are used to make PInvoke calls into functions that have function pointers as parameters. You'll learn the various data marshaling issues with PInvoke calls.

DllImport Attribute

To use the PInvoke service, managed components use an attribute called `DllImport` in the namespace `System::Runtime::InteropServices`. This attribute is used on a function prototype in managed components. There are two ways of authoring a function prototype that matches the corresponding exported global

or member function in a native DLL: global function prototype and static
member function prototype.

Global Function Prototype for an Exported Global Function

In the global function prototype approach, a global function that corresponds to
the native function is declared in a managed client. The DllImport attribute is
applied on this global function.

To invoke the function in the native DLL, it is called like a global function. No
special encoding is needed. The following code shows an example of this:

```
#using <mscorlib.dll>
using namespace System;
using namespace System::Runtime::InteropServices;

[DllImport("msvcr70", CharSet=CharSet::Auto)]
extern "C" int wcslen( String* pText );

int main() {
    String* str = S"Hello World!";
    int length = wcslen(str);
    Console::Write(S"Length of the string \"Hello World!\" is ");
    Console::WriteLine(length);
}
```

The output of the preceding program is as follows:

```
Length of the string "Hello World!" is 12
```

In this sample, the managed code calls the function wcslen defined in the
unmanaged DLL msvcr70.dll. The value CharSet::Auto for the CharSet parameter helps the PInvoke service determine how to marshal the String* argument.
We discuss the syntax and semantics of the DllImport attribute after the
next section.

Global Function Prototype for an Exported Member Function

Similar to a PInvoke declaration of a global function, functions that correspond
to the exported member functions of native C++ classes can be declared in

a managed client. The `DllImport` attribute is applied to all these functions in the managed client.

To make a call to a native function, the corresponding PInvoke global function is called like any other global function. The following code shows an example. We first create a native DLL that exports member functions and then use it in a managed client.

```
// file: NativeClass.cpp
#include <stdio.h>
class __declspec(dllexport) ExportedClass
{
public:
    int Func( int i ) { return i;}
};

extern "C" __declspec(dllexport) void CreateExportedClassObj(ExportedClass* obj) {
    obj = new  ExportedClass();
    printf("Object of ExportedClass Created\n");
}

extern "C" __declspec(dllexport)
void DeleteExportedClassObj( ExportedClass* instance ) {
    delete instance;
    printf("Object of ExportedClass Destroyed");
}
```

In the preceding code, the class `ExportedClass` exports the member function `Func`. The two methods `CreateExportedClassObj` and `DestroyExportedClassObj` are helper functions to create and destroy instances of the class `ExportedClass`. You can compile this code to generate a native DLL using the `/LD` compiler option.

The following code shows a managed client that makes PInvoke calls on the functions exported in the previous sample:

```
#using <mscorlib.dll>
using namespace System;
using namespace System::Runtime::InteropServices;
[ DllImport( "NativeClass.dll",
             EntryPoint="?Func@ExportedClass@@QAEHH@Z",
             CallingConvention=CallingConvention::ThisCall )]
extern "C" int CallFunc( IntPtr ths, int i );
```

```
[ DllImport( "NativeClass.dll" )]
extern "C" void CreateExportedClassObj(IntPtr ths);

[ DllImport( "NativeClass.dll" )]
extern "C" void DeleteExportedClassObj( IntPtr obj );

int main() {
    IntPtr pExport;
    CreateExportedClassObj(pExport);

    int result = CallFunc( pExport, 100 );
    Console::WriteLine( "Func() returned {0}", __box(result) );

    DeleteExportedClassObj( pExport );
}
```

In this code, the `CallFunc` method has the entry point `?Func@ExportedClass@@QAEHH@Z`. This entry point represents the member function Func of the class ExportedClass. You can obtain this string by using the `dumpbin.exe` utility with the `/exports` option on the native DLL `NativeClass.dll` from the previous sample. The `IntPtr` parameter can be used to pass the `this` pointer between managed and native components. The output of the program is as follows:

```
Object of ExportedClass Created
Func() returned 100
Object of ExportedClass Destroyed
```

Static Member Function Prototype

In the static member function prototype approach, a static member function that corresponds to the exported native function is declared in a managed class. The `DllImport` attribute is applied to the static member function. To make a call to the native function, the static member function of the managed class is called like any other static member function.

The following code shows the same example as shown in the earlier section, "Global Function Prototype for an Exported Global Function," with the prototype mapped to a static member function:

```
#using <mscorlib.dll>
using namespace System;
using namespace System::Runtime::InteropServices;
```

```
public __gc struct StringLibrary {
    [DllImport("msvcr70", CharSet=CharSet::Auto)]
    static int wcslen( String* pText );
};
int main() {
    String* str = S"Hello World!";
    int length = StringLibrary::wcslen(str);
    Console::Write(S"Length of the string \"Hello World!\" is ");
    Console::WriteLine(length);
}
```

In this sample, the gc class `StringLibrary` has a member function that repre-sents the `wcslen` function from the native `msvcr70.dll`. The managed client can invoke the `wcslen` function just like any other static member function of a class.

In the following section, we describe the various parameters required by the `DllImport` attribute used on both global and static functions.

Parameter Details

The `DllImport` attribute has one required (positional) parameter and six optional (named) parameters. The required parameter is the name of the unmanaged DLL without the extension. The optional parameters are as follows:

- `CallingConvention`: An enumeration parameter that defines the calling convention used. The default is `StdCall`. The other possible values are `Cdecl`, `FastCall` (not supported in the current version of the .NET Framework), `WinAPI`, and `ThisCall`.

- `CharSet`: Specifies which character set (ANSI or Unicode) should be used when marshaling string arguments. It is also used to modify the name of a function before it is looked up in the exported functions list of an unmanaged DLL. The default value is `CharSet::Ansi`. The other possible values are `Auto` and `Unicode`. These options are discussed in the next section.

- `EntryPoint`: Names the function to be called. The argument to this param-eter can be the name of a function or its ordinal number (an integer assigned to the function to represent it in a DLL) prefixed with the number sign (#).

- `ExactSpelling`: Boolean parameter that determines if the name of the function needs to be modified depending on the `CharSet` value. If

ExactSpelling is set to true, the name is not modified. Otherwise, if the CharSet value is Ansi, A is appended to the name of the function, and if the CharSet value is Unicode, W is appended to the name of the function.

- PreserveSig: If this Boolean parameter is set to true, the managed function signature should be used exactly as it is specified before making a PInvoke call. For those native DLL functions that return HRESULT, the value of this parameter should be set to false so that the function signature is modified to return HRESULT before making a PInvoke call. When the value is false and if the function returns a failure HRESULT, an exception will be thrown. The default value for PreserveSig is true.

- SetLastError: If set to true, this Boolean parameter indicates that the callee will call the Win32 API function SetLastError. The common language runtime (CLR) marshaler calls the GetLastError function of the Win32 API to determine if the PInvoke call failed during execution and saves the returned value so that it can be retrieved by the caller using the Marshaler::GetLastWinError method. The default value for this parameter is false.

Name Lookup

While matching the name of the function specified by the DllImport attribute to the function in the native DLL mentioned in the attribute, the CLR uses a *fuzzy pattern-matching* algorithm. In this section, we briefly explain the algorithm.

If the CharSet value is Ansi and the function is given the name Func, the lookup algorithm searches for Func. If Func is not available, it searches for FuncA. If both Func and FuncA are not found and the ExactSpelling parameter is not set, the algorithm searches for Func@n, where n is the size in bytes required for the parameter list for Func. If the search fails, the lookup fails.

If the CharSet value is Unicode (using the preceding example), the lookup algorithm first tries to find the function FuncW. In the absence of FuncW, the search continues for Func. In the absence of both FuncW and Func, and if the ExactSpelling parameter is not set, the search continues for Func@n, where n is the size in bytes required for the parameter list for Func. If the search fails, the lookup fails.

If the CharSet value is Auto, the search follows the previously mentioned rules for Ansi if the platform is Ansi. It follows the previously mentioned rules for Unicode if the platform is Unicode (Windows NT, Windows 2000, and Windows XP).

If the ExactSpelling parameter is set, the lookup tries for an exact match, Func.

PInvoke Using Delegates for Function Pointers

When invoked from a managed component, a function with function pointer parameters in a native DLL can itself call a managed function. Delegates are used for this purpose. A delegate representing the function to be called back is created and passed as the argument for the callback parameter (function pointer) of the unmanaged function. Here's an example:

```cpp
// file: export.cpp
// compile with /LD
#include <windows.h>
extern "C" {
  __declspec(dllexport)
  int AreYouDone(void (CALLBACK *callback)(const char* answer,
                                           const char* reason)) {
        callback("Not Done", "Project is too big");
        return 0;
  }
}
```

In the preceding sample, the export.cpp file defines the native function AreYouDone, which takes a function pointer as a parameter. This function is exported in a DLL file using the /LD compiler option.

The following code shows a sample that uses the exported function AreYouDone:

```cpp
#using <mscorlib.dll>
using namespace System;
using namespace System::Runtime::InteropServices;

__delegate bool CallBack (String* answer, String* reason);
__gc class Client {
  public:
    bool CallMeBack(String* answer, String* reason) {
        Console::WriteLine(S"Consultant says : {0}", answer);
        Console::WriteLine(S"Reason is : {0}", reason);
        return false;
    }
};

[DllImport("export", CharSet=CharSet::Ansi)]
extern "C" int AreYouDone( CallBack* call);
```

```
int main() {
    Client *c = new Client();
    CallBack *call = new CallBack(c, &Client::CallMeBack);
    AreYouDone(call);
    GC::KeepAlive(call);
}
```

In order to call this exported function from managed code, a delegate, CallBack, is defined. The gc class Client has a member function, CallMeBack, whose signature matches that of the CallBack delegate. An object of CallBack is created in the main function using an object of Client and the address of CallMeBack.

When the function AreYouDone is called with the delegate instance as an argument, the PInvoke service converts it into a function pointer before passing it to the native function implemented in the DLL file. The native function invokes the delegate call, which results in a call to the function CallMeBack.

The call to the method GC::KeepAlive prevents the object call from being garbage collected during the execution of the unmanaged function AreYouDone. The output of the program is as follows:

```
Consultant says : Not Done
Reason is : Project is too big
```

Data Marshaling

When an unmanaged function is called, there is a context change from managed to unmanaged. In this situation, you have to ensure that the data is properly marshaled. This is because types may have different or ambiguous representations and calling conventions are different between managed and unmanaged contexts. Similarly, when there is context change from unmanaged to managed (for example, when a call to an unmanaged function returns a value), data must be marshaled so that the native types are mapped to their counterparts on the managed side.

In the samples you have seen so far in this chapter, there was no need to explicitly specify how data should be marshaled. This is because most of the simple data types have the same representation in both native and managed contexts. Also, the default data marshaling rules usually do the correct marshaling.

The MarshalAs Custom Attribute and the UnmanagedType Enumeration

Nonprimitive types (such as strings) may need marshaling to ensure that both the managed and unmanaged sides agree on the data received. For example, a call from a managed component into a native component may pass the `System::String` object as an argument while the implementation of the function in the native component expects a Unicode string. For such types, the BCL provides a custom attribute to be attached to a type so that the managed object is marshaled to match the type expected on the native side. This holds true for return types and out parameters where the managed context expects a certain type and the native component passes a value with different representation. This attribute is called `MarshalAs` in the `System::Runtime::InteropServices` namespace.

The `MarshalAs` custom attribute is used to specify how to marshal a parameter or return type of a function or a field of a type. This attribute can be used for the Platform Invoke (PInvoke) service and interoperability between COM and .NET components. In this chapter we provide samples that use the PInvoke service. The `System::Runtime::InteropServices::UnmanagedType` enumeration is used to specify the data marshaling option when using the `MarshalAs` attribute. This enumeration has several members that are used for specifying data marshaling. The members of the `UnmanagedType` enumeration, which correspond to the basic types in native C++, are listed in Table 16-1. The number next to each .NET enumerator value (for example, the "1" in "I1") represents the number of bytes used for that type.

Table 16-1. UnmanagedType Enumerator Values and Their Corresponding C++ Types

.NET ENUMERATOR	NATIVE C++ TYPE
UnmanagedType::I1	char
UnmanagedType::U1	unsigned char
UnmanagedType::I2	short
UnmanagedType::U2	unsigned short
UnmanagedType::I4	int, long
UnmanagedType::U4	unsigned int, unsigned long
UnmanagedType::I8	__int64
UnmanagedType::U8	unsigned __int64
UnmanagedType::R4	float
UnmanagedType::R8	double

Primitive Types

The primitive types in native C++ have direct mapping to the types in the .NET Framework. For example, int maps to Int32, and float maps to Single. For these types there is no special marshaling required when changing context from managed to unmanaged or unmanaged to managed. Table 16-2 shows the mapping of the basic types from native C++ to the .NET types.

Table 16-2. Primitive Types in .NET and Native C++

.NET TYPE	NATIVE C++ TYPE
System::Void	void
System::SByte	char
System::Byte	unsigned char
System::Int16	short
System::UInt16	unsigned short
System::Int32	int, long
System::UInt32	unsigned int, unsigned long
System::Int64	__int64
System::UInt64	unsigned __int64
System::Single	float
System::Double	double

Simple types do not require special data marshaling. The CLR execution engine marshals these types correctly.

The following sample shows how to use the MarshalAs attribute on parameters of type double. Note that the attribute specification on simple data types is optional.

```
#using <mscorlib.dll>
using namespace System;
using namespace System::Runtime::InteropServices;

[DllImport("msvcr70", CharSet=CharSet::Auto)]
extern "C" double sin ([MarshalAs(UnmanagedType::R8)] double f);
                                            // attribute is optional
```

```
int main() {
    double pi = 3.1415926535;
    double sinPiBy2 = sin(pi/2);
    Console::WriteLine(sinPiBy2);
}
```

In the preceding example, the native math function `sin` is implemented in the `msvcr70.dll` file. This function expects a `double` parameter and returns a `double` value. The attribute attached to the parameter is `[MarshalAs(UnmanagedType::R8)]`. This attribute indicates that the parameter should be marshaled from a `double` to a floating-point number with a size of 8 bytes. However, we already know that the type `double` has a size of 8 bytes. Because the sizes are the same on the native as well as the managed side, the attribute is optional. The output of the preceding program is as follows:

```
1
```

Marshaling Value Classes

Only the data members of a value class are marshaled between managed and unmanaged contexts. Each data member of a value class can have the `MarshalAs` custom attribute attached to it. The following is a simple example that does not use the `MarshalAs` attribute on the members of the value types:

```
// file: export.cpp
// compile with /LD
extern "C" {
    struct Rectangle {
        int length, width;
    };
    // calculate the area of a rectangle
    __declspec(dllexport)
    int Area(Rectangle rec) {
        return rec.length*rec.width;
    }
}
```

The preceding sample declares a C function that takes the struct Rectangle as a parameter and returns the area based on the values of the fields in the argument. The following code shows how to calculate the area using a value type as a parameter:

```cpp
// file import.cpp
// compile with /clr
#using <mscorlib.dll>
using namespace System;
using namespace System::Runtime::InteropServices;

[StructLayout(Sequential)]
public __value struct Rec {
    int l;
    int w;
    String* Shape() {
        if (l == w) {
            return S"Square";
        }
        else {
            return S"Rectangle";
        }
    }
};

[DllImport("export")]
extern "C" int Area(Rec v);

int main() {
    Rec r;
    r.l = 3;
    r.w = 4;

    // call PInvoke function
    int a = Area(r);

    Console::WriteLine(S"Shape is {0}", r.Shape());
    Console::Write(S"Area is ");
    Console::WriteLine(a);
}
```

The preceding sample passes a value class instance as a parameter to the PInvoke function Area from export.dll. While marshaling the value class instance, the member function Shape is not marshaled (that is, it is not accessible on the native side) across managed and unmanaged contexts. The output of the program is as follows:

```
Shape is Rectangle
Area is 12
```

Marshaling Strings

Managed string objects of type System::String are marshaled by value.[1] This means that when the value of the argument changes inside the native function, it is not copied to the managed side. To get the in/out semantics where the modified value on the native side is copied back to the managed side, the System::Text::StringBuilder class must be used. It is always passed as an in/out argument.

The members of the UnmanagedType enumeration that are related to strings are LPStr (pointer to a NULL terminated array of ASCII characters), LPWStr (pointer to a NULL terminated array of Unicode characters), LPTStr (pointer to a NULL terminated array of platform-dependent characters), BStr (pointer to a COM BSTR with Unicode characters), AnsiBStr (pointer to a COM BSTR with ANSI characters), and TBstr (pointer to a COM BSTR with platform-dependent characters). Here's how:

```
#using <mscorlib.dll>
using namespace System;
using namespace System::Runtime::InteropServices;

[DllImport("msvcr70", CharSet=CharSet::Ansi)]
extern "C" int strlen( [MarshalAs(UnmanagedType::LPStr)] String* pText );

int main() {
    String* str = S"Hello World!";
    int length = strlen(str);
    Console::Write(S"Length of the string \"Hello World!\" is ");
    Console::WriteLine(length);
}
```

---

[1]   This is because managed strings are immutable.

In the preceding sample, with the specification of CharSet to Ansi, the CLR marshals the String objects from managed code to ANSI strings. The MarshalAs attribute is optional in this case, but when other string types such as a BSTR are involved, the attribute should be used. The output of the program is as follows:

```
Length of the string "Hello World!" is 12
```

The following sample shows an example of using the StringBuilder class from the System::Text namespace:

```
#using <mscorlib.dll>
using namespace System;
using namespace System::Text;
using namespace System::Runtime::InteropServices;

[DllImport("msvcr70", CharSet=CharSet::Ansi)]
extern "C" int strcat( StringBuilder* str1, String* str2 );

int main() {
    StringBuilder* str1 = new StringBuilder(S"Hello ");
    String* str2 = S"World!";
    Console::WriteLine(S"str1 : {0}", str1);
    Console::WriteLine(S"str2 : {0}", str2);
    strcat(str1, str2);
    Console::WriteLine(S"str1 after appending str2 : {0}", str1);
}
```

The two arguments to strcat are passed as in/out arguments. That is, values are passed in and modified values are copied back. In this sample, the first argument is modified. If you use the System::String class to achieve the same result, the first argument won't be modified.

The output of the preceding program is as follows:

```
str1 : Hello
str2 : World!
str1 after appending str2 : Hello World!
```

Marshaling Arrays

Arrays of both primitive and nonprimitive types can be marshaled between managed and unmanaged contexts. Arrays of primitive types are passed by copy-in/copy-out.[2] The following sample shows an example of arrays of primitive types being passed as arguments:

```cpp
// file: export.cpp
// Compile with /LD
extern "C" {
    /* exchange first element with the second */
    __declspec(dllexport)
    int Exchange(int arr[2]) {
        int tmp = arr[0];
        arr[0] = arr[1];
        arr[1] = tmp;
        return 0;
    }
}
```

This simple code exchanges the first element in an array with its second element. Compile this into a native DLL (export.dll) to be used by a managed client. The Exchange function is called as a PInvoke function from the following managed code:

```cpp
#using <mscorlib.dll>
using namespace System;
using namespace System::Runtime::InteropServices;

[DllImport("export", CharSet=CharSet::Ansi)]
extern "C" int Exchange( int arr __gc[]);

int main() {
    int  a __gc [] = { 10, 20};
    Console::WriteLine(S"Array before exchange");
    Console::WriteLine(a[0]);
    Console::WriteLine(a[1]);
    Exchange(a);
    Console::WriteLine(S"Array before exchange");
    Console::WriteLine(a[0]);
    Console::WriteLine(a[1]);
}
```

---

[2] For performance reasons, primitive arrays are not copied—they are pinned.

The elements of the array will be exchanged in the native function when it is called from the managed code. The output of the program is as follows:

```
Array before exchange
10
20
Array before exchange
20
10
```

The following code shows an example of an array of value types used as a parameter to a PInvoke function. In this sample, a native DLL exports a function that sorts an array of structs.

```
// file: NativeSort.cpp
#include <string.h>
struct Person {
    char* first;
    char* last;
};

extern "C" __declspec(dllexport)
void SortArrayOfStructs( Person* pPersonArray, int size ) {
    for( int i = 0; i < size; i++ ) {
        for (int j = i+1; j < size; j++) {
            if (strcmp(pPersonArray[i].last, pPersonArray[j].last) > 0) {
                // exchange pPersonArray[i] and pPersonArray[j]
                char* last = pPersonArray[i].last;
                char* first = pPersonArray[i].first;

                pPersonArray[i].last = pPersonArray[j].last;
                pPersonArray[i].first = pPersonArray[j].first;

                pPersonArray[j].last = last;
                pPersonArray[j].first = first;
            }
        }
    }
}
```

Compile the preceding code using the /LD compiler option to generate a native DLL.

The following managed code uses the SortArrayOfStructs function to sort an array of value types:

```
#using <mscorlib.dll>
using namespace System;
using namespace System::Runtime::InteropServices;

[ StructLayout( LayoutKind::Sequential, CharSet=CharSet::Ansi )]
public __value struct Person {
      String *first;
      String *last;
      Person( String *firstName, String *lastName ) {
            first = firstName;
            last = lastName;
      }
};

[ DllImport( "NativeSort.dll" )]
extern "C" int SortArrayOfStructs( [In, Out] Person personArray __gc[], int size );
int main() {
      Person persons __gc[]= { Person( S"John", S"Smith" ),
                               Person( S"Anthony", S"Marshal" ),
                               Person( S"Sara",S"Justice" )
                             };
      Console::WriteLine( "Person array before sorting by last name:" );
      for( int i = 0; i < persons->Length; i++ )
          Console::WriteLine( "last = {0}, first = {1}", persons[i].last,
                                                         persons[i].first );
      SortArrayOfStructs( persons, persons->Length );

      Console::WriteLine( "\nPerson array after sorting by last name:" );
      for( int i = 0; i < persons->Length; i++ )
          Console::WriteLine( "last = {0}, first = {1}", persons[i].last,
                                                         persons[i].first );
}
```

Notice that the first parameter in the PInvoke function declaration has In and Out attributes applied.[3] This is required when there are nonprimitive members in the value type used as the array element. Otherwise, the array will not be copied back.

---

[3]   See Chapter 11 for a discussion on the In and Out attributes.

The output of the program is as follows:

```
Person array before sorting by last name:
last = Smith, first = John
last = Marshal, first = Anthony
last = Justice, first = Sara

Person array after sorting by last name:
last = Justice, first = Sara
last = Marshal, first = Anthony
last = Smith, first = John
```

Summary

In this chapter, we described how the Platform Invoke (PInvoke) service is used to make function calls into the exported functions of native DLLs. We showed how the custom attribute `DllImport` and the enumeration `UnmanagedType` are used in making PInvoke function calls. We discussed how delegates are used to call methods with function pointers as parameters. Finally, we explained how to use the various data marshaling options in a PInvoke call. For a detailed description of the various marshaling options, refer to the .NET Framework documentation on PInvoke.

In the next chapter, we discuss how to access COM components from a .NET component.

CHAPTER 17

Accessing COM Components from .NET

ONE OF THE KEY REQUIREMENTS of the .NET Framework is to provide seamless integration between COM components and .NET components. To interact with a managed component, an unmanaged component need not be rewritten completely. Depending on the application, the unmanaged component, the managed component, or both can be tailored to work together.

In MC++, there are two ways to access COM components from a .NET component. You can use the directive `#import` to import a type library directly into the managed component. This directive generates C++ classes (and other declarations such as smart pointer and typedefs) for describing COM interfaces in the type library. You cannot inherit from them because inheritance between managed and unmanaged types is not allowed. If inheritance from the types in the type library is not a requirement in the managed component, the `#import` directive is the preferred way to use COM components. The reasons for this are that you don't need to use the wrappers that are required for interop assemblies (discussed in the next section), and the C++ header files generated for the type libraries can be part of precompiled header files, which results in faster importing.

The second way to access COM components from a .NET component is to generate interop assemblies for the type libraries and use them in .NET components.

In this chapter, we discuss the issues involved with accessing COM components from .NET components via interop assemblies.

Interop Assemblies

To access a COM type library from a .NET client, you must create an assembly that maps the types in a COM type library to managed types. This assembly is known as an *interop assembly.*

In an interop assembly, each type from the COM type library has a corresponding managed wrapper type that acts as a proxy and forwards all method invocations to the native type in the COM type library. These wrapper types collectively are known as a *Runtime Callable Wrapper (RCW)*. An RCW handles the creation of the COM object and provides the marshaling code required to transfer arguments and return types between an unmanaged component and a managed component. It also handles object identity and memory management. For an unmanaged component, this wrapper appears as a native client. For a managed component, this wrapper appears as a managed server. This wrapper is garbage collectible and it handles the reference count issues of the unmanaged component. Every COM object referenced will have a single RCW even if the COM object has multiple references. This assures that a single object identity is shared between the COM object and the RCW.

Interop assemblies can be private or shared. (Private and shared assemblies are described in Appendix C.) It is possible for multiple private assemblies with the same name to exist, but there can only be one shared assembly with a given strong name. Depending on the need, an interop assembly may or may not be generated to have a strong name. Typically, the producer of a type library creates a strong-named interop assembly known as the *primary interop assembly*. Only this primary interop assembly should be used by clients to avoid type incompatibilities that may result from using different assemblies for the same COM object.

There are three ways to generate an interop assembly:

- Use the Type Library Importer, or TlbImp (`tlbimp.exe`), from the .NET Framework SDK.

- Use the base class library (BCL) class `TypeLibConverter`.

- Use custom wrappers that are user-defined managed classes.

In the following sections, we discuss these approaches.

Interop Assembly Generation Using TlbImp and the TypeLibConverter Class

In this section, we briefly explain TlbImp and the `TypeLibConverter` class and then describe the steps involved in generating an interop assembly. Interop assemblies generated by TlbImp and the `TypeLibConverter` class for a given type library have the same metadata. The only difference is that TlbImp requires a persisted type library, whereas the `TypeLibConverter` class can generate an interop assembly in memory.

Type Library Importer

The .NET Framework SDK includes a tool called the Type Library Importer (TlbImp). This tool converts the types from a COM type library into managed types that act as proxies for the COM type library types. The syntax for using TlbImp is as follows:

```
tlbimp.exe tlbfile [options]
```

In the preceding command, `tlbfile` is a COM type library file. Several options can be used with `tlbimp.exe`. Some of the interesting options are as follows:

- `/asmversion:versionNumber`: This option specifies the version number to be used for the resulting interop assembly.

- `/help`: This option displays the command-line syntax for `tlbimp.exe`.

- `/keyfile:filename`: The file `filename` contains the strong name details (typically the public and private keys). This file can be generated using the strong name generation tool, `sn.exe`. This file is used to sign the resulting interop assembly.

- `/namespace:namespaceName`: The managed types generated for the type library types are enclosed in the namespace given with this option. The default namespace is the name of the type library.

- `/out:filename`: This option specifies the name of the assembly file to be generated. The default name is the name of the type library with the extension `.dll`.

- `/primary`: This option marks the generated interop assembly as the primary interop assembly. The assembly will contain the information that the publisher of the type library has created the interop assembly. Note that a primary interop assembly must contain a strong name.

- `/reference`: This option specifies the assembly to use for the referenced types defined outside the current type library. When this option is specified, the referenced types defined outside the current type library are looked up in the assembly. If they are not defined in the referenced assembly, the type libraries containing the definition are imported recursively.

- `/sysarray`: This option specifies that each COM `SafeArray` should be mapped as the type `System::Array`.

The following sample shows a COM server that implements an interface with one method. TlbImp converts the type library into an interop assembly.

```cpp
// a COM Server
// File: Publisher.cpp
#define _ATL_ATTRIBUTES
#include <atlbase.h>
#include <atlcom.h>
#include <stdio.h>
#include <comutil.h>

[module(name="Publisher",type="dll")];

// IPublisher interface with one method
[dual]
__interface IPublisher : IDispatch {
     [id(0x01)] HRESULT GetLatestBook([in] BSTR author, [out,retval] BSTR
*title);
};

// coclass CPublisher implements the interface IPublisher
[coclass, threading="both"]
class CPublisher: public IPublisher {
     HRESULT GetLatestBook(BSTR author, BSTR *title) {
        if (_bstr_t("Anonymous") == _bstr_t(author)) {
           *title = _bstr_t("The New Book").copy();
           return S_OK;
        }
        else {
           *title = _bstr_t("Error: Author Not Found").copy();
           return S_FALSE;
        }
     }
};
```

The Visual C++ .NET compiler generates a COM library file and a COM DLL file while compiling the preceding code with the /LD command-line option and linking with the comsupp.lib library, which provides marshaling functions to convert to and from BSTR. You can register the native COM DLL using the regsvr32.exe utility. The COM server is now available for use by its clients.

This sample shows a COM server that implements the interface IPublisher, has a single GetLatestBook method, and takes two BSTR parameters. The class CPublisher implements the IPublisher interface. The implementation of the

GetLatestBook method returns "The New Book" if the author parameter value happens to be "Anonymous". It returns "Error: Author Not Found" for any other value of the author parameter.

To generate an RCW, TlbImp is used. Because this server is a simple server, no special data marshaling is needed for the parameters of the member function GetLatestBook.

```
tlbimp.exe /out:PublisherLib.dll Publisher.dll
```

Upon successful completion, TlbImp generates the following message:

```
Type library imported to D:\work\comInterop\simple\PublisherLib.dll
```

The metadata generated in the PublisherLib.dll assembly is as follows:

```
.namespace PublisherLib {
  .class public auto ansi import CPublisherClass
         extends [mscorlib]System.Object
         implements PublisherLib.IPublisher,
                    PublisherLib.CPublisher  {
    .method public specialname rtspecialname
            instance void  .ctor() runtime managed internalcall {
    } // end of method CPublisherClass::.ctor

    .method public hidebysig newslot virtual
        instance string
        marshal( bstr)
      GetLatestBook([in] string  marshal( bstr) author)
                                 runtime managed internalcall {
      .override PublisherLib.IPublisher::GetLatestBook
    } // end of method CPublisherClass::GetLatestBook
  } // end of class CPublisherClass

  .class interface public abstract auto ansi import CPublisher
         implements PublisherLib.IPublisher {
  } // end of class CPublisher

  .class interface public abstract auto ansi import IPublisher {
    .method public hidebysig newslot virtual abstract
            instance string
            marshal( bstr)
            GetLatestBook([in] string  marshal( bstr) author)
                                      runtime managed internalcall {
```

```
        } // end of method IPublisher::GetLatestBook
      } // end of class IPublisher
} // end of namespace PublisherLib
```

The metadata in the `PublisherLib.dll` (the interface, the class, and their members) can be viewed using ILDasm (`ildasm.exe`). TlbImp generates the suffix `Class` for coclasses. Notice that the return type of the member function `GetLatestBook` is marked as a `String` and it has the custom attribute `marshal(bstr)` attached. Similarly, the parameter of the function is also defined as a `String` and it has the `marshal(bstr)` custom attribute attached to it. Note that the metadata listing shown here is a stripped-down copy of the actual metadata.

The generated `PublisherLib.dll` assembly can be used by a managed client like any other assembly. A sample is provided later in this chapter.

TypeLibConverter Class

The `System::Runtime::InteropServices` namespace provides a set of useful types that you can use for interoperability between COM type libraries and .NET clients. The `TypeLibConverter` class is from this namespace. You can use this class for converting type libraries into interop assemblies and assemblies into type libraries.

The method that converts a type library into an interop assembly is `ConvertTypeLibToAssembly`. This method returns a COM interface pointer. It is an overloaded method. The return type of the function is an instance of `AssemblyBuilder` in the `System::Reflection::Emit` namespace. The `AssemblyBuilder` class represents a dynamic assembly (that is, an assembly created in memory).

The parameters common to the two overloads are as follows:

- `typeLib`: The object that implements the `ITypeLib` interface. It represents the type library. It will be converted to metadata.

- `asmFileName`: The name of the file for the resulting interop assembly.

- `flags`: An enumerator of type `TypeLibExporterFlags`. The values of the enumerator are `PrimaryInteropAssembly`, `SafeArrayAsSystemarray`, and `UnsafeInterfaces`.

- `notifySink`: An interface of type `ITypeLibImporterNotifySink` implemented by the caller to get the status of the conversion process. This interface is also used when a reference to a type library needs to be resolved to an assembly.

- publicKey: This parameter represents a public key as a Byte array.

- keyPair: An object of type StrongNameKeyPair that contains the public and private cryptographic keys.

The parameter specific to the first overload is as follows:

- unsafeInterfaces: If this Boolean is true, expensive checks are not performed on type library interfaces. Otherwise, runtime checks are required for the type library interfaces.

The parameters specific to the second overload are as follows:

- asmNamespace: The namespace that will be used to generate the types in the interop assembly.

- asmVersion: An object of type System::Version that sets the version number of the generated interop assembly. If this parameter is null, the assembly version will be set based on the version number of the type library.

The following sample shows how to use the TypeLibConverter class to generate an interop assembly in memory and save it to a file:

```
#using <mscorlib.dll>
using namespace System;
using namespace System::Runtime::InteropServices;
using namespace System::Reflection;
using namespace System::Reflection::Emit;

public __value enum REGKIND
{
    REGKIND_DEFAULT = 0, // use default register behavior
    REGKIND_REGISTER,    // register the type library
    REGKIND_NONE         // don't register the type library
};

[DllImport("oleaut32.dll", CharSet=CharSet::Unicode)]
extern "C" void LoadTypeLibEx(
                    String *strTypeLibName,
                    REGKIND regKind,
                    [MarshalAs( UnmanagedType::Interface )] Object **TypeLib);
// Not used, other than to make ConvertTypeLibToAssembly compile.
```

```
public __gc class InnerSink : public ITypeLibImporterNotifySink {
public:
    Assembly *ResolveRef(Object *typeLib) { return 0; }
    void ReportEvent(ImporterEventKind eventKind, int eventCode,String *eventMsg)
{}
};

int main() {
    Object* tlb;
    Console::WriteLine(S"loading type library");
    LoadTypeLibEx("Publisher.dll",  REGKIND_NONE, &tlb);
    if(tlb == 0) {
        throw new TypeLoadException("TLB Not found" );
    }
    // Convert the COM TypeLib to a .NET Assembly
    TypeLibConverter *conv = new TypeLibConverter();
    InnerSink *eventHandler = new InnerSink();
    AssemblyBuilder *ab = conv->ConvertTypeLibToAssembly(
                tlb, "PublisherLib.dll", 0, eventHandler, 0,0,false);

    // Save out the Assembly into the cache ab->Save("assemblyName");
    ab->Save("PublisherLib.dll");
}
```

In this sample, it is assumed that the type library from previous section is generated and registered. The native method LoadTypeLibEx defined in oleaut32.dll is used to load a type library into memory. This method is invoked via the PInvoke service using the DllImport custom attribute. There are three parameters to this method: a string representing the type library name, an enumeration that indicates how the type library is to be registered, and a reference to the type library being loaded. Notice that the last parameter has a MarshalAs attribute that specifies that the argument should be converted to UnmanagedType::Interface during argument marshaling. The gc class InnerSink is a dummy class defined to make the call to ConvertTypeLibToAssembly succeed. It provides a dummy implementation for the two methods of the interface ITypeLibImporterNotifySink.

In the main method, the call to LoadTypeLibEx loads the type library into memory. If the call fails, the variable tlb will not be updated. Instances of TypeLibConverter and InnerSink are created in the next two statements. The call to ConvertTypeLibToAssembly creates the interop assembly and names it PublisherLib.dll. The in-memory interop assembly is saved to disk with the name PublisherLib.dll when the call to Save succeeds.

The output of the program is an assembly with the name `PublisherLib.dll` in the current directory.

Method Invocations on a COM Server

To invoke methods on a COM server from a managed client, an RCW is generated for the COM object. This RCW can be used to invoke methods on the corresponding COM objects. The steps involved in exposing a COM server to a managed client are as follows:

1. Register the COM server using the `regsvr32.exe` utility.

2. Use TlbImp or the `TypeLibConverter` class in the `System::Runtime::InteropServices` namespace to generate an assembly (a managed wrapper DLL) for the COM server. This assembly DLL is the interop assembly.

3. There are two ways of interacting with a COM server from a managed client: importing the interop assembly or using runtime type discovery.

    a. Use the `#using` directive in an MC++ client to import the metadata from the interop assembly and use the types from it. There are two ways of invoking methods on a type library: static invocation and dynamic invocation.

    b. Use the late-binding technique that uses the Reflection API provided by the .NET Framework to discover the type wrapped in an RCW, instantiate an object, and invoke methods on it.

After an interop assembly is created, the invocation of methods on the types in a COM type library is the same regardless of how the interop assembly is generated. The following subsections describe static invocation, dynamic invocation, and late binding, respectively.

Static Invocation

If a client of a COM server knows exactly which interface is implemented by a given object, the methods of the interfaces can be invoked on the object. This is known as *static invocation.*

The following sample shows how static invocation can be used on a COM server by a managed client using an interop assembly generated via TlbImp:

```
// .NET Client
#using<mscorlib.dll>
using namespace System;

// Import the metadata of the native Publisher.dll file
#using "PublisherLib.dll"
using namespace PublisherLib;

int main()
{
    // Create an instance of the COM object by creating
    // a Runtime Callable Wrapper object
    IPublisher *pub = new CPublisherClass;

    // Invoke a method on the RCW, which in turn forwards the call
    // to the COM object
    String *title = pub->GetLatestBook(S"Anonymous");

    // Print the result
    Console::WriteLine(title);
}
```

The preceding code shows a managed client. To use the type from the unmanaged DLL, the managed client should import the metadata from the interop assembly PublisherLib.dll using the #using directive. When an instance of the wrapper is created, it in turn loads the COM object. You do not need to use the CoCreateInstance or QueryInterface functions that are needed in COM programming. The invocation of the GetLatestBook method on the wrapper instance generates a call to the GetLatestBook method of the COM object by providing appropriate data marshaling (conversion of String to BSTR in this sample). If there is a failure in the COM object, the HRESULT values are converted to .NET exceptions in the managed code.

The output of the preceding program is as follows:

```
The New Book
```

Dynamic Invocation

To see if an interface is supported by an unmanaged object, you can make use of the QueryInterface solution in COM programming. For managed types, it simply translates to doing a type cast to the interface in question. In MC++, you can use __try_cast to achieve this. If a given object does not implement the interface to which a cast is tried, the runtime throws an exception that can be handled by using try-catch blocks.

The following sample shows a revised managed client from the example given in the previous section:

```
// .NET Client
#using<mscorlib.dll>
using namespace System;

// Import the metadata of the native Publisher.dll file
#using "PublisherLib.dll"
using namespace PublisherLib;

int main()
{
    // Create an instance of the Runtime Callable Wrapper (RCW)
    CPublisher *pPub = new CPublisherClass;
    IPublisher* pIPub = 0;
    try {
        pIPub = __try_cast<IPublisher*>(pPub);
    }
    catch(InvalidCastException *e) {
        Console::WriteLine(S"Cpublisher does not implement IPublisher");
        return 1;
    }

    // Invoke a method on the RCW, which in turn forwards the call
    // to the native dll
    String *title = pIPub->GetLatestBook(S"Anonymous");

    // Print the result
    Console::WriteLine(title);
}
```

In this sample, the __try_cast keyword is used to cast the managed object of CPublisher to a pointer to the interface IPublisher. If the CPublisher object implements the IPublisher interface, the cast succeeds and it will not generate any exceptions. If the cast fails, it generates the System::InvalidCastException object. In the current sample, the cast succeeds. The output is the same as that of the previous managed client:

```
The New Book
```

Late Binding

The previous sections have shown static and dynamic invocation of methods on a COM object. In both cases, the metadata for the COM object is available at compile time to a managed client via an RCW. In the absence of the metadata at compile time, you can use the late binding technique with the help of the Reflection API provided by the .NET Framework. This involves finding out if a COM server exists for a given programmatic identifier (ProgID, a registry entry that can be associated with a class) using the method GetTypeFromProgID. This method returns a pointer to Type*. If the returned pointer is not null, the server object can be created using the Activator::CreateInstance method. A method can be invoked on the server object using the InvokeMember method on the object. When late binding is used, the RCW instance will have the type System::__ComObject.

Although the late binding technique gives you the flexibility to do a method invocation by discovering the type at runtime, it is less efficient than static and dynamic invocations.

The following sample shows a managed client that uses the late binding technique for invoking a method on the COM server object from previous sections:

```
#using<mscorlib.dll>
using namespace System;
using namespace System::Reflection;
int main()
{
    Object *objPublisherLateBound;
    Type *objTypePublisher;

    // get type of the wrapper
    objTypePublisher = Type::GetTypeFromProgID("CPublisher.CPublisher");
```

```
    if (objTypePublisher == 0) {
        Console::WriteLine(S"GetTypeFromProgID() failed");
    }
    else {
     // create an instance of the wrapper, which in turn creates the COM object
        objPublisherLateBound = Activator::CreateInstance(objTypePublisher);
    try {
            // prepare the parameter list
            Object *params [] = {S"Anonymous"};
            // invoke the method GetLatestBook
            String *title = __try_cast<String *>
                    (objTypePublisher->InvokeMember(S"GetLatestBook",
                    BindingFlags::InvokeMethod,
                    0,
                    objPublisherLateBound,
                    params));
            //  print the result
            Console::WriteLine(title);
        }
        catch(InvalidCastException* e) {
            Console::WriteLine(e);
        }
    }
}
```

In this sample, the ProgID of the COM server object is
`CPublisher.CPublisher`. This ProgID is passed to the `GetTypeFromProgID`
Reflection API call. In the current example, this routine returns
a non-zero value. The COM server object is then instantiated using the
`Activator::CreateInstance` method. Then, a method on the object is invoked
using the `InvokeMember` method. The output of the program is as follows:

```
The New Book
```

Using Connection Points in COM from a .NET Client

Connections points are one of the main bidirectional communication mechanisms used in COM. They are similar to events in the .NET Framework. Event
source components in COM have an interface that has the attribute [source] on

it in the coclass. This interface is called an *outgoing interface*. Event receivers implement this outgoing interface. An interface pointer to this outgoing interface is passed to the event source by the event receivers. The event source maintains a list of interface pointers to the event receivers. When the event source raises an event, it notifies the event receivers by calling the corresponding method on the outgoing interface implemented by the event receivers. See the Visual C++ .NET documentation for more details.

The following sample shows how connection points in COM servers are used by managed clients. In this sample, we assume that `sample.dll` (a COM server) implements connection points for a Publisher application. The example from the previous sections can be extended to implement an event where the Publisher application is extended to have an event that fires whenever a new book is published. Customers can register with the Publisher application to be notified when a new book is published. Customers can unregister whenever they'd like.

The following listing shows the `sample.idl` file generated using the ATL COM AppWizard in Visual Studio 6.0:

```
// sample.idl : IDL source for sample.dll
// This file will be processed by the MIDL tool to
// produce the type library (sample.tlb) and marshaling code.
import "oaidl.idl";
import "ocidl.idl";
[
    object,
    uuid(CO9626DA-8AEA-4CA7-AAAE-9E7A73C77FEC),
    dual,
    helpstring("IConnection Interface"),
    pointer_default(unique)
]
interface IConnection : IDispatch
{
    [id(1), helpstring("method GetBook")]
    HRESULT BookPublished([in] BSTR author, [in] BSTR title);
};
[
    uuid(C742AD61-8170-49C8-B7D4-C33D57966ABF),
    version(1.0),
    helpstring("sample 1.0 Type Library")
]
library SAMPLELib
{
    importlib("stdole32.tlb");
    importlib("stdole2.tlb");
```

```
    [
        uuid(C9965E85-3F68-4D7E-BDCA-9A104D4E307D),
        helpstring("_IConnectionEvents Interface")
    ]
    dispinterface _IConnectionEvents {
        properties:
        methods:
            [id(1), helpstring("method InformMe")]
            HRESULT InformCustomer([in] BSTR author, [in] BSTR title);
    };


    [
        uuid(CE27FF4F-273D-4094-9B00-130A4F2CCB5C),
        helpstring("Connection Class")
    ]
    coclass Connection {
        [default] interface IConnection;
        [default, source] dispinterface _IConnectionEvents;
    };
};
```

When the BookPublished method is called, the implementation calls the InformCustomer method on registered clients.

We assume that TlbImp is used on the COM server (sample.dll) to generate the interop assembly sampleLib.dll. This RCW is imported by a managed client and used to register to and unregister from events. The following listing shows the partial output of ILDasm when it is applied on sampleLib.dll:

```
.namespace SAMPLELib
{
  .class interface public abstract auto ansi import _IConnectionEvents  {
    .method public hidebysig newslot virtual abstract
            instance int32
            marshal( error)
            InformCustomer([in] string  marshal( bstr) author,
                           [in] string  marshal( bstr) title)
                                 runtime managed preservesig internalcall {
    } // end of method _IConnectionEvents::InformCustomer
  } // end of class _IConnectionEvents


  .class public auto ansi sealed _IConnectionEvents_InformCustomerEventHandler
        extends [mscorlib]System.MulticastDelegate
```

```
                {
                } // end of class _IConnectionEvents_InformCustomerEventHandler

                .class public auto ansi import ConnectionClass
                        extends [mscorlib]System.Object
                        implements SAMPLELib.IConnection,
                                   SAMPLELib.Connection,
                                   SAMPLELib._IConnectionEvents_Event
                {
                    .method public specialname rtspecialname
                            instance void  .ctor() runtime managed internalcall
                    {
                    } // end of method ConnectionClass::.ctor

                    .method public hidebysig newslot virtual
                            instance void  BookPublished([in] string  marshal( bstr) author,
                                                         [in] string  marshal( bstr) title)
                                                             runtime managed internalcall {
                      .override SAMPLELib.IConnection::BookPublished
                    } // end of method ConnectionClass::BookPublished

                    .method public hidebysig newslot virtual
                            instance void  add_InformCustomer(
                            class   SAMPLELib._IConnectionEvents_InformCustomerEventHandler A_1)
                                runtime managed internalcall    {
                      .override SAMPLELib._IConnectionEvents_Event::add_InformCustomer
                    } // end of method ConnectionClass::add_InformCustomer

                    .method public hidebysig newslot virtual
                            instance void  remove_InformCustomer(
                              class SAMPLELib._IConnectionEvents_InformCustomerEventHandler A_1)
                                 runtime managed internalcall {
                      .override SAMPLELib._IConnectionEvents_Event::remove_InformCustomer
                    } // end of method ConnectionClass::remove_InformCustomer

                    .event SAMPLELib._IConnectionEvents_InformCustomerEventHandler InformCustomer
                    {
                       .addon instance void SAMPLELib.ConnectionClass::add_InformCustomer(
                                class SAMPLELib._IConnectionEvents_InformCustomerEventHandler)
                       .removeon instance void SAMPLELib.ConnectionClass::remove_InformCustomer(
                                class SAMPLELib._IConnectionEvents_InformCustomerEventHandler)
                    } // end of event ConnectionClass::InformCustomer
```

```
    } // end of class ConnectionClass
}
```

This listing shows the event definition for `InformCustomer` in the class
`ConnectionClass`.[1] The delegate used to implement this event is
`_IConnectionEvents_InformCustomerEventHandler`. The following code shows
a managed client that uses this event from the `sampleLib.dll` interop assembly:

```
// client.cpp
// Compile with /clr
#using <mscorlib.dll>
using namespace System;
#using "sampleLib.dll"
using namespace sampleLib;

[event_receiver(managed)] // optional
__gc class Customer {
   public:
      void InformMe(String* author, String* title){
                Console::WriteLine(S"author: {0}", author);
                Console::WriteLine(S"title: {0}", title);
      }
      void SubscribeToPublisher(ConnectionClass* publisher) {
       // The += operator calls the Advise method
         publisher->InformCustomer  += new
    _IConnectionEvents_InformCustomerEventHandler(
                                             this, &Customer::InformMe);
      }
      void UnsubscribeToPublisher(ConnectionClass* publisher) {
         // The -= operator calls the UnAdvise method
         publisher->InformCustomer  -= new
    _IConnectionEvents_InformCustomerEventHandler (
                                             this, &Customer::InformMe);
      }
};

int main() {
        // create an instance of the server
        ConnectionClass* pSource =  new ConnectionClass();
        // Create an instance  of the customer
        Customer* pCustomer = new Customer();
```

---

[1]   For a detailed discussion on how events are defined and used, refer to Chapter 13.

```
        // Register the customer with the server
        pCustomer->SubscribeToPublisher(pSource);

        // fire the event
        String* author = S"Anonymous";
        String* title = S"Great Book";
        pSource->BookPublished(author, title);

        // Unregister the customer with the server
        pCustomer->UnsubscribeToPublisher(pSource);
    }
```

In this sample, the generated wrapper using TlbImp has all types enclosed in the namespace SAMPLELib. The class Customer has three methods: InformMe, SubscribeToPublisher, and UnsuscribeToPublisher. The InformMe method has a signature that matches the signature of the InformCustomer method in the COM server. The SubscribeToPublisher method has code that uses the += operator of events. The InformCustomer variable is an unmanaged equivalent of a delegate in the COM server. To subscribe to the event, the += operator is used along with the creation of the delegate object of _IConnectionEvents_InformCustomerEventHandler (from sampleLib.dll). Similarly, the -= operator is used to unsubscribe to the events.

In the main function, a server object is created first, followed by a client object. The client is registered with the server using the SubscribeToPublisher method. The BookPublished event of the server is fired. This event calls the InformMe method of the client. The client is unregistered with the server using the UnsubscribeToPublisher method. At this point, the client's InformMe method will not be called even after firing the BookPublished event. The output of the program is as follows:

```
author: Anonymous
title: Great Book
```

Interop Assembly Generation Details

We briefly discuss the details of interop assembly generation in this section.

A type library can have more than one module with constants and methods. The constants are imported as members of a managed type with the same name as that of the module. The methods that are not part of any class are not imported.

While an interface is imported, the methods from `IUnknown` and `IDispatch` are not imported. The .NET runtime automatically provides an alternative implementation for them. The interface identifier (IID) is copied via the custom attribute `Guid`.

While a coclass is imported, TlbImp generates an interface with the name of the coclass and a managed class with the name of the coclass suffixed with `class` (in the sample from the previous section, the coclass `Connection` has a managed class `ConnectionClass` in the interop assembly). The members of this class consist of member methods of each of the interface that the coclass implements. In case of name collisions with names from multiple interfaces implemented by the coclass, the name of the interface is prefixed to the name of the member. A default constructor will also be generated for the managed type. If the imported coclass is marked with a `noncreatable` type library attribute, a default constructor is not generated for the corresponding managed class. `DispIds` are copied while importing. Collisions with `DispIds` are resolved by assigning `DispIds` to the members of the coclass' default interface.

The types introduced using the `typedef` keyword are not imported by TlbImp. It replaces the usage of `typedef` with the actual underlying type. The original name of the imported member is saved using `ComAliasNameAttribute`.

Properties are imported as managed properties. A getter and/or a setter is created if a getter and/or setter is available for the property from the type library. The managed property getter and setter will have the prefixes get_ and set_, respectively.

Inheritance and Containment of COM Types

It is possible that a managed client can inherit from or contain a COM type after it is wrapped by a managed type (RCW) via TlbImp or the `System::Runtime::InteropServices::TypLibConverter` class.

Inheriting from a COM Type

COM types can be inherited by managed types. However, they can only be inherited from their corresponding mappings in the interop assembly. Requirements for a COM type to be a base type are as follows:

- It must be creatable.

- It must be aggregatable.

- It should have metadata generated for it.

COM Interface Inheritance

While importing COM interfaces that use inheritance, the generated derived managed interface will contain the methods of the base interface.

Interfaces in the type library:

```
__interface Base : IDispatch {
        HRESULT method1();
};
__interface Derived: public Base {
        HRESULT method2();
};
```

Interfaces in the interop assembly:

```
__gc __interface Base {
void method1();
};
__gc __interface Derived: public Base {
        void method1();
        void method2();
};
```

In this sample, the derived interface `Derived` is a wrapper interface for the COM interface. It supports two methods: `method1` from the `Base` interface and `method2` from the `Derived` interface.

Containment

Containment is the typical wrapping technique used while wrapping unmanaged types with managed types.

Managed types can have COM types as members. However, you cannot directly use COM types as members; when importing interop assemblies, the public types from interop assemblies can be used as the members of managed types. The COM objects created programmatically using the `Activator::CreateInstance` method on types obtained from the `Type::GetTypeFromProgID` method can be members of managed types.

Limitations of Exposing COM Components to Managed Clients

Some of the limitations of generating metadata for type libraries are as follows:

- The HRESULTs that represent success are not reported to the .NET components, whereas the HRESULTs that represent failures are reported as runtime exceptions. If successful HRESULTs are needed, the custom attribute PreserveSigAttribute must be used.

- Variable length arrays can be parameters of a method in a type library. Typically, the length of the array is passed as a separate argument. There is no direct way to link the array length and the array together. This is because the type library does not capture this information (even if the IDL does). This may cause problems in marshaling variable length arrays. The recommended way to add length information is in the MarshalAs attribute.

- TlbImp may not generate the right metadata when void* or union is used as a parameter of a method. Incorrect metadata may also be generated if a method uses a buffer and the size of the buffer as parameters.

In such cases, the output of TlbImp can be disassembled with ILDasm (ildasm.exe), modified with the necessary attributes, and then reassembled with ILAsm (ilasm.exe). The following section explains this process.

Customizing Interop Assemblies

Sometimes the default marshaling supported by TlbImp is not enough to marshal user-defined types. This can happen if not all details from the IDL are propagated to the type library. In such situations, it is the programmer's responsibility to provide implementation for marshaling the data between managed and unmanaged contexts. In order to customize the interop assembly generated for a COM type library, the descriptions of coclasses and interfaces should be available. Knowledge of data marshaling rules is required. As this description indicates, customizing interop assemblies is an advanced technique that is not used in typical applications.

Customization can be done at two places: at the native source descriptions of COM types and at the metadata description generated in interop assemblies.

COM Source Customization

On the COM side, the custom keyword and the type library attributes can be used to customize the COM types. Note that in the custom attribute, the key and value pair of an attribute must be represented as UUIDs and their corresponding values. A custom attribute can be applied to interfaces, coclasses, members, and parameters. This attribute attaches information into the type library that can be used by the type library importers that generate interop assemblies.

Consider the following sample:

```
// a COM Server
// Compile with /LD
#define _ATL_ATTRIBUTES
#include <atlbase.h>
#include <comdef.h>
#include <atlcom.h>


[module(name="PublisherLib",type="dll")];

[custom(0F21F359-AB84-41e8-9A78-36D110E6D2F9, "PublisherLibrary.PubInterface")]
// IPublisher interface with one method
[object]
__interface IPublisher
{
    [id(0x01)]HRESULT GetLatestBook([in] BSTR author, [out,retval] BSTR *title);
};


// class CPublisher implements the interface IPublisher
[custom(0F21F359-AB84-41e8-9A78-36D110E6D2F9, "PublisherLibrary.PubCoClass")]
[coclass, threading(both)]
class CPublisher: public IPublisher
{
    HRESULT GetLatestBook(BSTR author, BSTR *title)
    {
        if (_bstr_t("Anonymous") == _bstr_t(author)) {
        *title = _bstr_t("The New Book").copy();
        return S_OK;
        }
        else {
        *title = _bstr_t("Error: Author Not Found").copy();
        return S_FALSE;
        }
    }
};
```

In this sample, the `custom` attribute is applied to an interface and a coclass at the native source level. The GUID, `0F21F359-AB84-41e8-9A78-36D110E6D2F9`, is defined in the .NET Framework SDK include file `cor.h` (`GUID_ManagedName`). The second parameter to the `custom` attribute specifies mapping for the name of the type in an interop assembly. When the resulting type library is converted into an interop assembly, the `IPublisher` interface is mapped to the `PubInterface` interface in the `PublisherLibrary` namespace and the `CPublisher` coclass is mapped to the `PubCoClass` gc class in the `PublisherLibrary` namespace. The generated metadata for the interop assembly can be viewed using ILDasm (`ildasm.exe`).

```
.module PublisherLib.dll
// stripped information
.namespace PublisherLibrary
{
  .class public auto ansi import PubCoClass
         extends [mscorlib]System.Object
         implements PublisherLibrary.PubInterface
  {
      // stripped details
  } // end of class PubCoClass
  .class interface public abstract auto ansi import PubInterface
  {
    // stripped details
  } // end of class PubInterface
} // end of namespace PublisherLibrary
```

Refer to the .NET documentation for a detailed discussion of type library attributes.

Metadata Customization

To apply customization to the metadata of an interop assembly, you can save the metadata of the assembly into a file using ILDasm (`ildasm.exe`). The necessary interop attributes can be applied to interfaces, methods, classes, and parameters. The modified metadata can be assembled again into an interop assembly using ILAsm (`ilasm.exe`).

The following sample shows an example where TlbImp does not generate the expected signature for a method of a COM object in the interop assembly. Let's suppose that the Publisher type library in the previous section has an additional method, GetAuthorIDs, that updates a given integer array with author IDs. The following code shows the source code used to generate the COM type library:

```cpp
// file: Publisher.cpp
#define _ATL_ATTRIBUTES
#include <atlbase.h>
#include <atlcom.h>
#include <stdio.h>
#include <comutil.h>

[module(name="Publisher",type="dll")];

// IPublisher interface with two methods
[dual]
__interface IPublisher : IDispatch {
    [id(0x01)] HRESULT GetLatestBook([in] BSTR author,
        [out,retval] BSTR *title);
    [id(0x02)] HRESULT GetAuthorIDs([in] BSTR author,
        [in] int numIDs,
        [out, size_is(numIDs)] long IDs[]);
};

// coclass CPublisher implements the interface IPublisher
[coclass, threading="both"]
class CPublisher: public IPublisher {
    HRESULT GetAuthorIDs(BSTR author, int numIDs, long IDs[]) {
        if (_bstr_t("Anonymous") == _bstr_t(author)) {
            for (int i = 0; i < numIDs; i++)
                IDs[i] = i+1;
            return S_OK;
        }
        else {
            for (int i = 0; i < numIDs; i++)
                IDs[i] = 0;
            return S_FALSE;
        }
    }
}
```

```
HRESULT GetLatestBook(BSTR author, BSTR *title) {
    if (_bstr_t("Anonymous") == _bstr_t(author)) {
        *title = _bstr_t("The New Book").copy();
        return S_OK;
    }
    else {
        *title = _bstr_t("Error: Author Not Found").copy();
        return S_FALSE;
    }
}
};
```

As you can see, the second and third parameters of the GetAuthorIDs method represent an IDs integer array with its length represented by the numIDs parameter. You can generate a type library for this code by using the /LD compiler option and linking with comsupp.lib.

When you try to use an interop assembly generated using TlbImp from the type library for the preceding code, it will not work because the signature for the GetAuthorIDs method is incorrect in the interop assembly. TlbImp maps the last parameter of the method incorrectly as [out] int32& IDs.

To fix this problem, you need to edit the metadata. Metadata can be generated using ILDasm on the interop assembly. You need to replace the third parameter of the GetAuthorIDs method with [out] int32[] marshal([]) IDs.

The following listing shows the modified metadata for this method:

```
.namespace PublisherLib
{
  .class public auto ansi import CPublisherClass
          extends [mscorlib]System.Object
          implements PublisherLib.IPublisher,
                     PublisherLib.CPublisher
  {
    .method public hidebysig newslot virtual
            instance void  GetAuthorIDs(
                              [in] string  marshal( bstr) author,
                              [in] int32 numIDs,
                              [out] int32[] marshal([])  IDs
                          ) runtime managed internalcall
    {
      .override PublisherLib.IPublisher::GetAuthorIDs
    } // end of method CPublisherClass::GetAuthorIDs

  } // end of class CPublisherClass
```

```
.class interface public abstract auto ansi import IPublisher
{
    .method public hidebysig newslot virtual abstract
            instance void  GetAuthorIDs(
                                [in] string  marshal( bstr) author,
                                [in] int32 numIDs,
                                [out] int32[] marshal([]) IDs
                            ) runtime managed internalcall
    {
    } // end of method IPublisher::GetAuthorIDs
} // end of class IPublisher
```

The modified metadata can be reassembled using ILAsm. The following code uses the modified metadata (reassembled in the file PublisherLib.dll). Note that the file Publisher.dll should be registered for the sample to work.

```
// .NET Client
#using<mscorlib.dll>
using namespace System;

// Import the metadata of the native Publisher.dll file
#using "PublisherLib.dll"
using namespace PublisherLib;

int main()
{
    // Create an instance of the Runtime Callable Wrapper (RCW)
    IPublisher *pub = new CPublisherClass;

    // Invoke a method on the RCW, which in turn forwards
    // the call to the native dll
    int IDs __gc[] = new int __gc [3];
    pub->GetAuthorIDs(S"Anonymous", 3, IDs);

    // Print the result
    for (int i=0; i < 3; i++)
        Console::WriteLine(IDs[i]);
}
```

The output of the program is as follows:

```
1
2
3
```

Some of the other cases where metadata customization is needed are In/Out C-style arrays, multidimensional C-style arrays, and nonzero bound SAFEARRAYs. Refer to the .NET documentation for a discussion on how to modify interop assemblies containing these types.

Summary

In this chapter, we introduced interop assemblies. We showed various techniques of generating interop assemblies for COM servers. You saw samples for using TlbImp and the TypeLibConverter class. We discussed how methods in a COM server can be called statically, dynamically, and using late binding. We explained how to customize standard wrappers with source changes on the COM side as well as how to modify and reassemble assemblies.

In the next chapter, we show how .NET components can be accessed from COM components.

CHAPTER 18

Accessing .NET Components from COM

IN THE PREVIOUS CHAPTER, you learned how COM components are exposed to .NET clients. This chapter discusses how .NET components are exposed to COM clients.

While developing applications for the .NET platform, existing software components can be accessed by .NET clients. It is equally as important to be able to access .NET components from COM clients, depending on the application requirements.

To access a .NET component from a COM client, the .NET component is mapped to a type library. We use the terms "assembly" and ".NET component" interchangeably in this chapter. The COM clients can then use the generated type library to interact with the managed components. For a COM client, the generated type library appears like any other COM server. All method invocations are forwarded to the managed component by the wrapper.

Similar to a Runtime Callable Wrapper (RCW), each type from a managed component will have a corresponding wrapper type in the type library. These wrapper types collectively are known as a *COM Callable Wrapper (CCW)*.

There are four ways to generate type libraries for .NET components:

- Use the Type Library Exporter (`tlbexp.exe`) tool.

- Use the Assembly Registration utility (`regasm.exe`). (This utility calls `tlbexp.exe` internally.)

- Use the gc class `TypeLibConverter` from the `System::Runtime::InteropServices` namespace.

- Use the .NET services installation tool (`regsvcs.exe`).

Of these four techniques, the last one, `regsvcs.exe`, is used for interoperability between .NET components and COM+ 1.0 services. When applied to an assembly, this tool executes the following actions: It loads and registers the assembly, and it generates, registers, and installs the type library corresponding to the assembly into a specified COM+ 1.0 application. For more details on this tool, refer to the .NET documentation.

In this chapter, we discuss the techniques used to generate type libraries from .NET assemblies, and we explain the three ways of invoking methods on the generated types.

Type Library Generation

In this section, we discuss three techniques used to generate type libraries from an assembly. In all three techniques, the steps involved in exposing a .NET component to a COM client are as follows:

1. Register the .NET component using the Register Assembly (`regasm.exe`) utility (also known as the RegAsm utility).

2. Use the Type Library Exporter (`tlbexp.exe`) tool (also known as the TlbExp tool) or the `TypeLibConverter` class to generate wrapper classes for the types in the .NET component so that they can be accessed by a COM client.

3. Use the `#import` directive in the client application source code to import the type library generated in step 2 and use the types from it.

Note that RegAsm is a superset of TlbExp. Registration and type library creation can be done in one step using RegAsm.

The following sample shows the code for an assembly that uses a book publisher server responding to the invocation of the `GetLatestBook` method from a customer:

```
// .NET Component
// File: Publisher.cpp
#using <mscorlib.dll>
using namespace System;
using namespace System::Runtime::InteropServices;
[ClassInterface(ClassInterfaceType::AutoDual)]
public __gc class CPublisher
```

```
{
public:
      // Simple method that just knows about "Anonymous"
      [returnvalue: MarshalAs(UnmanagedType::LPStr)]
      String*  GetLatestBook(String* author) {
            if (String::Equals(author, new String("Anonymous"))) {
                return (new String("The New Book"));
            }
            else {
                return (new String("Error: Author Not Found"));
            }
      }
};
```

This sample implements the gc class CPublisher with one method, GetLatestBook. This method has String* as a parameter and a return type. Note that the class has a custom attribute, ClassInterface, indicating that the generated type library should contain a dual class interface that contains all methods that include inherited methods of the class CPublisher. A class interface has the same name as the class but with an underscore (_) prefix (in the preceding sample, it would be _CPublisher). The return value of the function has a custom attribute, MarshalAs, that specifies how the return type should be marshaled between managed and unmanaged contexts.

Note that the use of AutoDual as a class interface value is discouraged because it does not version well. This is because it exposes a class interface to COM clients and they can bind to a specific interface layout that is subject to change. We used AutoDual to illustrate method invocations (shown later) on a .NET component. You should try to use the None value where possible. This value indicates that no class interface is generated for the gc class. The gc class only supports late binding for COM clients.

TlbExp

The .NET Framework SDK provides the TlbExp tool, which is used to generate type libraries for assemblies. The syntax is as follows:

```
Tlbexp.exe [options] assemblyName
```

The options are as follows:

- `/help` or `/?`: Prints the Help file text.

- `/names:fileName`: The `fileName` file is an input text file that specifies the capitalization of names in the type library that will be generated.

- `/nologo`: Suppresses the banner text.

- `/out:fileName`: Keeps the generated type library in the file `fileName`.

- `/silent`: Suppresses the output text generated by `tlbexp.exe`.

- `/verbose`: Generates detailed output from `tlbexp.exe`.

To generate a type library for the previous sample, you can use `tlbexp.exe` as follows:

```
tlbexp.exe /out:PublisherLib.dll Publisher.dll
```

In this command, `Publisher.dll` is the assembly. This command generates the type library but doesn't register it.

RegAsm

The .NET Framework SDK provides an assembly registration utility called RegAsm (`regasm.exe`). The primary purpose of this utility is to register assemblies so that they can be used by COM components. This utility is also used to generate type libraries from assemblies. The syntax is as follows:

```
regasm.exe [options] assemblyName
```

The options are as follows:

- `/codebase filePath`: This option creates a code base entry (`filePath`) in the system registry. This entry identifies the location of the assembly. The assembly used as the argument to `regasm.exe` must be a strong-named assembly. Note that if the assembly is going to be added to the global assembly cache, the `/codebase` option should not be used.

- `/help` or `/?`: This option prints the Help file text.

- `/nologo`: This option suppresses the banner text.

- /regfile [:regFile]: This option creates a registry file (regFile) that can be used to update the registry when needed. Note that the registry file doesn't contain any information that would be added to the registry as part of the custom user registration functions.

- /silent: This option suppresses the messages emitted during the operation of tlbexp.exe.

- /tlb [:typeLibFile]: This option generates a type library file corresponding to the assembly passed as the argument to regasm.exe and registers it. This type library is also registered. This is required if cross-apartment context or process calls are to be made on methods of interfaces (or class interfaces) defined in the assembly.

- /u or /unregister: This option suppresses the registration of the creatable classes in the assembly, which can be used by the COM clients.

- /v or /verbose: This option prints detailed output generated by regasm.exe.

If a given assembly references other assemblies, a type library for each one is generated recursively. Note that TlbExp cannot be used on the interop assembly created using TlbImp or the TypeLibCoverter class.

For the previous sample, RegAsm can be used as follows:

```
regasm.exe /tlb:PublisherLib.dll Publisher.dll
```

This command registers the assembly, generates the type library file PublisherLib.dll, and registers the file.

TypeLibConverter Class

The System::Runtime::InteropServices namespace provides a set of useful types that can be used for interoperability between COM type libraries and .NET clients. The TypeLibConverter class belongs to this namespace. Similar to generating assemblies from type libraries (discussed in the previous chapter), this class can be used for converting assemblies to type libraries.

The method that converts an assembly into a type library is ConvertAssemblyToTypeLib. This method returns a pointer to UnmanagedType::Interface. The parameters are as follows:

- assembly: The name of the assembly to be converted.

- typeLibName: The name of the type library file to be generated.

251

- flags: An enumerator of type TypeLibExporterFlags. The value of the enumerator is OnlyReferenceRegistered.

- notifySink: An interface of type ITypeLibExporterNotifySink implemented by the caller to get the status of the conversion process.

The following sample shows how to use the TypeLibConverter class to generate type libraries from assemblies. It assumes that the assembly DLL Publisher.dll is available in the current directory.

```
#using <mscorlib.dll>
using namespace System;
using namespace System::Reflection;
using namespace System::Reflection::Emit;
using namespace System::Runtime::InteropServices;

[ComImport,
InterfaceTypeAttribute( ComInterfaceType::InterfaceIsIUnknown ),
GuidAttribute( "00020406-0000-0000-C000-000000000046" )
]
public __gc __interface UCOMICreateITypeLib {
        void CreateTypeInfo();
        void SetName();
        void SetVersion();
        void SetGuid();
        void SetDocString();
        void SetHelpFileName();
        void SetHelpContext();
        void SetLcid();
        void SetLibFlags();
        void SaveAllChanges();
};
public __gc class ConversionEventHandler : public ITypeLibExporterNotifySink {
public:
        void ReportEvent( ExporterEventKind eventKind,
                                          int eventCode,
                                          String* eventMsg ) { }

        Object *ResolveRef( Assembly* asmbly ) {  return 0; }
};
```

```
int main() {
    Assembly *asmbly = Assembly::LoadFrom( "Publisher.dll" );
    TypeLibConverter *converter = new TypeLibConverter();
    ConversionEventHandler *eventHandler = new ConversionEventHandler();

    UCOMICreateITypeLib *typeLib =
    __try_cast<UCOMICreateITypeLib*>
    (
        converter->ConvertAssemblyToTypeLib(
                                    asmbly,
                                    "PublisherLib.dll",
                                    (TypeLibExporterFlags)0,
                                    eventHandler )
    );
    typeLib->SaveAllChanges();
    }
```

In this sample, the `UCOMICreateITypeLib` interface has a few custom attributes. The `ComImport` attribute indicates that the interface has been implemented in a COM type library. `InterfaceTypeAttribute` indicates that the current interface should be exposed to COM as an interface inheriting from `IUnknown`. The gc class `ConversionEventHandler` is used to implement the `ItypeLibExporterNotifySink` interface. This interface is used to inform the caller of events and to have him or her resolve referenced assemblies to type libraries. The implementation of the methods is not noteworthy for this example.

In the main function, the assembly `Publisher.dll` is loaded into memory using the `LoadFrom` static method of the `Assembly` class. The assembly is converted into a type library using the `ConvertAssemblyToTypeLib` function of the `TypeLibConverter` class. The return value of this function is an object that implements the `UCOMICreateITypeLib` interface. The type library is saved to disk with the name `PublisherLib.dll`, using the `SaveAllChanges` function.

Method Invocations on a .NET Component

An instance of a managed class can be created and invoked from COM in three ways: static invocation, dynamic invocation, and late-bound invocation through `IDispatch`. The first two samples in this section assume that you have created the DLL `PublisherLib.dll` in the current directory. The last sample assumes that you have registered the assembly `Publisher.dll` using RegAsm.

Static Invocation

Static invocation requires a method name and its signature be known at compile time. In the following sample, the GetLatestBook method is invoked on a server using static method invocation.

```
// COM Client
#include <stdio.h>
#import "PublisherLib.dll" auto_search auto_rename

using namespace Publisher;

int main()
{
    CoInitialize(NULL);

    // Create an instance of the managed object. This will automatically create
    // the COM Callable Wrapper (CCW) object
    _CPublisherPtr pub(__uuidof(CPublisher));

    BSTR author = ::SysAllocString(L"Anonymous");

    // Invoke a method on the managed object; this call will go through the CCW
    const char* book = pub->GetLatestBook(author);

    // Print the result
    printf("%s\n", book);
    SysFreeString(author);
    CoUninitialize();
}
```

In this sample, the type library created in the previous section is imported using the #import statement. An instance of the managed object is created using _CpublisherPtr. The invocation of GetLatestBook on the variable pub is a static method invocation. The output of the program is as follows:

```
The New Book
```

Dynamic Invocation

The standard QueryInterface solution for COM works for dynamic invocation on .NET components. After a COM component (a type library) is generated from a .NET component, a COM client can treat that type library as a native type library. The CCW corresponding to a type library is responsible for creating managed objects and invoking methods on them with proper marshaling of the parameters.

The following example shows how to invoke the GetLatestBook method dynamically on a .NET component:

```
// COM Client
#include <stdio.h>
#import "PublisherLib.dll" auto_search auto_rename
using namespace Publisher;
int main()
{
    CoInitialize(NULL);
    IUnknown* pUnk=0;
    _CPublisher* pPub=0;
    CoCreateInstance(__uuidof(CPublisher), 0, CLSCTX_ALL,
                     IID_IUnknown, (void **) &pUnk);
    pUnk->QueryInterface(__uuidof(_CPublisher), (void **) &pPub);

    BSTR author = ::SysAllocString(L"Anonymous");
    // Invoke a method on the managed object. This will go through the CCW
    const char* book = pPub->GetLatestBook(author);
    // Print the result
    printf("%s\n", book);
    SysFreeString(author);
    CoUninitialize();
}
```

In this sample, an instance of the managed object is created using the CoCreateInstance method. The CCW calls into the managed server to create an instance of the Cpublisher class. The QueryInterface method is called to get an interface pointer that supports the GetLatestBook method. Then the method is invoked on the interface pointer. This method is forwarded to the object of CPublisher.

Late-Bound Invocation

Similar to dynamic invocation, late-bound invocation on the .NET components from COM can be achieved by using IDispatch as in COM programming. The following example shows how to create and invoke methods on a .NET component without importing the corresponding type library:

```
// COM Client
#include <stdio.h>
#include <atlbase.h>

int main()
{
    CoInitialize(NULL);

    CLSID classId;
    CLSIDFromProgID(L" CPublisher", &classId);

    // create an instance of the CCW
    IDispatch* pDisp;
    CoCreateInstance(classId, 0, CLSCTX_ALL, IID_IDispatch, (void **) &pDisp);

    // Get the DispID of the function GetLatestBook
    DISPID disp = 0;
    BSTR newStr = ::SysAllocString(L"GetLatestBook");
    pDisp->GetIDsOfNames(IID_NULL, &newStr, 1, 0, &disp);


    // prepare to invoke the method GetLatestBook
    CComVariant author("Anonymous");
    CComVariant returnValue;

    // prepare the arguments list
    DISPPARAMS d;
    d.rgvarg = &author;
    d.rgdispidNamedArgs = 0;
    d.cArgs = 1;
    d.cNamedArgs = 0;

    // invoke the method
    pDisp->Invoke(disp, IID_NULL, 0, DISPATCH_METHOD, &d, &returnValue, 0, 0);

    // print the result
    wprintf(L"%s\n", returnValue.bstrVal);

    SysFreeString(newStr);
    CoUninitialize();
}
```

In this sample, the ProgID `CPublisher` is used to get the ClassID for the `CPublisher` class. The ClassID is used to create an instance of the managed object. The methods supported by the managed object are found by calling the `GetIDsOfNames` method. The argument list is prepared using the structure `DISPPARAMS`. The `GetLatestBook` method is called using the `Invoke` method. Note that the `returnValue` variable contains a wide character string. The output of the program is as follows:

```
The New Book
```

Type Library Generation Details

While using the type libraries generated from a .NET component using TlbExp, RegAsm, or the `TypeLibConverter` class, either the `#import` option `raw_interfaces_only` should be used or `mscorlib.tlb` should also be imported using `#import`. An important point to note is that .NET assembly names are case insensitive. Two assemblies that differ only in the case of the name are treated as two different assemblies from the perspective of native C++. During the type library creation, the assembly name is used as the type library name as well as the namespace name that encloses the types.

If there are types that have members with the same name as that of the type, the common case for that name will be the first name encountered while generating the type library. For example, if the class name is `Customer` and a method name is `Customer`, the name `Customer` appears for both the class name and the method name in the type library. You can control how the name appears in the type library by using the /names option of TlbExp.

You are not allowed to apply TlbExp on a .NET component generated with TlbImp. An assembly is identified by the combination of the name of the assembly, the originator key (public/private key pair), the culture (locale of the assembly), and the version (a string consisting of the major, minor, build, and revision numbers). When generating a type library ID (TLBID), the name of the assembly, originator key, and the product portion (major and minor) of the version are used. The build number and revision number are saved as the version number of the type library. The assembly culture is converted to an LCID.

The `AssemblyDescriptionAttribute` contents are mapped to the help string. Types are usually exported without the qualified name, but when there is a name collision, the qualified name is used for the translation. The period (.) character in a qualified name is translated to an underscore (_) character. The managed types that are creatable will have a ProgID (usually the qualified name of the type). The ProgID is not stored in the type library; however, it will be added to the registry when you run RegAsm on the assembly.

Each public managed class is exported to the type library unless it is restricted to be exported with the custom attribute `ComVisibleAttribute`.[1] The coclass generated implements all interfaces implemented by the managed type. A `GuidAttribute` attribute on managed classes is used if available. If it is absent, a GUID is generated automatically. Managed classes that are not creatable (abstract) are marked with the `noncreatable` attribute.

All managed interfaces are exported as dual interfaces with `IDispatch` as their base class. `InterfaceTypeAttribute` can be used to identify the type of the interface (`dual`, `non-dispatch`, and `dispatch`). All generated interfaces are marked with `odl` and `oleautomation` type library attributes. The inheritance hierarchy of interfaces is flattened while exporting. For example, if managed interface `IDerived` inherits from managed interface `IBase`, in the generated type library `IDerived` does not inherit from `IBase`. This makes it difficult for a COM client to use polymorphism and pass `IDerived` where `IBase` is expected.

For each managed class, a dispatch-only class interface is generated. The name of the class interface is the same as the managed class, except it is prefixed with an underscore (_). This will become the default interface. A class interface contains all public, nonstatic members of the managed class. This is a useful interface for COM clients, but it should be used with caution because it doesn't support any versioning.

The custom attribute `ClassInterfaceAttribute` controls the generation of the class interface.

- If `ClassInterface(ClassInterfaceType::AutoDual)` is specified, a dual class interface will be generated (which does not version). This will become the default interface.

- If `ClassInterface(ClassInterfaceType::None)` is specified, no class interface is generated and the first implemented interface will be the default interface. `ClassInterfaceType::None` is the recommended option.

Value classes are exported as C-style structs. Member functions of value classes are not exported and are not callable from COM clients.

Enumerations are exported with the enumeration name followed by an underscore attached as a prefix for each enumerator. This is to avoid name conflicts.

Managed types that reference unmanaged types originally exported from a COM component get a direct reference. They don't access the unmanaged types via CCW.

---

[1] This attribute has no affect on interfaces with the `ComImport` attribute.

Methods in .NET and COM are different in the sense that COM methods use HRESULTs. Each exported method will have a .NET signature and a COM signature. The return value of a method is converted to an out, retval parameter in the COM signature. The method signature is preserved in COM when the custom attribute System::Runtime::InteropServices::PreserveSig is attached.

Overloaded methods are exported so that they have unique names. An ordinal number with an underscore prefix is attached to the end of the overloaded method name. COM clients must use decorated names when calling overloaded methods.

Default values for parameters are exported so that the generated parameter will have the defaultvalue type library attribute.

Managed properties are exported to have propget and propput type library attributes.

Mapping Events

Managed event sources can have COM event clients. While mapping managed events, the public delegates are mapped to interfaces with the same name but with an underscore (_) prefix. The interfaces have the members from the System::MultiCastDelegate class and the Invoke method.

The public event members are mapped to two methods: add_X and remove_X (where X is the name of the event). These are added as members of the class interface. The unmanaged clients of the event use the add_X and remove_X methods to register and unregister.

In order to use COM connection point clients, the preceding mechanism cannot be used. A separate event interface must be generated in the managed component. The custom attribute ComSourceInterfacesAttribute must be used on this event interface. This attribute contains the event interfaces that the class uses as source interfaces. The attribute GuidAttribute can be used on the event interface. In the absence of this attribute on an event interface, the runtime will generate the GUID automatically. The event interface members have the names of the public events and they have the same signature of the corresponding delegates. When generating the type library, this event interface is marked as a source interface for the coclass corresponding the managed type that contains the events.

When mapping the event interface, TlbExp generates the wrapper that implements the IConnectionPointContainer interface. A connection point is generated for each source interface marked with the ComSourceInterfaces attribute. The unmanaged clients must implement the event interface.

Aggregation and Containment

Managed objects can be contained or aggregated in COM objects. The requirement on the managed classes is that they must have public accessibility with a default public constructor.

A managed object can be contained in a COM object as a member. As shown in earlier chapters, managed classes can be pointer members of unmanaged classes. The outer object forwards calls to the contained objects as needed.

A managed object can be aggregated in a COM object. The unmanaged COM object creates the managed object by calling CoCreateInstance and passing its own IUnknown as the OuterUnknown parameter. The aggregated managed object caches the parameter. When queried for an interface not supported by the managed object, it passes the calls to the cached interface. All calls to the managed object's AddRef and Release methods are passed to the cached interface.

Customizing Standard Wrappers

Similar to customizing the standard wrappers for COM to .NET interoperability, it is sometimes necessary to customize the standard wrappers for .NET to COM interoperability. In order to achieve this, custom attributes can be used at the source code of the assemblies. In the previous chapter, you saw how interop attributes are applied to the disassembled code. The interop attributes can be applied to the source code of assemblies. For example, the MarshalAs attribute can be applied to the System::String* parameter of a method when a COM client expects to see a wide character string. Chapter 19 contains more information on the MarshalAs attribute.

Summary

In this chapter, we discussed various techniques for creating a type library from an assembly, including using TlbExp, using RegAsm, using the TypeLibConverter class, and using regsvcs.exe. We showed samples for generating type libraries using the first three options. You saw method invocations on a managed object from a COM client using a CCW for static invocation, dynamic invocation, and late binding.

In the next chapter, we examine the various data marshaling options used for method invocations between COM and .NET components.

CHAPTER 19

Data Marshaling between COM and .NET

TRANSPORTING DATA FROM ONE SYSTEM to another and converting it to its proper representation on the target system is called *data marshaling.* The data marshaling techniques we describe in this chapter apply to the interoperability between COM and .NET components.

Similar to the Platform Invoke (PInvoke) service, where data marshaling is required when there is a context change between managed and unmanaged components, data marshaling is also required when there is a transition from a managed context to an unmanaged COM context (for example, when a COM object's method is called from a managed client). Similarly, in case of a transition from an unmanaged context to a managed context (for example, when a call to a COM method returns a value), data must be marshaled so that the native types are translated to match the size expected by the corresponding managed types.

Note that the custom attribute MarshalAs and the enumeration UnmanagedType are used to specify data marshaling for the PInvoke service as well as interoperability between COM and .NET components. For primitive types and some string types, the marshaling behavior for PInvoke is the same as COM and .NET component interoperability. However, there are more options for COM and .NET interoperability.

In this chapter we extend the discussion on the MarshalAs custom attribute from Chapter 16 and show you the various options for marshaling types between COM and .NET components.

Primitive Types

Primitive types do not require marshaling specifications when they are used as function parameters or returns. The reason for this is that primitive types have the same size and representation in both managed and native contexts. The common language runtime (CLR) execution engine marshals these types correctly.

Among the primitive types, Boolean has multiple representations in unmanaged contexts. Data marshaling is required between a managed context where the size of a Boolean is 4 bytes and the native context where the size could be 1, 2, or 4 bytes. Also, nonprimitive types may require special handling to ensure that data representation is matched between the managed and unmanaged sides. For such types, the BCL provides a custom attribute called `MarshalAs` in the `System::Runtime::InteropServices` namespace. In the following section, this attribute is described in detail with regard to COM and .NET interoperability.

MarshalAs Custom Attribute

The `System::Runtime::InteropServices::MarshalAs` custom attribute is used to specify how to marshal a parameter or a return type of a function or a field of a type. This attribute can be used for PInvoke and interoperability between COM and .NET components. The `MarshalAs` attribute is introduced in Chapter 16.

The enumeration `System::Runtime::InteropServices::UnmanagedType` is used to specify data-marshaling options. In the following sections, we discuss how the `MarshalAs` attribute is used to specify marshaling options for various types used in COM and .NET components.

Marshaling Interfaces

Interfaces are marshaled as COM interfaces. All interfaces used by COM and .NET components have definitions in both managed and native components. They share the same identity, a universal unique identifier (UUID). The native interface is visible only to COM components, whereas the managed interface is visible only to .NET components.

The following is an example of a managed interface:

```
#using <mscorlib.dll>
using namespace System;
using namespace System::Runtime::InteropServices;
[Guid(S"70E88C4A-3BC4-4925-9CAE-359FC4173DA9")]
public __gc __interface Publisher {
    String* GetLatestBook(String* author);
};
```

To see how this interface is exposed to a COM client, you can compile the code into an assembly and use TlbExp to generate a type library from it.

The following code shows a matching interface in the type library corresponding to the assembly for the preceding code[1]:

```
[
     odl,
     uuid(70E88C4A-3BC4-4925-9CAE-359FC4173DA9),
     version(1.0),
     dual,
     oleautomation,
     custom(0F21F359-AB84-41E8-9A78-36D110E6D2F9, Publisher)
]
interface Publisher : IDispatch {
        [id(0x60020000)] HRESULT GetLatestBook( [in] BSTR author,
                                                [out, retval] BSTR* pRetVal);
};
```

Note that the name of the interface is the same as the one from the managed code. The identity (UUID) is also the same. The parameter and return value of the GetLatestBook method are marshaled as a BSTR. We explain the marshaling of strings later in this chapter.

Marshaling Gc Classes

Similar to value types, you can specify the layout of a gc class using the StructLayout attribute. The gc classes with a user-specified layout are called *formatted* gc classes, whereas the gc classes without the StructLayout attribute are called *unformatted* gc classes. We discuss marshaling formatted gc classes and value types later in this chapter.

In this section, we discuss how an unformatted gc class is marshaled as a COM interface. This interface is called a *class interface* and it implements all public, nonstatic methods of the class, including the methods from the base classes. The name of this interface is the same as the name of the class prefixed with an underscore (_). A class interface inherits from IDispatch.

The following code shows an example of a gc class:

```
#using <mscorlib.dll>
using namespace System;
using namespace System::Runtime::InteropServices;
```

---

[1] You can view type library contents by using the tool OleView (oleview.exe) from the platform SDK.

```
[ClassInterface(ClassInterfaceType::AutoDual)]
public __gc struct Publisher {
    String* GetLatestBook(String* author) {
        String* book = S"";
        // retrive the book name and set the variable book
        return book;
    }
};
```

In this code, the Publisher class implements a public method that uses System::String as a parameter and a return type. You need to use the ClassInterface attribute to expose the Publisher class to COM components.[2] You can use the tool TlbExp (tlbexp.exe) to generate a type library corresponding to the assembly for the preceding code.

The following listing shows the class interface from the type library for the preceding code:

```
interface _Publisher : IDispatch {
  [id(00000000), propget] HRESULT ToString([out, retval] BSTR* pRetVal);
  [id(0x60020001)] HRESULT Equals([in] VARIANT obj,
                                  [out, retval] VARIANT_BOOL* pRetVal);
  [id(0x60020002)] HRESULT GetHashCode([out, retval] long* pRetVal);
  [id(0x60020003)] HRESULT GetType([out, retval] _Type** pRetVal);
  [id(0x60020004)] HRESULT GetLatestBook([in] BSTR author,
                                         [out, retval] BSTR* pRetVal);
};
```

Note that the name of the interface is prefixed with an underscore (_). The parameter and return type of the GetLatestBook method are marshaled as a BSTR. The methods other than GetLatestBook are from the base class of Publisher. Using this class interface, it is possible to call any method of the managed object because all methods including those from the base classes are flattened into one interface in the type library.

---

[2] Refer to the .NET documentation on the ClassInterface attribute for other ways of using this attribute on classes. The recommended value is ClassInterfaceType::None. The value ClassInterfaceType::AutoDual is not conducive to versioning because COM clients can potentially depend on the interface layout, which can change between versions. This is discussed in Chapter 18.

Marshaling Formatted Managed Types

Formatted managed types are value types and gc classes with the StructLayout attribute on them. Individual members of value classes can have the MarshalAs custom attribute attached to them. When marshaled to the native side, only the data members are marshaled—the member functions are not available to the native side.

The following code shows how a simple value type is marshaled when it is used as a parameter:

```
#using <mscorlib.dll>
using namespace System;
using namespace System::Runtime::InteropServices;

[StructLayout(Sequential)]
public __value struct Rec {
    int l;
    int w;
    String* Shape() {
        if (l == w)
            return new String(S"Square");
        else
            return new String(S"Rectangle");
    }
};

[ClassInterface(ClassInterfaceType::AutoDual)]
public __gc struct GeometricShape {
    String* GetName (Rec r) {
        return r.Shape();
    }
};
```

In this sample, the value type Rec is used as a parameter in the function GetName. In the type library for this code (generated from its assembly using TlbExp), the value type will have a matching type.

```
struct tagRec {
    long l;
    long w;
} Rec;
```

```
interface _GeometricShape : IDispatch {
[id(00000000), propget] HRESULT ToString([out, retval] BSTR* pRetVal);
[id(0x60020001)] HRESULT Equals( [in] VARIANT obj,
                                        [out, retval] VARIANT_BOOL* pRetVal);
    [id(0x60020002)] HRESULT GetHashCode( [out, retval] long* pRetVal);
      [id(0x60020003)] HRESULT GetType( [out, retval] _Type** pRetVal);
      [id(0x60020004)] HRESULT GetName( [in] Rec r,
                                        [out, retval] BSTR* pRetVal);
};
```

Notice that the type `Rec` does not have any member functions. The method `GetName` in the class interface has a parameter of type `Rec`.

Marshaling Booleans

As mentioned earlier, Boolean types have multiple representations on the native side. There are 1-, 2-, and 4-byte representations for Booleans. For example, `VARIANT_BOOL` is represented with 2 bytes. On the managed side, a Boolean is represented with 4 bytes. When you pass a Boolean value from managed to unmanaged or unmanaged to managed contexts, it should be marshaled to match the size. The `UnmanagedType` enumeration has three values to represent Booleans: `Bool`, `VariantBool`, and `U1`. Depending on the application context, one of these three options can be used to marshal a Boolean. The default value for marshaling a Boolean is `UnmanagedType::Bool`.

The following sample shows how to use the `MarshalAs` attribute on a Boolean:

```
#using <mscorlib.dll>
using namespace System;
using namespace System::Runtime::InteropServices;

[ClassInterface(ClassInterfaceType::AutoDual)]
public __gc class EmployeeDatabase
{
    int earnedIncome;
public:
    int  GetEarnedIncome([MarshalAs(UnmanagedType::VariantBool)] bool salaried)
    {
        if (salaried) {
            // calculate salary and update the variable 'earnedIncome'
        }
```

```
        else {
            // calculate wages and update the variable 'earnedIncome'
        }
        return earnedIncome;
    }
};
```

In the preceding code, the parameter of the `GetEarnedIncome` method is
a Boolean. It has the `MarshalAs` attribute on it. The marshaling option
`UnmanagedType::VariantBool` instructs the CLR marshaler to marshal the argument as `VariantBool` with a size of 2 bytes.

Applying `tlbexp.exe` on the assembly for the preceding code generates a type
library for it. The following code shows the COM interface generated for the
`EmployeeDatabase` class:

```
interface _EmployeeDatabase : IDispatch {
    [id(00000000), propget] HRESULT ToString([out, retval] BSTR* pRetVal);
    [id(0x60020001)] HRESULT Equals( [in] VARIANT obj,
                                     [out, retval] VARIANT_BOOL* pRetVal);
    [id(0x60020002)] HRESULT GetHashCode([out, retval] long* pRetVal);
    [id(0x60020003)] HRESULT GetType([out, retval] _Type** pRetVal);
    [id(0x60020004)] HRESULT GetEarnedIncome([in] VARIANT_BOOL salaried,
                                     [out, retval] long* pRetVal);
};
```

Notice the parameter type `VARIANT_BOOL` in the method `GetEarnedIncome`. For
a COM client, the method takes a 2-byte Boolean (`VARIANT_BOOL`) as a parameter.
During a method invocation, the CLR data marshaler converts the 2-byte value
into a 4-byte value.

Marshaling Strings

In the .NET Framework, strings are represented by the type `System::String`.
There are different representations of strings (such as ANSI strings and Unicode
strings) in C++ and in COM (such as `BSTR` and `LPTStr`). The enumeration
`System::Runtime::InteropServices::UnmanagedType` has several members that
represent strings in different unmanaged contexts, such as when a string is used
in a PInvoke function, as a member of an interface, and as a member of
a structure.

The members of `System::Runtime::InteropServices::UnmanagedType` that are common to all unmanaged contexts (such as a PInvoke function, strings in structures, and strings in interfaces) are as follows:

- `UnmanagedType::BStr`: Unicode character string that is a length-prefixed double byte

- `UnmanagedType::LPStr`: ANSI character string with each character being a single byte

- `UnmanagedType::LPWStr`: a double-byte Unicode character string

The following code shows a gc class that implements a method whose parameter type and return type are the same (`System::String*`):

```
#using <mscorlib.dll>
using namespace System;
using namespace System::Runtime::InteropServices;
[ClassInterface(ClassInterfaceType::AutoDual)]
public __gc class CPublisher
{
public:
    // Simple method that just knows about "Anonymous"
    [MarshalAs(UnmanagedType::LPWStr)]
    String*  GetLatestBook( [MarshalAs(UnmanagedType::LPWStr)] String* author ) {
        if (String::Equals(author, S"Anonymous"))
            return (S"The New Book");
        else
            return (S"Error: Author Not Found");
    }
};
```

In this sample, both the return type and the parameter have the same `MarshalAs` attribute with the option `UnmanagedType::LPWStr` on them. When a type library is generated from the assembly for the preceding code, the return type and parameter type are exposed as `LPWSTR`.

The following listing shows the contents of the type library for the preceding code:

```
interface _CPublisher : IDispatch {
        [id(00000000), propget, custom(54FC8F55-38DE-4703-9C4E-250351302B1C, 1)]
        HRESULT ToString([out, retval] BSTR* pRetVal);
        [id(0x60020001)] HRESULT Equals( [in] VARIANT obj,
                                          [out, retval] VARIANT_BOOL* pRetVal);
        [id(0x60020002)] HRESULT GetHashCode([out, retval] long* pRetVal);
        [id(0x60020003)] HRESULT GetType([out, retval] _Type** pRetVal);
        [id(0x60020004)] HRESULT GetLatestBook( [in] LPWSTR author,
                                          [out, retval] LPWSTR* pRetVal);
    };
};
```

Notice the return type and parameter type for the last `GetLatestBook` method.

For managed strings used in value types, there is an additional marshaling option, `UnmanagedType::ByValTStr`, that is a fixed-length array of characters. The type of the character in this array is same as that of the enclosing value type (specified in the `StructLayout` attribute on the value type).

Marshaling Arrays

There are three options for marshaling arrays between COM and .NET:

- `UnmanagedType::LPArray`: Array with its size calculated at runtime based on the argument

- `UnmanagedType::SafeArray`: Self-describing array that carries the type, rank, and bounds of the array data

- `UnmanagedType::ByValArray`: Array embedded inside the structure in which it is defined

In the following sections we first describe how arrays are marshaled from COM to .NET, and then we describe how they are marshaled from .NET to COM.

COM to .NET: SafeArrays

A SafeArray is a self-describing array that carries the type of element, rank, and bounds of the array. When imported from a type library, a SafeArray is converted as a single-dimensional array. The rank is 1 and the lower bound of the array is 0.

The following code shows an example of a SafeArray used as a parameter in a COM server:

```
#define _ATL_ATTRIBUTES
#include <atlbase.h>
#include <atlcom.h>
#include <stdio.h>
#include <comutil.h>
[module(name="Publisher",type="dll")];
[dual]
__interface IPublisher : IDispatch {
    [id(0x01)]HRESULT GetBooks([in] BSTR author,
                               [in, out, satype(BSTR)] SAFEARRAY *titles);
};


[coclass, threading="both"]
class CPublisher: public IPublisher {
    HRESULT GetBooks(BSTR author, SAFEARRAY *titles) {
        // code to retrieve books
        // . . .
        return S_OK;
    }
};
```

The metadata for the IPublisher interface in the assembly generated (using TlbImp) for the preceding type library is as follows:

```
.class interface public abstract auto ansi import IPublisher
{
.method public hidebysig newslot virtual abstract
 instance void  GetBooks([in] string  marshal( bstr) author,
  [in][out] string[]  marshal( safearray bstr) titles) runtime managed
internalcall
    // text stripped
 {
    // text stripped
 } // end of method IPublisher::GetBooks
} // end of class IPublisher
```

The parameter has the `MarshalAs` attribute on it.

Refer to the .NET documentation for details on how to marshal multidimensional or nonzero-based arrays.

COM to .NET: C-Style Arrays

For C-style arrays, the lower bound is 0. You can marshal single-dimensional or multidimensional C-style arrays. Multidimensional arrays are imported as single-dimensional arrays in column-major order (elements are listed as first column elements, followed by second column elements, and so on).

TlbImp can only import fixed-length arrays as arrays on the managed side. You must manually edit the managed signature using the technique of disassembling and reassembling metadata in an assembly (see Chapter 17 for details on how to dissemble and reassemble an assembly).

The following code shows an example of a C-style array being used as a parameter:

```
#define _ATL_ATTRIBUTES
#include <atlbase.h>
#include <atlcom.h>
#include <stdio.h>
#include <comutil.h>

[module(name="Publisher",type="dll")];

[dual]
__interface IPublisher : IDispatch {
    [id(0x01)] HRESULT GetAuthorIDs([in] BSTR author,
        [in] int numIDs,
        [out, size_is(numIDs)] long IDs[]);
};

// coclass CPublisher implements the interface IPublisher
[coclass, threading="both"]
class CPublisher: public IPublisher {
    HRESULT GetAuthorIDs(BSTR author, int numIDs, long IDs[]) {
        return S_OK;
    }
};
```

The parameter IDs for the method GetAuthorIDs is an array of integers with its length represented by numIDs. The assembly generated for a type library corresponding to the preceding code contains the following metadata:

```
.class interface public abstract auto ansi import IPublisher
{
    .method public hidebysig newslot virtual abstract
            instance void  GetAuthorIDs([in] string  marshal( bstr) author,
                                        [in] int32 numIDs,
                                        [out] int32& IDs
                             ) runtime managed internalcall
    {
    } // end of method IPublisher::GetAuthorIDs

} // end of class IPublisher
```

Notice that TlbImp maps the last parameter of the method incorrectly as [out] int32& IDs. You need to disassemble and reassemble metadata by replacing the third parameter of the GetAuthorIDs method with [out] int32[] marshal([]) IDs.

For more details on how TlbImp imports arrays and how to encode variable-length arrays (such as int a[]), refer to the .NET documentation.

.NET to COM: SafeArrays

Managed arrays can be marshaled either as SafeArrays or as C-style arrays. The following code shows an example of a managed array being passed as a SafeArray (which is the default):

```
#using <mscorlib.dll>
using namespace System;
using namespace System::Runtime::InteropServices;
[ClassInterface(ClassInterfaceType::AutoDual)]
public __gc class CPublisher {
    int IDs __gc [];
public:
    int GetAuthorIDs()__gc[] {
      return IDs;
    }
};
```

In this code, the GetAuthorIDs method returns a managed array of integers. The type library generated from an assembly corresponding to the preceding code contains the following class interface:

```
interface _CPublisher : IDispatch {
    [id(00000000), propget, custom(54FC8F55-38DE-4703-9C4E-250351302B1C, 1)]
                        HRESULT ToString([out, retval] BSTR* pRetVal);
    [id(0x60020001)] HRESULT Equals( [in] VARIANT obj,
                                    [out, retval] VARIANT_BOOL* pRetVal);
    [id(0x60020002)] HRESULT GetHashCode([out, retval] long* pRetVal);
    [id(0x60020003)] HRESULT GetType([out, retval] _Type** pRetVal);
    [id(0x60020004)] HRESULT GetAuthorIDs(
                                    [out, retval] SAFEARRAY(long)* pRetVal);
};
```

In the last method, the parameter is a SafeArray of long values.

.NET to COM: C-Style Arrays

The following sample shows an example of a C-style array used as a parameter:

```
#using <mscorlib.dll>
using namespace System;
using namespace System::Runtime::InteropServices;

[ClassInterface(ClassInterfaceType::AutoDual)]
public __gc class CPublisher {
    int IDs __gc [];
public:
    [MarshalAs(UnmanagedType::LPArray)] int GetAuthorIDs()__gc[] {
        return IDs;
    }
};
```

The return value of the GetAuthorIDs method is a managed array. It has the MarshalAs attribute on it with LPArray as the marshaling option. This option is to marshal managed arrays as C-style arrays.

The type library for the preceding code (generated from its assembly) contains the following class interface:

```
interface _CPublisher : IDispatch {
    [id(00000000), propget, custom(54FC8F55-38DE-4703-9C4E-250351302B1C, 1)]
                    HRESULT ToString([out, retval] BSTR* pRetVal);
    [id(0x60020001)] HRESULT Equals( [in] VARIANT obj,
                                    [out, retval] VARIANT_BOOL* pRetVal);
    [id(0x60020002)] HRESULT GetHashCode([out, retval] long* pRetVal);
    [id(0x60020003)] HRESULT GetType([out, retval] _Type** pRetVal);
    [id(0x60020004)] HRESULT GetAuthorIDs([out, retval] long** pRetVal);
};
```

Marshaling System::Object*

When the type System::Object* is explicitly used as a parameter or a return type, or as a field, it is exposed to the unmanaged context as either a COM Variant or an interface pointer. The default is COM Variant. The following list contains the options to marshal System::Object*:

- UnmanagedType::IDispatch: COM IDispatch pointer

- UnmanagedType::Interface: COM IUnknown pointer

- UnmanagedType::IUnknown: COM IUnknown pointer

- UnmanagedType::Struct: COM Variant

The following sample shows an example of using the marshaling option UnmanagedType::Interface:

```
#using <mscorlib.dll>
using namespace System;
using namespace System::Runtime::InteropServices;
public __gc struct Record {
    String* name;
    int ID;
};
[ClassInterface(ClassInterfaceType::AutoDual)]
public __gc class Employees {
```

```
public:
    void GetEmployeeRecord( int idNum,
                            [MarshalAs(UnmanagedType::Interface)]
                            System::Object* rec ) {
        try {
            Record* r = __try_cast<Record*>(rec);
            // fetch the record from a database and
            // update the record object pointed to by r
        }
        catch(System::Exception* e) {
            Console::WriteLine(e);
        }
    }
};
```

In the preceding code, the rec parameter of the GetEmployeeRecord method has the MarshalAs attribute with the UnmanagedType::Interface marshaling option.

The type library for the preceding code (generated from its assembly) contains the following class interface:

```
interface _Employees : IDispatch {
        [id(00000000), propget] HRESULT ToString([out, retval] BSTR* pRetVal);
        [id(0x60020001)] HRESULT Equals( [in] VARIANT obj,
                                          [out, retval] VARIANT_BOOL* pRetVal);
        [id(0x60020002)] HRESULT GetHashCode([out, retval] long* pRetVal);
        [id(0x60020003)] HRESULT GetType([out, retval] _Type** pRetVal);
        [id(0x60020004)] HRESULT GetEmployeeRecord( [in] long idNum,
                                                     [in] IUnknown* rec);
    };
```

Notice that the second parameter of GetEmployeeRecord has the type IUnknown*.

Marshaling Delegates

Delegates from managed code can be marshaled either as COM interfaces or as function pointers. The marshaling options are UnmanagedType::FunctionPtr and UnmanagedType::Interface.

The following sample shows how the two marshaling options are used on delegates used as parameters:

```
#using <mscorlib.dll>
using namespace System;
using namespace System::Runtime::InteropServices;

// delegate declaration
public __delegate  void ControlAirFlow(int flowLevel);

public __gc __interface AirFlowController {
    void FlowControl1([MarshalAs(UnmanagedType::Interface)]Delegate* del);
    void FlowControl2([MarshalAs(UnmanagedType::FunctionPtr)]Delegate* del);
};
```

Both member functions have the MarshalAs attribute applied on their parameters. The following listing shows the contents of a corresponding type library for this code:

```
[
     odl,
     uuid(E401B73A-F286-3BFD-9007-99AB165A09B2),
     version(1.0),
     dual,
     oleautomation,
     custom(0F21F359-AB84-41E8-9A78-36D110E6D2F9, AirFlowController)

]
interface AirFlowController : IDispatch {
        [id(0x60020000)] HRESULT FlowControl1([in] _Delegate* del);
        [id(0x60020001)] HRESULT FlowControl2([in] int del);
};
```

Notice that the FlowControl1 method has a parameter of type _Delegate, indicating that delegate marshaling should be done as an interface, whereas the FlowControl2 method has a parameter of type int, indicating that delegate marshaling should be done as a function pointer.

Summary

In this chapter, we discussed how to use the `MarshalAs` attribute to marshal Booleans, strings, value types, gc classes, interfaces, arrays, and delegates. As you have seen, specifying different data marshaling options is an important interoperability technique.

In the next chapter, we explore another interoperability technique: writing managed wrappers for native C++ classes.

CHAPTER 20

Managed Wrappers for Native Types

FOR NATIVE APPLICATIONS TO TAKE advantage of the facilities in the .NET Framework or for managed applications to interact with native C++ objects, sometimes it is beneficial (in terms of flexibility and performance) to create a *managed wrapper*—a managed class that acts as a proxy for a native class and provides the same functionality of the native class by forwarding all member-function calls to the native C++ class.

You have seen in the previous chapters that you can use the PInvoke service and tools such as TlbImp (`tlbimp.exe`) and TlbExp (`tlbexp.exe`) to interoperate between managed and native components. The disadvantage of the PInvoke service is that separate methods have to be provided for creating and destroying instances of exported classes from a native DLL. You need to remember to use these methods instead of constructors and destructors.

You can use the TlbImp tool to create interop assemblies for COM type libraries. The main disadvantage of this tool is that you cannot selectively expose a type. When you use TlbImp, an interop assembly is created for a type library. It is not possible to create an interop assembly for a subset of types from a type library. Another problem is that if there is a native C++ class that you want to expose to a managed client and you want to use TlbImp, you must create a COM interface for the native C++ class, generate a type library, and then use TlbImp to create a Runtime Callable Wrapper (RCW) for the native class in an assembly. You then reference the assembly into the managed client (with the `#using` directive) and use the functionality of the native C++ class via the RCW.

MC++ addresses these problems and provides effective solutions. MC++ allows wrapping of individual native types. This approach gives more control to the user in deciding precisely what needs to be wrapped. Using this approach, you can eliminate the overhead of going through an RCW and a COM interface when accessing a native C++ object. In some cases, it is possible to have both the wrapper class and the native C++ class in the same executable, thus avoiding the overhead of going out of the managed component boundary to call a method of the native C++ class. MC++ also allows you to call native APIs directly without requiring any explicit data marshaling. In some cases, it is possible to have both a native function and the managed client that uses the native C++ function in the same executable.

Chapter 15 presents a few basic wrapping techniques. In this chapter, we discuss how to provide a managed wrapper for a simple native C++ class and describe how to use the BCL class `Marshal` in writing proxy methods for native C++ member functions. We also describe the issues and workarounds in writing proxy methods for native C++ types.

A Simple Managed Wrapper

A C++ class can have methods and data in `private`, `protected`, and `public` sections of the class. When you write a wrapper class, it is not necessary to provide proxy methods for private methods and helper member methods of an unmanaged type that are not called by the managed components.

The following sample shows how to wrap a simple native C++ class:

```
#using <mscorlib.dll>
#include <stdio.h>
// unmanaged class
class Unmanaged {
    void PrivateFunc() { printf("Unmanaged::PrivateFunc\n"); }
  protected:
    void ProtectedFunc() { printf("Unmanaged::ProtectedFunc\n"); }
  public:
    void HelperFunc() { printf("Unmanaged::HelperFunc\n"); }
    void PublicFunc() {
        HelperFunc();
        printf("Unmanaged::PublicFunc\n");
    }
};
// Wrapper class
public __gc class Managed {
    Unmanaged *pU;
    public:
        Managed() { pU = new Unmanaged(); }
        ~Managed() { delete pU; }
        void PublicFunc() { pU->PublicFunc();}
};

int main() {
   Managed *m = new Managed();
   m->PublicFunc();
  }
```

This sample has an unmanaged class with `public`, `private`, and `protected` member functions. Assume that the managed clients do not use the function `HelperFunc`. Only the method `PublicFunc` of `Unmanaged` needs to have a proxy method.

The gc class `Managed` is the wrapper class for the unmanaged type `Unmanaged`. The assembly access specifier `public` on `Managed` is needed because when a managed client imports the assembly containing the wrapper, all private types will not be imported. The class `Managed` contains a `private` data member pointing to the variable pU of type `Unmanaged`. The member `PublicFunc` of `Managed` is a proxy method that forwards calls to `PublicFunc` of pU. Note that the return type of the function is `void`, which is same in both MC++ and native C++.

The wrapper object of `Managed` controls the lifetime of an object of `Unmanaged`: The constructor of `Managed` creates the object of `Unmanaged` on the C++ heap and the destructor of `Managed` deletes it. It is the application's responsibility to do this because the garbage collector cannot collect unmanaged objects.

The output of the program is as follows:

```
Unmanaged::HelperFunc
Unmanaged::PublicFunc
```

Marshal Class

As discussed in Chapter 5, the .NET Framework defines value classes that represent basic C++ types. For example, `System::Int32` represents int, `System::Single` represents `float`, and `System::Byte` represents char. If a nonprimitive type, such as a struct, class, or array, is used as a parameter or a return type of a public method in an unmanaged class, that nonprimitive type must also have a mapping in managed form.

The BCL class `System::Runtime::InteropServices::Marshal` provides a wide range of methods to marshal data between unmanaged and managed contexts. The following sample shows how a native string parameter is wrapped using one such method:

```
#using <mscorlib.dll>
using namespace System;
using namespace System::Runtime::InteropServices;
#include <stdio.h>

class Unmanaged {
   public:
     void PrintString(const char* str) {
        printf("%s\n", str);
     }
```

```
};
// wrapper class
public __gc class Managed {
    Unmanaged *pU;
    public:
        Managed() { pU = new Unmanaged(); }
        void PrintString(String *str) {
            char *pNativeStr = NULL;
            try {
                pNativeStr = static_cast<char*>
                                (Marshal::StringToHGlobalAnsi(str).ToPointer());
            }
            catch (Exception *e) {
                Console::WriteLine("String conversion to char* failed");
            }

            pU->PrintString(pNativeStr);

            Marshal::FreeHGlobal(pNativeStr);
        }
        ~Managed() { delete pU; }
};
int main() {
    Managed *m = new Managed();
    m->PrintString("An invitation from Managed World");
}
```

In this sample, the native C++ class Unmanaged has a PrintString method that takes const char* as a parameter. The wrapper class Managed implements the PrintString method with the parameter of type System::String*. In this proxy method, the argument is converted to a char* string using the StringToHGlobalAnsi static method of the Marshal class. This method raises exceptions if the conversion fails. The exceptions are handled inside the proxy method itself. After passing the argument to the native PrintString method, the proxy method frees the memory allocated for the native char* string.

An important point to note here is that we have both a native class and a managed class in the same file. As you have seen before, MC++ allows managed and native classes to coexist. At execution time, since both managed and native objects are in the same executable, the cost of making a transition from a managed to unmanaged context is minimal because it just involves a few additional instructions. If the native class were implemented in a different DLL, there would have been an additional cost to cross the assembly boundary.

Some of the static methods of the `Marshal` class are as follows:

- `AddRef`: Increments the reference count on an interface

- `AllocHGlobal`: An overloaded method that allocates a chunk of memory using `GlobalAlloc`

- `Copy`: An overloaded method that copies data between an unmanaged pointer and a managed array

- `CreateAWrapperOfType`: Creates a wrapper class of a given managed type for a given COM object

- `FreeBSTR`: Deletes the memory in a `BSTR` using the `SysFreeString` method

- `FreeHGlobal`: Deletes the memory allocated on a C++ heap with `AllocHGlobal`

- `IsComObject`: Specifies whether a given object is a COM object or not

- `IsTypeVisibleFromCOM`: Specifies whether a managed type should be visible to COM or not

- `NumParamBytes`: Specifies the number of bytes required to hold the parameters of a function

- `PtrToStringBSTR`: Copies a Unicode string from a native C++ heap to a managed string

- `ReadByte`: Reads a byte from a native pointer

- `StringToBSTR`: Allocates a BSTR object and copies the contents of a managed string into it

- `StringToHGlobalUni`: Copies the contents of a managed string into a native C++ heap

- `WriteByte`: Writes a single byte into a native C++ heap

Refer to the .NET documentation on the `System::Runtime::InteropServices` namespace for more information on the `Marshal` class.

Issues and Workarounds with Wrapping Native Types

In Chapter 15, we discuss the various aspects of what to consider when wrapping a native type with a managed type. In this section, we discuss the issues involved with writing proxy methods for some of the member functions of native classes and we provide workarounds for them.

Methods with a Variable Number of Arguments

Methods that can be called with a variable number of arguments are known as *varargs* methods. The last parameter of a varargs method is an ellipsis (...). The current implementation of the MC++ compiler does not support managed varargs methods as members of managed types. As a workaround, a varargs method can be mapped to a number of overloaded proxy methods. For instance, suppose that the managed clients won't pass more than four arguments at any time. If the variable parameters start with the second parameter, the overloaded methods can have two, three, and four parameters.[1]

The following sample shows how to wrap a native C++ class that has a varargs member function:

```
#using <mscorlib.dll>
#include <stdio.h>
#include <stdarg.h>

class NativePrinter {
    public:
    void PrintNumbers(int count, ... ) {
        printf("count is %d; numbers are ", count);
        va_list numbers;
        va_start(numbers, count);  // Initialize variable arguments
        for (int i = 0; i< count; i++) {
            printf("%d ", va_arg(numbers, int));
        }
        printf("\n");
        va_end(numbers);
    }
};
```

---

[1] The recommended solution in the .NET Framework is to have overloaded methods for one, two, and three parameters. To handle more than three parameters, you can use an array (with element type System::Object*) as the fourth parameter and get the remaining arguments from that array. When calling this method, you can create an array of arguments starting from the fourth argument and pass that array as the fourth argument.

```
// Managed Wrapper
public __gc class ManagedPrinter {
    NativePrinter *pU;
    public:
        ManagedPrinter() { pU = new NativePrinter(); }
        ~ManagedPrinter() { delete pU; }
        void PrintNumbers(int count, int num1) {
            pU->PrintNumbers(count, num1);
        }
        void PrintNumbers(int count, int num1, int num2) {
            pU->PrintNumbers(count, num1, num2);
        }
        void PrintNumbers(int count, int num1, int num2, int num3) {
            pU->PrintNumbers(count, num1, num2, num3);
        }
};

int main() {
    ManagedPrinter *m = new ManagedPrinter();
    m->PrintNumbers(1, 10);
    m->PrintNumbers(2, 10, 20);
    m->PrintNumbers(3, 10, 20, 30);
}
```

In this sample, the native class NativePrinter has the varargs method PrintNumbers. The second parameter of this method is an ellipsis. The managed code calling this function passes a maximum of four parameters. In the wrapper class ManagedPrinter, there are three overloaded methods that represent the native class method PrintNumbers. These overloaded methods take two, three, and four parameters respectively and call the PrintNumbers method on the native class pointer pU. The output of the program is as follows:

```
count is 1; numbers are 10
count is 2; numbers are 10 20
count is 3; numbers are 10 20 30
```

Methods with Default Arguments

In the current version of the MC++ compiler, it is not possible to use methods with default arguments. However, default arguments are a useful feature of C++ and they are commonly found in native C++ applications. To wrap native C++ classes that have methods with default arguments, you can use overloaded methods. For each default argument, an additional overloaded method is used in the managed wrapper.

The following sample shows a native C++ class with a member function that has one default argument being wrapped by a managed class:

```
#using <mscorlib.dll>
using namespace System;
using namespace System::Runtime::InteropServices;
#include <stdio.h>

class NativeAdder {
    public:
// method with a default argument
    int CumulativeSum(int delta, int currentTotal = 0) {
        return currentTotal + delta;
    }
};

public __gc class ManagedAdder {
    NativeAdder *pU;
    public:
        ManagedAdder () { pU = new NativeAdder (); }
        ~ ManagedAdder () { delete pU; }
        int CumulativeSum(int delta, int currentTotal) {
            return pU->CumulativeSum(delta, currentTotal);
        }
        int CumulativeSum(int delta) {
            return pU->CumulativeSum(delta, 0);
        }
};
int main() {
    ManagedAdder *m = new ManagedAdder ();
    int sum = m->CumulativeSum(10);
    sum = m->CumulativeSum(20, sum);
    Console::Write("10 + 20 = ");
    Console::WriteLine(sum);
}
```

In this sample, the native C++ class NativeAdder has a member function, CumulativeSum, that takes the default argument currentTotal with a value of 0. The gc class ManagedAdder is a wrapper for NativeAdder. This class contains a pU pointer to the NativeAdder class as a private data member. It has a constructor

that creates an object of `NativeAdder` on the C++ heap and a destructor that
deletes the object on the C++ heap.

There are two overloaded member functions of `ManagedAddr` that represent
the method `CumulativeSum` of `NativeAdder`. The first method takes two parameters and calls the `CumulativeSum` method on the object pointed to by `pU`. The
second method takes one parameter and calls the same `CumulativeSum` method
on the native object via `pU`. The second argument value in this case is `0`. The output of the program is as follows:

```
10 + 20 = 30
```

Explicit Constructors

In C++ you can use the `explicit` keyword on constructors that take at most one
parameter without a default value. Such a constructor is called an *explicit constructor.* An explicit constructor creates objects in the same way as a regular
constructor, but does so only when direct initialization or casts are explicitly
used. In native C++, a constructor with one argument is called a *conversion constructor.* A conversion constructor with the `explicit` keyword attached cannot be
used for implicit conversions.

The following sample compiles with an error message because the constructor `C` is an explicit constructor:

```
// compile with /c
class C {
 public:
   explicit C(int i) { /* . . . */} // conversion constructor
   void Func() {
      C p = 1; // error
   }
};
```

MC++ does not support the `explicit` keyword on managed types.
Conversion constructors of native C++ classes are implemented as constructors
in the wrapper class. They are also implemented as the managed conversion
operators, `op_Implicit` or `op_Explicit` static member functions (these operators
are introduced in Chapter 10). To provide a managed conversion operator for an
explicit constructor, the name `op_Explicit` should be used.

The use of the operator `op_Explicit` instead of conversion constructors helps
other .NET languages to recognize it as an operator.

The following sample shows how to wrap a native C++ class that has an explicit constructor:

```cpp
#using <mscorlib.dll>
using namespace System;
class Native {
   int m_i;
 public:
   explicit Native(double f): m_i((int)f) {}; // conversion constructor
   Native(int i): m_i(i) {}; // conversion constructor
};
// wrapper class
public __gc class Managed {
   Native *pU;
   public:
   Managed(double f) { pU = new Native(f); }
   Managed(int i) { pU = new Native(i); }
   ~Managed() { delete pU; }

   static Managed* op_Explicit(double f) {
     return new Managed(f);
   }
   static Managed* op_Implicit(int i) {
     return new Managed(i);
   }
};
int main() {
   Managed *pM1 = new Managed(10);
   Managed *pM2 = Managed::op_Explicit(20.0);
}
```

In this sample, the Native class has an explicit constructor taking a float parameter and a nonexplicit constructor taking an int parameter. The wrapper class provides a constructor and the managed conversion operator op_Explicit corresponding to the explicit constructor. This operator takes a float as a parameter and returns an object of the wrapper type Managed by calling its constructor.

Both statements in the main function create managed objects of the wrapper class. By defining the managed conversion operator op_Explicit, the wrapper class enforces the explicit constructor semantics on other .NET languages that use this wrapper class. They have to use the explicit conversion to Managed to create an object of Managed class from a float.

Destructors

The proxy methods for destructors of native C++ class are simple methods that just forward function calls to their native C++ counterparts. A call to the `delete` operator on a managed wrapper object destroys the native object on the C++ heap. The garbage collector deletes the wrapper object. Refer to Chapter 3 for the discussion on how destructors are handled in gc classes.

Copy Constructors

Managed classes are not allowed to have copy constructors. The reason for this is that the common language runtime (CLR) does not support copy constructors. To wrap a native C++ class with a copy constructor, a managed wrapper class should provide a method that mimics the semantics of the copy constructor. The managed interface `System::ICloneable` has a `Clone` method. The wrapper classes that need to implement a copy constructor can inherit from this interface and implement the `Clone` method.

The following sample shows how to wrap a native C++ class that has a user-defined copy constructor:

```
#include <stdio.h>
#using <mscorlib.dll>
using namespace System;

class Unmanaged {
    int m_i;
    public:
    Unmanaged() : m_i(10){}
    Unmanaged(const Unmanaged& u) { *this = u; }
    void Print() { printf("%d\n", m_i); }
};

public __gc class Managed : public ICloneable{
    Unmanaged *pU;
    public:
        Managed() { pU = new Unmanaged(); }
        ~Managed() { delete pU; }
        Unmanaged* GetPU() { return pU; }
        void Print() { pU->Print(); }
        virtual Object* Clone() {  // copy constructor wrapper
            Managed* pM = new Managed();
            Unmanaged* pTmpU = pM->GetPU();
```

```
            *pTmpU = *pU; // calls copy constructor of Unmanaged
            return pM;
        }
};
int main() {
    Managed *m1 = new Managed();
    Managed *m2 = dynamic_cast<Managed *>(m1->Clone());
    m2->Print();
}
```

In this sample, the native C++ class Unmanaged has a copy constructor. There is a member function, Print, that prints the value of the private data member m_i of Unmanaged. The wrapper class Managed inherits from the System::ICloneable interface and implements the Clone method, which returns a System::Object* pointer.

The wrapper class also has a helper method that returns the pointer pU. The copy constructor of the Unmanaged class is called in the Clone method. The Clone method returns an instance of Managed as a pointer to System::Object. The output of the program is as follows:

10

Public Data Members and Accessor Methods

It is a common practice to use accessor methods (such as GetX and SetX) to get and set values of a data member (X) or declare the data member as public and access it directly. While wrapping an unmanaged class, you can use properties to map public data members and accessor functions.

The following sample shows how to wrap a native C++ class that has data accessor methods:

```
#using <mscorlib.dll>
using namespace System;

class Unmanaged {
    int m_count;
    public:
     int m_total;
     Unmanaged() : m_count(0), m_total(0){}
     int GetCount() { return m_count; }
     void SetCount(int i) { m_count = i; }
};
```

```
public __gc class Managed {
    Unmanaged *pU;
    public:
        Managed() { pU = new Unmanaged(); }
        ~Managed() { delete pU; }
        __property int get_count() { return pU->GetCount(); }
        __property void set_count(int i) { pU->SetCount(i); }
        __property int get_total() { return pU->m_total; }
        __property void set_total(int n) { pU->m_total = n; }
};

int main() {
    Managed *m = new Managed();
    m->count = 20;
    m->total = m->count + 30;
    Console::WriteLine(m->count);
    Console::WriteLine(m->total);
}
```

In this sample, the native C++ class Unmanaged has two data members: the private data member m_count and the public data member m_total. There are two accessor functions, GetCount and SetCount. The wrapper class Managed has two properties corresponding to the two data members of Unmanaged. There are four property accessor methods in the wrapper class Managed: get_count (which returns m_count of the native object via GetCount), set_count (which sets the m_count of the native object via SetCount), get_total (which returns m_total of the native object directly), and set_total (which sets m_total of the native object directly).

In the main function, the properties are accessed like data members. The output of the program is as follows:

```
20
50
```

Operators

Managed classes are allowed to have operators. These operators are called *managed operators*. The native C++ operator definition syntax cannot be used to define managed operators—they must be defined as static member functions with predefined names. For example, the addition (+) and subtraction (-) operators are named op_Addition and op_Subtract, respectively. Operators are introduced in Chapter 10.

In the following sample, we show how to wrap the binary operator +:

```
#using <mscorlib.dll>
using namespace System;
class Unmanaged {
    public:
      int m_number;
      Unmanaged(int i) : m_number(i){}
      Unmanaged* operator+(const Unmanaged *u) {
          m_number += u->m_number;
          return this;
      }
};
// wrapper class
public __gc class Managed {
    Unmanaged *pU;
    public:
        Managed(int i) { pU = new Unmanaged(i); }
        ~Managed() { delete pU; }
        __property int get_number() { return pU->m_number; }
        Unmanaged* GetPU() { return pU;}
        static Managed* op_Addition(Managed* m1, Managed* m2) {
            Unmanaged* u = m1->GetPU();
            u = *u + m2->GetPU();
            return m1;
        }
};
int main() {
    Managed *m1 = new Managed(20);
    Managed *m2 = new Managed(30);
    m1 = Managed::op_Addition(m1, m2);
    Console::WriteLine(m1->number);
}
```

In this sample, the native C++ class Unmanaged has the binary operator + defined. In the wrapper class Managed, the operator is defined as a static member function with the name op_Addition. The only way to call operators on gc classes is to use the static member function. Unlike value classes, the infix notation (for example, a + b) is not allowed on gc classes. The output of the program is as follows:

50

Passing Delegates to Native Functions As Function Pointers

The current implementation of the BCL class `Marshal` does not have support to pass a delegate to a native function expecting a function pointer. The following sample shows a workaround for this.

In this sample, a delegate is passed to the PInvoke function `lstrcpyn` from `kernel32.dll`. The return value of this function is an address that can be used from unmanaged code to execute a delegated function.

```cpp
#using <mscorlib.dll>
using namespace System;
using namespace System::Runtime::InteropServices;
#include <stdio.h>
typedef void (*FuncPtr)();
// native function that expects a function pointer as a parameter
void NativeFunc(FuncPtr f) {
  printf("Entered NativeFunc\n");
  f();
  printf("Exiting NativeFunc\n");
}


// delegate declaration
__delegate void CallBackFunc();
// managed class whose method is used as a delegated function
__gc struct ManagedClass {
  void ManagedFunc() {
    Console::WriteLine("ManagedClass::ManagedFunc()");
  }
};
// use the string copy function from kernel32 DLL.
// This basically returns the address of a delegated funcion
[DllImport("kernel32")]
extern "C" int lstrcpyn(Delegate* d1, int passMeZero, int passMeAnotherZero);
int main() {
  ManagedClass __gc* pM = new ManagedClass();
  // create a delegate
  CallBackFunc __gc* callBack = new CallBackFunc(pM, &ManagedClass::ManagedFunc);
  // pin the delegate so that it won't be garbage collected while the native
  // function is using it
  CallBackFunc __pin* pcallBack = callBack;
```

```
// get the address of the code to execute the delegated function
// Note: This is a workaround because this functionality is currently
// not directly supported in the .NET Framework
int addr = lstrcpyn(callBack, 0, 0);
// pass the address to the native function expecting a function pointer
NativeFunc((FuncPtr)addr);
}
```

In this sample, NativeFunc is the native function that has a function pointer, FuncPtr, as a parameter type. The member function ManagedFunc of ManagedClass is used as a delegated function for the delegate CallBackFunc. The function lstrcpyn from the native DLL kernel32.dll is used to get the starting address of the code that can be executed from a native function to call a delegated function. Before calling the native function NativeFunc, the delegate is pinned to make sure that the CLR does not garbage collect it while the native function is executing.

The output of the program is as follows:

```
Entered NativeFunc
ManagedClass::ManagedFunc()
Exiting NativeFunc
```

Miscellaneous

Multiple inheritance of gc classes is not supported in the .NET Framework. To wrap classes with multiple inheritance, you can use interfaces because a gc class is allowed to inherit from multiple interfaces.

The current version of the MC++ compiler has a performance problem with calling methods via function pointers or methods that are virtual in native C++ classes. There is extraneous overhead involved during calls to such functions. Even though the code is managed (code compiled with /clr and source code for the methods is not covered by #pragma unmanaged), the compiler introduces a transition from managed to native and native to managed. To avoid this overhead, it may be useful to reimplement the native class as a managed class or compile the native C++ class to generate native code (using #pragma unmanaged).

When you are wrapping the public methods of native classes, if a method takes a nonprimitive type as a parameter or a return type, that type should also be wrapped and exposed as a public type, unless there is a direct mapping that can be used by the BCL class System::Runtime::InteropServices::Marshal.

When you are wrapping unmanaged types, if the managed clients require the instance of the object to be allocated on the stack, value classes can be used to wrap the unmanaged types. Refer to Chapter 15 for an example.

Summary

In this chapter we discussed the disadvantages of the PInvoke service and TlbImp, and we demonstrated how to use managed wrappers to overcome these difficulties. We detailed the various issues of and workarounds for wrapping native C++ classes with managed wrappers.

APPENDIX A
Compiling the Code

THIS APPENDIX DESCRIBES the compiler options commonly used when compiling source code files written using Managed Extensions for C++ (MC++). You can type **cl /?** or **cl /help** at the command line to see a complete list of the options supported by the compiler.

When you compile code written in Visual C++, the generated code can be an MSIL binary or a native binary depending on the compiler options used.

/clr Compiler Option

You use the /clr compiler option to generate a managed image. You must use this option for compiling any source code that uses MC++ or any native C++ code for which an MSIL image is to be generated. /clr takes an optional argument, :noAssembly, which we explain later in this appendix.

Note that /clr implies /MT.

Generating a Managed EXE

The compiler will produce an EXE file when /clr is specified without /LD. A starting point, such as main or WinMain, must be present to generate a managed executable. All managed executables are assemblies. Assemblies are explained in Appendix C.

The following sample shows how to write a simple output statement in MC++:

```
// file: hello.cpp
#using <mscorlib.dll>
using namespace System;
int main() {
  Console::WriteLine(S"Hello from Managed World!");
}
```

The following command line shows how to compile hello.cpp:

```
cl /clr hello.cpp
```

If the `main` function is defined in the file `hello.cpp`, the MC++ compiler generates a managed executable with the name `hello.exe`.

Generating a Managed DLL

The `/clr` and `/LD` compiler options are used to generate an assembly as a managed DLL file.

The following code is a simple example of source code that will be used to generate an assembly as a DLL file:

```
// file: automobile.cpp
#using <mscorlib.dll>
using namespace System;

public __gc struct Automobile {
 /* declarations */
 void PrintName() {
   Console::WriteLine(S"Automobile");
 }
};
```

The file `automobile.cpp` can be compiled to a DLL using the following command:

```
cl /clr /LD automobile.cpp
```

The resulting DLL can be referenced (with the `#using` directive in MC++) into other managed applications and the public types from it can be used.

```
// file: managedApp.cpp
#using <mscorlib.dll>
#using "automobile.dll"
int main() {
  Automobile *pAuto = new Automobile();
  pAuto->PrintName();
}
```

Use the following command line to compile `managedApp.cpp` into an executable file:

```
cl /clr managedApp.cpp
```

Generating a Netmodule

When you compile a file with the /clr and /LD compiler options, an assembly is generated as a managed DLL. To generate a netmodule, you can use the compiler option /clr:noAssembly. This option must be accompanied by /c or /LD. With the /c option, an object file (a file with an .obj extension) is generated, and with the /LD option, a DLL file is generated. Netmodules are discussed in Appendix C.

To reference an assembly or a netmodule, use the #using statement in a source code file. For example, to import the assembly mscorlib.dll, you would use the following code:

```
#using <mscorlib.dll>
```

Separate Compilation and Linking

The command-line option /c when used with /clr generates an MSIL object (.obj) file. The following code samples show you how to use the /c option.

This code contains a global function, Func, defined in the file sample_part1.cpp:

```
// file: sample_part1.cpp
#using <mscorlib.dll>
using namespace System;
void Func() { Console::WriteLine(S"sample_part1.cpp:Func()"); }
```

The following code shows the function Func being used in a different file:

```
// file: sample_part2.cpp
extern void Func();
int main() {
  Func();
}
```

In this code, the main function calls the external function Func. The following command sequence shows how the /c option is used and how object files are linked:

```
cl /clr /c sample_part1.cpp
cl /clr /c sample_part2.cpp
link /out:sample.exe sample_part1.obj sample_part2.obj
```

The link command generates the executable sample.exe. The linker options used to generate managed code are as follows:

- /ASSEMBLYMODULE:fileName: Adds a module to the current managed EXE or DLL being generated. The public types in this added module are not available to the other modules in the same assembly (because they didn't use the #using directive to import the module), but they are available to the applications that import the assembly containing the module. Note that when the #using statement refers to a netmodule, the /ASSEMBLYMODULE option is automatically passed to the linker.

- /ASSEMBLYRESOURCE:fileName: Adds a resource file to the current assembly being generated.

- /NOASSEMBLY: Generates the image as a module. Note that when /clr:noAssembly is used to compile a program, the /NOASSEMBLY option is automatically passed to the linker.

Mixing Native and Managed Object Files

It is possible to mix MSIL and native .obj files in the same image. To do this, compile a native .obj with the /c option and another .obj with the /clr and /c options and link them together to generate a final executable image.

The following code shows a function with print statement in native C++:

```
// file: native.cpp
extern "C" int printf( ... );
void Func() {
    printf("native function Func\n");
}
```

This code can be compiled into a native object file using the following command:

```
cl /c native.cpp
```

The following code shows the use of the function Func defined in the native code:

```
// file: managed.cpp
extern void Func();
int main() {
    Func();
}
```

A managed object file for this code can be generated using the following command:

```
cl /clr /c managed.cpp
```

Both native and managed object files can be linked together using the following command to generate an executable in the file sample.exe:

```
link native.obj managed.obj /out:sample.exe /nodefaultlib:libc.lib
```

Building Assemblies Using al.exe

The .NET Framework SDK provides the tool al.exe to create an assembly from one or more MSIL modules. Note that al.exe requires a static member function of a managed type as a starting function for EXE assemblies.

Compile the following code to a module using the /clr:noAssembly compiler option:

```
// file: automobile.cpp
#using <mscorlib.dll>
using namespace System;

public __gc struct Automobile {
public:
 /* declarations */
 static void PrintName() {
   Console::WriteLine(S"Automobile");
 }
};
```

The following command generates an EXE assembly from a single module. Note that the resulting assembly consists of two PE files: sample.exe (which contains the manifest and other assembly metadata) and automobile.dll.

```
al /target:exe /out:sample.exe automobile.dll /main:Automobile.PrintName
```

Refer to the .NET documentation for more details on al.exe.

Other Compiler Options Related to Managed Code

So far, you have seen how to use the compiler options /clr and /LD. In this section, we explain how to use other compiler options related to managed code.

/FU (Force #using) Compiler Option

To reference an assembly without using the #using statement, you can use the /FU compiler option. You already know that to use the classes from the System namespace, you must import the BCL file mscorlib.dll. The following code uses the System::Console class without importing mscorlib.dll. However, at compilation time, you can import this file using /FU.

```
//file: hello.cpp
int main() {
   System::Console::WriteLine(S"Hello from Managed World!");
}
```

The following command generates the executable hello.exe:

```
cl /FU mscorlib.dll /clr hello.cpp
```

Note that the assembly or module being referenced must be in the path.

/AI (Assembly Include) Compiler Option

To add a directory to the search path for finding an assembly, you can use the /AI option. Assume that the file hello.cpp uses the assembly random.dll, and random.dll is in the c:\tmp directory. The following compilation succeeds in finding the assembly random.dll while parsing the file hello.cpp:

```
cl /AI c:\tmp /clr hello.cpp
```

The preceding command searches the c:\tmp directory if the regular search fails for any assembly imported via the #using directive in the file hello.cpp. Refer to Appendix C for more information on how assemblies are searched by the compiler and the runtime.

/EHsc Compiler Option

Use the /EHsc option to enable C++ exception handling along with structured exception handling exceptions.

/O1 and /O2 Compiler Options

You can use the usual optimization options /O1 (minimize space) and /O2 (maximize speed) when compiling managed code.

/Zi Compiler Option

To generate debug information for managed code, use the compiler option /Zi. You can also use this option to produce debug information in a native C++ compilation.

The following command generates a .pdb file that can be used to debug an application:

```
cl /clr /Zi sample.cpp
```

/Fx Compiler Option

To view the compiler-injected code when attributes, delegates, or events are used in the source code, use the /Fx switch.

Restrictions on the Use of the /clr Compiler Option

Some compiler options are not supported by /clr, including the runtime check options RTC1, RTCc, RTCs, and RTCu; the precompiled header file option /YX; the /ZI option (Edit and Continue is not supported in the current version of the Visual Studio .NET); and the buffer overrun detection option /GS.

For more details on compiler option restrictions and other relevant details, refer to the Visual C++ .NET documentation.

Summary

In this appendix, we discussed the various compiler options to use when you're working with managed code. In Appendix B, we discuss metadata.

Metadata

METADATA IS A REPRESENTATION of managed application information in binary form. Metadata includes information about assembly identity, referenced assemblies, security access details of the assembly, types referenced and defined in the assembly, and custom attributes used to modify the behavior of the types in the assembly or the behavior of the assembly itself. Metadata is an integral part of a file compiled to MSIL. The common language runtime (CLR) uses metadata to discover information about the types used in a managed application.

When a managed application is compiled, a portable executable file is generated. This file contains the following information:

- *Portable Executable (PE) header:* This header contains index entries for all sections in the file. It is used by the CLR to find out where the execution starts in that program.

- *Metadata:* This part contains the metadata for the application.

- *MSIL:* This is the code in intermediate form. This code is translated to native code using Just In Time compilers (JITters) before the execution starts.

In this appendix, we show how the metadata looks when an assembly or module is generated for an MC++ program. We start with a "Hello, World!" sample. We discuss in detail the metadata for various types, members (including data and functions), properties, delegates, and events.

Hello, World!

The .NET Framework SDK provides a tool called `ildasm.exe` that you can use to view the metadata in a file. This tool disassembles managed binary images into MSIL with metadata. The following sample shows a "Hello, World!" program:

```
// file: hello.cpp
#using <mscorlib.dll>
using namespace System;
```

```
int main() {
    Console::WriteLine(S"Hello from Managed World!");
}
```

You can save the `ildasm.exe` output of the executable for the preceding program to a file using the following command:

```
ildasm /out=hello.ildasm /tokens /source hello.exe
```

The metadata in the following listing shows a stripped-down version of the output from the file `hello.ildasm`. Note that the assemblies, `mscorlib.dll` and `Microsoft.VisualC.dll`, must be available to compile any program that uses Managed Extensions for C++. References to these assemblies can be seen in the metadata of every assembly generated by the MC++ compiler.

```
.assembly extern /*23000001*/ mscorlib
{
    /* text stripped */
}
.assembly extern /*23000002*/ Microsoft.VisualC
{
    /* text stripped */
}
```

All program entities (types, methods, references, and so on) in an assembly get their own tokens (indices into the various tables in the assembly) in the metadata. A *token* is a 4-byte value whose most significant byte represents the type of the token and whose least significant 3 bytes constitute an index into the table corresponding to that type of token. For example, in the following metadata output, the assembly `mscorlib.dll` has a token value of `23000001`. The keyword `extern` indicates that this assembly is referenced in the current assembly. The following output shows the assembly `hello` with the token `20000001`:

```
.assembly /*20000001*/ hello
{
    /* text stripped */
}
```

The following metadata output shows the `main` method, which has `public` visibility and is a `static` method returning an `int`. This method has an attribute representing the calling convention used. This method is the managed entry point into the program.

```
.method /*06000001*/ public static int32 modopt([mscorlib/* 23000001 */]
      System.Runtime.CompilerServices.CallConvCdecl/* 01000004 */)
          main() cil managed
{
/* code stripped */
}
```

In order for the CLR to do the CRT initialization, all MC++ executables contain an unmanaged entry point with the name _mainCRTStartup. This method returns an unsigned int. For an explanation of the options for this Platform Invoke (PInvoke) specification, refer to Chapter 16.

```
.method /*06000002*/ public static pinvokeimpl(/* No map */)
        unsigned int32  _mainCRTStartup() native unmanaged preservesig
{
  .entrypoint
  .custom /*0C000001:0A000003*/ instance void [mscorlib/* 23000001 */]
      System.Security.SuppressUnmanagedCodeSecurityAttribute/* 01000006 */
*/::.ctor()
          /* 0A000003 */ = ( 01 00 00 00 )
  // Embedded native code
  //  Disassembly of native methods is not supported.
  //  Managed TargetRVA = 0x106f
} // end of global method _mainCRTStartup
```

Since the method _mainCRTStartup is a native method, the CLR cannot verify the code. The verification is suppressed by using the custom attribute System.Security.SuppressUnmanagedCodeSecurityAttribute.

CorTokenType

You can find the various token types in the .NET Framework in the header file corhdr.h in the Platform SDK include files. The following enumerator shows the token types based on the most significant byte of a token value:

```
typedef enum CorTokenType
{
    mdtModule              = 0x00000000,
    mdtTypeRef             = 0x01000000,
    mdtTypeDef             = 0x02000000,
    mdtFieldDef            = 0x04000000,
    mdtMethodDef           = 0x06000000,
```

```
        mdtParamDef              = 0x08000000,
        mdtInterfaceImpl         = 0x09000000,
        mdtMemberRef             = 0x0a000000,
        mdtCustomAttribute       = 0x0c000000,
        mdtPermission            = 0x0e000000,
        mdtSignature             = 0x11000000,
        mdtEvent                 = 0x14000000,
        mdtProperty              = 0x17000000,
        mdtModuleRef             = 0x1a000000,
        mdtTypeSpec              = 0x1b000000,
        mdtAssembly              = 0x20000000,
        mdtAssemblyRef           = 0x23000000,
        mdtFile                  = 0x26000000,
        mdtExportedType          = 0x27000000,
        mdtManifestResource      = 0x28000000,
        mdtString                = 0x70000000,
        mdtName                  = 0x71000000,
        mdtBaseType              = 0x72000000,
} CorTokenType;
```

Types

We use the following sample to show how metadata for types is represented in a PE image. In this sample, an interface, a value type, and a gc class that implement the interface are used. A native type is also defined and used in a member function of the gc class.

```cpp
// file: types.cpp
#using <mscorlib.dll>
using namespace System;

// interface definition
public __gc __interface IFace {
  void MemFunc();
};

// value type definition
public __value class ValueClass : public IFace{
    int m_i;
    static float m_f;
```

```
  public:
    void memFunc() {
      String *str = "Hello";
    }
};

// native type definition
class UnmanagedClass {
  // declarations
};

// gc class definition
public __gc struct GcClass : public IFace {
  private:
    UnmanagedClass PrivateMemFunc() {
        UnmanagedClass u;
        // code
        return u;
    }
  public:
    void MemFunc(){
      UnmanagedClass u = PrivateMemFunc();
      // code that uses u
    }
};
```

This sample can be compiled into a managed DLL using the following command:

```
cl /clr /LD types.cpp
```

The metadata in the DLL `types.dll` can be saved to a file using the following command:

```
ildasm /out=types.meta types.dll /tokens /source
```

The metadata for the interface `IFace` is as follows:

```
.class /*02000002*/ interface public abstract auto ansi IFace
{
  .method /*06000002*/ public newslot virtual abstract
          instance void  MemFunc() cil managed
```

```
    {
    } // end of method IFace::MemFunc
} // end of class IFace
```

The metadata token for the interface is 02000002. The first byte (02) of the token indicates that it is a type definition token. The token for the method MemFunc is 06000002. The first byte (06) indicates that it is a method definition token. The newslot keyword indicates that there will be a new slot for the MemFunc method in the vtable layout of the IFace interface. The accessibility of public on the method and the interface indicates that they are accessible outside the assembly.

The metadata for the value type ValueClass is as follows:

```
.class /*02000003*/ public sequential ansi sealed ValueClass
       extends [mscorlib/* 23000001 */]System.ValueType/* 01000005 */
       implements IFace/* 02000002 */
{
  .field /*04000002*/ private int32 m_i
  .field /*04000003*/ private static float32 m_f
  .method /*06000003*/ public virtual instance void
          MemFunc() cil managed
  {
    // Code stripped
  } // end of method ValueClass::MemFunc
  .method /*06000004*/ public specialname rtspecialname
          instance void  .ctor() cil managed
  {
    // Code stripped
  } // end of method ValueClass::.ctor
  .method /*06000005*/ private specialname rtspecialname static
          void  .cctor() cil managed
  {
    // Code stripped
  } // end of method ValueClass::.cctor
} // end of class ValueClass
```

The sequential keyword indicates that the value type has a sequential layout. The fields are laid out in a sequential order. The auto keyword (not shown in this listing) indicates that the runtime should provide the layout for the class. The sealed keyword indicates that this type cannot be a base class. All value types extend the type ValueType in the System namespace. The type ValueType is used (it has a typeref token indicated by its token's most significant byte, 01) from the referenced assembly mscorlib.dll (indicated by the first byte 23 of the assembly token). All implemented interfaces are listed after the implements keyword. The data member m_i is marked as private. ValueClass has a static data member, m_f, and it does not have a user-defined static constructor. The MC++ compiler generates a class constructor (cctor in the previous metadata) for this type. This is behavior similar to gc classes. The cil keyword (which stands for Common Intermediate Language) indicates that the MemFunc method has MSIL implementation as opposed to native code. The MC++ compiler generates a default constructor for value types in the absence of a user-defined constructor. Constructors and destructors are marked with specialname and rtspecialname keywords in the metadata.

The following is the partial metadata for the native class UnmanagedClass:

```
.class /*02000006*/ private sequential ansi sealed UnmanagedClass
        extends [mscorlib/* 23000001 */]System.ValueType/* 01000005 */
{
  .pack 1
  .size 4
} // end of class UnmanagedClass
```

Unmanaged types are mapped to value types in the metadata. They are marked as private. The members of unmanaged types are not mapped to the metadata. Instead, only the size and packing information is passed in the metadata. The size of the type UnmanagedClass is 4, as it has just one integer member. The custom attributes (not shown) in the metadata are internal to the compiler.

The metadata for the gc class GcClass is as follows:

```
.class /*02000005*/ public auto ansi GcClass
        extends [mscorlib/* 23000001 */]System.Object/* 01000004 */
        implements IFace/* 02000002 */
{
  .custom /*0C000004:0A000003*/ instance void [Microsoft.VisualC/* 23000002 */]
        Microsoft.VisualC.MiscellaneousBitsAttribute/* 01000008 */::.ctor(int32)
           /* 0A000003 */ = ( 01 00 01 00 00 00 00 00 )
  .method /*06000005*/ private instance valuetype UnmanagedClass/* 02000006 */
        PrivateMemFunc() cil managed
  {
    // code stripped
  } // end of method GcClass::PrivateMemFunc

  .method /*06000006*/ public virtual instance void
        MemFunc() cil managed
```

```
  {
    // code stripped
  } // end of method GcClass::MemFunc

  .method /*06000007*/ public specialname rtspecialname
          instance void  .ctor() cil managed
  {
    // code stripped
  } // end of method GcClass::.ctor
} // end of class GcClass
```

All gc classes have the Object class from the System namespace as their top-most base class in the ancestor class chain. The GcClass class extends the Object class and implements the IFace interface. This class has a private member function, PrivateMemFunc, whose return type is UnmanagedClass. The MC++ compiler generates a default constructor for GcClass. There is no static constructor generated for this class because there are no static data members. Since GcClass is a struct, the custom attribute MiscellaneousBitsAttribute is used to indicate that.

Native strings are given a unique name and are encoded as private value types in the metadata. The member function MemFunc of the value type ValueClass uses a native string to create a String* object. This native string is represented as a private value type with a special unique name.

The following listing shows the metadata representation for the native string "hello":

```
.class /*02000004*/ private explicit ansi sealed $ArrayType$0x6047384f
       extends [mscorlib/* 23000001 */]System.ValueType/* 01000005 */
{
  .pack 1
  .size 6
  .custom /*0C000003:0A000002*/ instance void [Microsoft.VisualC/* 23000002 */]
          Microsoft.VisualC.DebugInfoInPDBAttribute/* 01000007 */::.ctor()
            /* 0A000002 */ = ( 01 00 00 00 )
} // end of class $ArrayType$0x6047384f
```

The string "hello" used in the function MemFunc of ValueClass is represented as the native type $ArrayType$0x6047384f. The size of this type is equal to the length of the native string.

Nested types will be represented in the metadata with the nested keyword. They will also have their enclosing type noted in their metadata. Typically, all DLL assemblies have a default entry point called __DllMainCRTStartup@12. This function contains native start-up code for the DLL.

Members

Members of managed classes include data members, member functions, properties, and events. All types can have custom attributes attached to them. We use
the following sample to show how metadata is encoded for members of
managed types:

```cpp
// file: members.cpp
#using <mscorlib.dll>
#using <system.dll>
using namespace System;
using namespace System::ComponentModel;

// delegate declaration
public __delegate int MyDelegate (int first, int second);

public __gc class ManagedClass {
 public private:
    [DefaultValue(10)]
    int privateData;
    int privateMethod(float f) { return 0; }

 private protected:
    int protectedData;
    int protectedMethod(char c) { return 0; }

 protected public:
    int publicData;
    int publicMethod(String* s) { return 0; }

 public private:
    __property int get_Prop() { return privateData; }
    __property void set_Prop(int i) { privateData = i; }

 public public:
    // event declaration
    __event MyDelegate *delegateOne;
};
```

In this sample, the MyDelegate delegate is defined. The members of the gc
class ManagedClass include a few data members, a few member functions, an
event, and a property.

The metadata for the data members and the property is as follows:

```
.field /*04000001*/ assembly int32 privateData
.custom /*0C000002:0A000002*/ instance void [System/* 23000002 */]
    System.ComponentModel.DefaultValueAttribute/* 01000009 */::.ctor(int32)
        /* 0A000002 */ = ( 01 00 0A 00 00 00 00 00 )
.field /*04000002*/ famandassem int32 protectedData
.field /*04000003*/ famorassem int32 publicData
.field /*04000004*/ private class MyDelegate/* 02000002 */ delegateOne
.property /*17000001*/ specialname instance int32
        Prop()
{
  .set /*0600000A*/ instance void ManagedClass/* 02000003 */::set_Prop(int32)

  .get /*06000009*/ instance int32 ManagedClass/* 02000003 */::get_Prop()

} // end of property ManagedClass::Prop
```

The data member privateData has assembly access because it is marked with public private access specifiers in the source code. We know that the more restrictive of the two access specifiers becomes the assembly access for the member, so the member privateData is accessed only within the assembly and not beyond. The same data member has a custom attribute, DefaultValueAttribute, attached to it. The default value is 10. The other data members include protectedData with FamilyAndAssembly access, publicData with FamilyOrAssembly access, and the delegate delegateOne (generated by the compiler for the event member delegateOne) with private access. The Prop property is defined using the property keyword. Both getter and setter are part of this declaration.

The metadata for user-defined member methods is as follows:

```
.method /*06000006*/ assembly instance int32
        privateMethod(float32 f) cil managed
{
  // Code stripped
} // end of method ManagedClass::privateMethod


.method /*06000007*/ famandassem instance int32
      protectedMethod(int8 modopt([Microsoft.VisualC/* 23000003 */]
          Microsoft.VisualC.NoSignSpecifiedModifier/* 0100000A */) c) cil
managed
{
  // Code stripped
} // end of method ManagedClass::protectedMethod
```

```
.method /*06000008*/ famorassem instance int32
        publicMethod(string s) cil managed
{
  // Code stripped
} // end of method ManagedClass::publicMethod
.method /*06000009*/ assembly specialname
        instance int32  get_Prop() cil managed
{
  // Code stripped
} // end of method ManagedClass::get_Prop

.method /*0600000A*/ assembly specialname
        instance void  set_Prop(int32 i) cil managed
{
  // Code stripped
} // end of method ManagedClass::set_Prop
```

The user-defined methods include privateMethod with private access,
protectedMethod with FamilyAndAssembly access, and publicMethod with
FamilyOrAssembly access. The property methods include get_Prop, which has
assembly visibility, and set_Prop, which also has assembly access. Property
methods are marked with specialname. The managed keyword in all of the methods indicates that managed code is generated for them.

The metadata for the delegate at the beginning of the source code is
as follows:

```
.class /*02000002*/ public auto ansi sealed MyDelegate
       extends [mscorlib/* 23000001 */]System.MulticastDelegate/* 01000004 */
{
  .method /*06000002*/ public specialname rtspecialname
          instance void   .ctor(object __unnamed000,
                                native int __unnamed001) runtime managed forwardref
  {
  } // end of method MyDelegate::.ctor

  .method /*06000003*/ public newslot virtual
          instance int32   Invoke(int32 first,
                                  int32 second) runtime managed forwardref
  {
  } // end of method MyDelegate::Invoke
```

```
    .method /*06000004*/ public newslot virtual
            instance class [mscorlib/* 23000001 */]System.IAsyncResult/* 01000007
*/
            BeginInvoke(int32 first,
                        int32 second,
                        class [mscorlib/* 23000001 */] System.AsyncCallback
                           /* 01000008 */ __unnamed002,
                              object __unnamed003) runtime managed forwardref
    {
    } // end of method MyDelegate::BeginInvoke

    .method /*06000005*/ public newslot virtual
        instance int32  EndInvoke(class [mscorlib/* 23000001 */]
            System.IAsyncResult/* 01000007 */ __unnamed000) runtime managed
forwardref
    {
    } // end of method MyDelegate::EndInvoke
} // end of class MyDelegate
```

The MC++ compiler injects code for the MyDelegate class while parsing the delegate declaration. The MyDelegate class extends the gc class MulticastDelegate in the System namespace. It is sealed, meaning that other gc classes cannot inherit from MyDelegate.

The methods injected into the class are the constructor, Invoke, BeginInvoke, and EndInvoke. All of these methods have the newslot keyword, which means that these methods get a new entry in the vtable layout of the MyDelegate class.

The gc class ManagedClass has an event as a member. The metadata for the event is as follows:

```
    .method /*0600000B*/ public instance void
            add_delegateOne(class MyDelegate/* 02000002 */ eh) cil managed
    {
      // Code stripped
    } // end of method ManagedClass::add_delegateOne

    .method /*0600000C*/ public instance void
            remove_delegateOne(class MyDelegate/* 02000002 */ eh) cil managed
    {
      // Code stripped
    } // end of method ManagedClass::remove_delegateOne

    .method /*0600000D*/ family instance int32
            raise_delegateOne(int32 i1,
                                int32 i2) cil managed
```

```
  {
    // Code stripped
  } // end of method ManagedClass::raise_delegateOne

  .event /*14000001*/ specialname MyDelegate/* 02000002 */ /*02000002*/
delegateOne
  {
    .addon instance void ManagedClass/* 02000003 */::add_delegateOne(
                      class MyDelegate/* 02000002 */) /* 0600000B */
    .fire instance int32 ManagedClass/* 02000003 */::raise_delegateOne(int32,

int32) /* 0600000D */
    .removeon instance void ManagedClass/* 02000003 */::remove_delegateOne(
                      class MyDelegate/* 02000002 */) /* 0600000C */
  } // end of event ManagedClass::delegateOne
```

The MC++ compiler generates three methods corresponding to an event: add_delegateOne, remove_delegateOne, and raise_delegateOne. In addition, an event is shown in the metadata as an event member using the event keyword.

Summary

In this appendix, we showed how the metadata looks when an MC++ program is compiled into an assembly or a module. In Appendix C, we discuss assemblies.

APPENDIX C
Assemblies

APPLICATION DEVELOPMENT FOR the Windows platform has become increasingly diffi-cult due to problems such as DLL hell and complex deployment. The term *DLL hell* refers to a second version of a DLL replacing the first version of the same DLL, and existing applications that depend on the first version ceasing to function properly. The *complex deployment* problem refers to applications that have various components at multiple locations on the same machine and that require modifying the registry, which often results in conflicts with other applications or other versions of the same application's components. Assemblies in the .NET Framework address problems such as DLL hell.

Simply put, an *assembly* is a set of one or more files that are used to run a managed application in the .NET Framework. Assemblies are the basic deployment units that are versionable in the .NET Framework. They support side-by-side execution, meaning that multiple versions of the same application can coexist. Applications depending on an earlier version of an assembly can continue to use that assembly whereas other applications that depend on a newer version can use the newer version. Each assembly can be deployed as a single implementation unit that may contain one or more files. Assemblies are self-describing in the sense that each assembly contains metadata that describes the assembly. You don't need to work with registry entries to deploy an assembly. The assembly manifest (the description of the assembly in metadata) contains information that is required by the common language runtime (CLR) to load and execute the application. This is a key point to note because it is this capability of assemblies that simplifies the application deployment process.

An assembly contains a collection of one or more of the following: metadata, executable code, and resources. If all the contents of an assembly are in one file, it is called a *single-file assembly*. An assembly that has more than one file is called a *multifile assembly*. In this appendix, we use the term "assembly" to refer to both single-file and multifile assemblies, unless otherwise specified.

To be an assembly, the metadata must contain a description of the assembly called the *assembly manifest*. Without the assembly manifest, a managed PE image is called a *netmodule*. It can contain type definitions but it cannot be an independent entity in the .NET Framework—that is, you cannot load and execute a netmodule or deploy it as an implementation unit in the .NET Framework. It has to be part of an assembly.

As mentioned in Appendix B, an assembly contains a Portable Executable (PE) header, Microsoft Intermediate Language (MSIL), and metadata.

The contents of an assembly can be categorized as follows:

- *Assembly manifest:* Contains information about the assembly identity, version, culture information, strong name identification, and type reference (used by the runtime to locate the type), as well as a list of all modules in the assembly, and a list of all referenced assemblies.

- *Metadata:* Binary description for types (referenced as well as defined) and custom attributes. Netmodules can also contain a list of referenced assemblies and referenced modules.

- *MSIL:* Code for the managed methods defined in the assembly.

- *A set of resources:* Typically used for localization.

An assembly manifest can be stored as a stand-alone portable executable file that just contains the manifest information, or it can be stored along with the MSIL code in one of the other portable executable files that make up the assembly. An assembly can be a single DLL that you plan to reference from source code, a single executable, several DLLs (this is a multifile assembly, with the file containing the manifest referred to as the assembly manifest file), or an executable with additional DLL netmodules (this is also a multifile assembly, but the executable must contain the manifest and thus is always the assembly manifest file). Note that the MC++ compiler generates DLL netmodules, whereas other .NET-targeted languages generate netmodules with the file extension `.netmodule`. An executable assembly must contain a starting point such as `main` or `WinMain`. You can view the contents of an assembly using the .NET Framework SDK tool Microsoft Intermediate Language Disassembler (ILDasm) `ildasm.exe`.

You can create assemblies using a compiler or the .NET Framework SDK tool `al.exe`. You can also generate assemblies programmatically using the classes from the namespace `System::Reflection::Emit`.

In this appendix, we discuss different types of assemblies that can be generated by the MC++ compiler.

Single-File versus Multifile Assemblies

As mentioned before, the contents of an assembly can all be in a single file (assuming that no resource files are used), in which case it is called a single-file assembly, or the contents can be in multiple files, in which case it is called a multifile assembly. One of the major benefits of having multifile assemblies is that netmodules from different languages can be part of a single assembly.

Single-File Assemblies

The "Hello, World!" example you have seen in this book is a simple example of an assembly composed of a single file.

```
// filename: hello.cpp
#using <mscorlib.dll>
int main() {
  System::Console::WriteLine(S"Hello From Managed World!");
}
```

You can use the `/clr` compiler option to generate an assembly for the preceding sample.

```
cl /clr hello.cpp /out:hello.exe
```

This command creates the application `hello.exe`, which is a single-file assembly.

Multifile Assemblies

A multifile assembly contains multiple files that can include netmodules, resources, and an assembly manifest. The file that contains the manifest is called the *assembly manifest file*. When other assemblies want to reference this assembly, they only need to reference the assembly manifest file, not all the other files. The following code shows how to create a multifile assembly:

```
// filename: file1.cpp
#using <mscorlib.dll>
public __gc class Managed {
   int m_i;
 public:
   __property int get_i() {
      return m_i;
   }
   __property void set_i(int val) {
      m_i = val;
   }
};
```

Compile this code to generate a module with the following command:

```
cl /clr:noAssembly /LD file1.cpp
```

The following code shows a second module:

```
// filename: file2.cpp
#using <mscorlib.dll>
public __value struct V {
    int m_j;
};
```

Compile this code to generate a module with the following command:

```
cl /clr:noAssembly /LD file2.cpp
```

The following code shows an assembly that imports the previous two modules:

```
// filename: assem.cpp
#using <mscorlib.dll>
#using "file1.dll"
#using "file2.dll"
using namespace System;

int main() {
  Managed *m = new Managed();
  m->i = 10;
  Console::WriteLine(m->i);
  V v;
  v.m_j = 20;
  Console::WriteLine(v.m_j);
}
```

You can compile the preceding code to generate an assembly using the /clr option.

```
cl /clr assem.cpp /out:assem.exe
```

Note that the assembly assem.exe references the modules file1.dll and file2.dll.

Suppose that you just want to create an assembly that has the modules `file1.dll` and `file2.dll`. You can use the .NET Framework SDK's Assembly Generation Tool (`al.exe`) for this purpose.

This command generates the assembly `assem.dll`, which contains references to the modules `file1.dll` and `file2.dll`:

```
al.exe file1.dll file2.dll /out:assem.dll
```

Application Private Assemblies versus Shared Assemblies

Assemblies in the .NET Framework can be categorized as application private assemblies or shared assemblies. An *application private assembly* is private to an application and to other applications in the same directory or a subdirectory of the directory that contains the assembly. It is typically located in the directory where the application resides. A *shared assembly* can be shared by applications in any directory on that machine.

The advantage of shared assemblies over application private assemblies is that one copy of the assembly can be shared by multiple applications. A shared assembly must have a strong name (described in the next section). An example of a shared assembly is `mscorlib.dll`. All shared assemblies typically reside in a global directory called the global assembly cache (GAC), which we discuss later in this appendix.

Strong-Named Assemblies

A *strong name* is a unique name given to an assembly. It consists of an assembly identity, a public key, and a digital signature. An assembly identity is its textual name, version number, and culture information. You can use the .NET Framework SDK's Strong Name Tool (`sn.exe`) to create a key file.

```
sn.exe /out:myKey.snk
```

This command generates a key in the file `myKey.snk`. To assign this key to an assembly, you can either use the .NET Framework SDK's Assembly Generation Tool (`al.exe`) or the custom attribute `AssemblyKeyFileAttribute`.

Creating a Strong-Named Assembly with a Custom Attribute

The following sample shows how to create a strong-named assembly using the custom attribute AssemblyKeyFileAttribute in the namespace System::Reflection:

```
// filename: assem.cpp
#using <mscorlib.dll>
using namespace System::Reflection;
[assembly:AssemblyKeyFileAttribute(S"myKey.snk")];
public __value struct V {
    int m_i;
};
```

When compiled into an assembly, the assembly will have a strong name with the key from myKey.snk.

The following command generates the assembly assem.dll with a strong name:

```
cl /clr /LD assem.cpp
```

Warning: The filename as it appears in the custom attribute will be stored in the metadata. You should use caution to ensure that the filename does not contain any sensitive information (such as user names or account names).

Creating a Strong-Named Assembly with al.exe

You can use the al.exe tool to generate a strong-named assembly. In this case, you don't need to use the custom attribute. You first create a key file using sn.exe and then use al.exe to sign it with a strong name, as follows:

```
// filename: module.cpp
#using <mscorlib.dll>
public __value struct V {
    int m_i;
};
```

The following command generates a module:

```
cl /clr:noAssembly  /LD module.cpp
```

The following command signs the multifile assembly `assem.dll` with a strong name:

```
al.exe module.dll /out:assem.dll /keyfile:myKey.snk
```

Dynamic Assemblies

Assemblies that are generated programmatically are called *dynamic assemblies.* The BCL classes from the `System::Reflection::Emit` namespace can be used to create dynamic assemblies. The BCL classes from the `System::Reflection` namespace are used to load an assembly into memory and inspect the types from the assembly.

Assembly Creation

Suppose that you want to generate an assembly with a public gc class that contains a public method, `SayHello`. Assume that this method is supposed to print the string `"Hello, World!"`. The following code shows how a dynamic assembly is created for this scenario:

```
#using <mscorlib.dll>
using namespace System;
using namespace System::Reflection;
using namespace System::Reflection::Emit;
// Build and save a dynamic assembly using Reflection Emit API.
void CreateDynamicAssembly(AppDomain *domain) {
  // set the assembly name
  AssemblyName *assemblyName = new AssemblyName();
  assemblyName->Name = S"DynAssembly";
  // define the assembly
  AssemblyBuilder *assemblyBuilder =
      domain->DefineDynamicAssembly(assemblyName, AssemblyBuilderAccess::Save);
  // define a module for the assembly
  ModuleBuilder *moduleBuilder =
      assemblyBuilder->DefineDynamicModule(S"DynModule", S"DynModule.mod");
    // define a public type
    TypeBuilder *typeBuilder =
                moduleBuilder->DefineType(S"MyType", TypeAttributes::Public);
    // define a public method for the type
```

```
    MethodBuilder *methodBuilder =
                    typeBuilder->DefineMethod(S"SayHello",
                                            MethodAttributes::Public,
                                            CallingConventions::Standard,
                                            __typeof(void),
                                            0);
        // add code for the body of the method
    ILGenerator *ilGenerator = methodBuilder->GetILGenerator();
    ilGenerator->EmitWriteLine(S"Hello, World!");
    ilGenerator->Emit(OpCodes->Ret);
    // create the type and get the assembly
    AssemblyBuilder* obj =
        dynamic_cast<AssemblyBuilder*>(typeBuilder->CreateType()->Assembly);
    // save the assembly
    assemblyBuilder->Save(S"DynAssembly.dll");
}
int main() {
    AppDomain *currentDomain = AppDomain::CurrentDomain;
    CreateDynamicAssembly(currentDomain);
}
```

In this sample, the method `CreateDynamicAssembly` creates and saves an assembly `DynAssembly` with a module `DynModule`. This module defines a `public gc` class `MyType` with a public method `SayHello` that prints the message `Hello, World!`.

In order to create an assembly, an application domain is obtained for the current application. This is used to define a dynamic assembly. This dynamic assembly is used to create a dynamic module. The dynamic module is used to define a type. A method along with a method body is added to the type. All of the types used to create an assembly are from the `System::Reflection::Emit` namespace. This namespace and the types defined in it provide the functionality needed to define assemblies.

The assembly created by the program is saved into the file `DynAssembly.dll`.

To generate an executable, the method `AssemblyBuilder::SetEntryPoint` must be called to specify the entry point method for the assembly. Refer to the .NET documentation on dynamic assemblies for more details.

Reflection

The `System::Reflection` namespace contains types that can be used to inspect an assembly. The process of inspecting a type, its members, and its attributes is called *reflection*.

The following sample shows how reflection is used to examine the assembly created in the previous example. This program queries the user for an assembly name and lists all public types and their members.

```cpp
#using <mscorlib.dll>
using namespace System;
using namespace System::Reflection;
using namespace System::IO;

void ListAllTypesAndMembers(Assembly *a) {
    Console::WriteLine("Method: ListAllTypesWithMembers");
    Console::WriteLine("Types for {0}", a->FullName);
    Type *types __gc[] = a->GetTypes();
    for (int i = 0; i < types->Length; i++) {
        Console::WriteLine("   {0}", types[i]);
        MemberInfo *members __gc[] = types[i]->GetMembers();
        Console::WriteLine("      Members for {0}", types[i]->FullName);
        for (int j = 0; j < members->Length; j++) {
            Console::WriteLine("         {0}", members[j]);
        }
    }
    Console::WriteLine("\n");
}
int main() {
    Assembly *a = 0;
    try {
        Console::WriteLine("Type an assembly name without .dll");
        String* assemblyName = Console::ReadLine();
        a = Assembly::Load(assemblyName);
        ListAllTypesAndMembers(a);
    }
    catch(FileNotFoundException *e) {
        Console::WriteLine(e->Message);
    }
}
```

In this code, the method `Assembly::Load` is used to load an assembly into the memory. The method `ListAllTypesAndMembers` iterates through all public types in the assembly and lists public members of each type. The method `GetTypes` of the type `Assembly` returns an array of types. The method `GetMembers` of the class `Type` returns an array of all public members of a type.

Assuming that the input is DynAssembly, the output of the program is as follows:

```
Type an assembly name without .dll
DynAssembly
Method: ListAllTypesWithMembers
Types for DynAssembly, Version=0.0.0.0, Culture=neutral, PublicKeyToken=null
    MyType
        Members for MyType
        Int32 GetHashCode()
        Boolean Equals(System.Object)
        System.String ToString()
        Void SayHello()
        System.Type GetType()
        Void .ctor()
```

Refer to the System::Reflection namespace in the .NET documentation for more details on the Reflection API.

Global Assembly Cache

Shared assemblies are typically kept in a common place so that the CLR knows where to find them. This common place is the global assembly cache (GAC), which resides under the directory Assembly that exists under the operating system installation directory (the directory windows on the Windows XP platform). You can use the platform SDK tool gacutil.exe to view and manipulate the contents of the GAC.

How Are Assemblies Located?

When an assembly is imported into a file (without an absolute path), the search algorithms used by the MC++ compiler and the CLR are different.

Compiler Search

The MC++ compiler searches for an assembly (when the absolute path is not used) as follows in priority order:

- Current directory

- CLR installation directory

- Directories specified by the /AI option

- Directories specified with the LIBPATH environment variable

In the current version of the compiler, there is no distinction between using angle brackets (< >) and double quotes ("") for an imported filename.

Common Language Runtime Search

In this section we briefly discuss how the CLR locates assemblies. Refer to the .NET documentation for a detailed discussion.

Given an assembly reference, the CLR first applies version policy on the assembly (version policies are set by the application in a configuration file, or by the assembly publisher, or by the administrator). After deciding which version of the assembly to load, the CLR looks for a codebase (file location) entry from the assembly configuration files. If a codebase is not present and if the assembly has a strong name, the CLR searches in the GAC, then in the current directory, and finally in the CLR installation directory. If the assembly does not have a strong name, the search starts in the current directory followed by the CLR installation directory. For a detailed description on how the CLR locates assemblies, refer to the .NET documentation.

Miscellaneous

In this section we describe various issues related to the assemblies generated by the MC++ compiler.

Required Assemblies for MC++

There are two assemblies that must always be available to any managed executable generated from the MC++ compiler: mscorlib.dll and Microsoft.VisualC.dll. The first assembly contains the BCL type definitions. The second assembly contains a custom attribute and several custom modifiers that are specific to MC++. You need to make sure that these two assemblies are available in the CLR installation directory.

Case Sensitivity

Assemblies in .NET are case insensitive, but they are case sensitive in MC++. You must take care when you write managed components that interoperate with other .NET-targeted languages.

Private versus Public Types

While you import an assembly, none of the private types defined in an assembly are imported into the client code. While you import a nonassembly netmodule, all private types are accessible to the importing component. Note that types in a module must be defined in the same file. The current MC++ compiler will not allow the definition of a type to be split across modules.

Unverifiable Code

By default, the current MC++ compiler generates unverifiable code. It cannot be used where code verification is an important criterion for a managed application.

Importing Assemblies

When importing assemblies, transitivity is not followed. For example, if assembly A imports assembly B, and assembly B imports assembly C, assembly C is not automatically imported by assembly A. You need to explicitly import assembly C in assembly A if types from assembly C are needed.

Summary

In this appendix, we discussed different types of assemblies, including single-file and multifile assemblies, shared and private assemblies, strong-named assemblies, and dynamic assemblies. We showed how to create and inspect a dynamic assembly. We also discussed the differences among the search methods used by the compiler and the CLR.

Index

Announcing *About VS.NET*—
the *free* Apress .NET e-newsletter with great .NET news, information, code—and attitude

We guarantee that this isn't going to be your typical boring e-newsletter with just a list of URLs (though it will have them as well).

Instead, *About VS.NET* will contain contributions from a whole slate of top .NET gurus, edited by award-winning, best-selling authors Gary Cornell and Dan Appleman. Upcoming issues will feature articles on:

- Best coding practices in ADO.NET

- The hidden "gotchas" in doing thread programming in VB.NET

- Why C# is (not) a better choice than VB.NET

- What Java can learn from C# and vice versa

About VS.NET will cover it all!

This *free* e-newsletter will be the easiest way for you to get up-to-date .NET information delivered to your Inbox every two weeks—more often if there's breaking news!

Apress Titles

ISBN	PRICE	AUTHOR	TITLE
1-893115-73-9	$34.95	Abbott	Voice Enabling Web Applications: VoiceXML and Beyond
1-893115-01-1	$39.95	Appleman	Appleman's Win32 API Puzzle Book and Tutorial for Visual Basic Programmers
1-893115-23-2	$29.95	Appleman	How Computer Programming Works
1-893115-97-6	$39.95	Appleman	Moving to VB. NET: Strategies, Concepts, and Code
1-893115-09-7	$29.95	Baum	Dave Baum's Definitive Guide to LEGO MINDSTORMS
1-893115-84-4	$29.95	Baum, Gasperi, Hempel, and Villa	Extreme MINDSTORMS: An Advanced Guide to LEGO MINDSTORMS
1-893115-82-8	$59.95	Ben-Gan/Moreau	Advanced Transact-SQL for SQL Server 2000
1-893115-48-8	$29.95	Bischof	The .NET Languages: A Quick Translation Guide
1-893115-67-4	$49.95	Borge	Managing Enterprise Systems with the Windows Script Host
1-893115-28-3	$44.95	Challa/Laksberg	Essential Guide to Managed Extensions for C++
1-893115-44-5	$29.95	Cook	Robot Building for Beginners
1-893115-99-2	$39.95	Cornell/Morrison	Programming VB .NET: A Guide for Experienced Programmers
1-893115-72-0	$39.95	Curtin	Developing Trust: Online Privacy and Security
1-59059-008-2	$29.95	Duncan	The Career Programmer: Guerilla Tactics for an Imperfect World
1-893115-71-2	$39.95	Ferguson	Mobile .NET
1-893115-90-9	$44.95	Finsel	The Handbook for Reluctant Database Administrators
1-893115-85-2	$34.95	Gilmore	A Programmer's Introduction to PHP 4.0
1-893115-36-4	$34.95	Goodwill	Apache Jakarta-Tomcat
1-893115-17-8	$59.95	Gross	A Programmer's Introduction to Windows DNA
1-893115-62-3	$39.95	Gunnerson	A Programmer's Introduction to C#, Second Edition
1-893115-30-5	$49.95	Harkins/Reid	SQL: Access to SQL Server
1-893115-10-0	$34.95	Holub	Taming Java Threads
1-893115-04-6	$34.95	Hyman/Vaddadi	Mike and Phani's Essential C++ Techniques
1-893115-96-8	$59.95	Jorelid	J2EE FrontEnd Technologies: A Programmer's Guide to Servlets, JavaServer Pages, and Enterprise JavaBeans
1-893115-49-6	$39.95	Kilburn	Palm Programming in Basic
1-893115-50-X	$34.95	Knudsen	Wireless Java: Developing with Java 2, Micro Edition
1-893115-79-8	$49.95	Kofler	Definitive Guide to Excel VBA

ISBN	PRICE	AUTHOR	TITLE
1-893115-57-7	$39.95	Kofler	MySQL
1-893115-87-9	$39.95	Kurata	Doing Web Development: Client-Side Techniques
1-893115-75-5	$44.95	Kurniawan	Internet Programming with VB
1-893115-46-1	$36.95	Lathrop	Linux in Small Business: A Practical User's Guide
1-893115-19-4	$49.95	Macdonald	Serious ADO: Universal Data Access with Visual Basic
1-893115-06-2	$39.95	Marquis/Smith	A Visual Basic 6.0 Programmer's Toolkit
1-893115-22-4	$27.95	McCarter	David McCarter's VB Tips and Techniques
1-893115-76-3	$49.95	Morrison	C++ For VB Programmers
1-893115-80-1	$39.95	Newmarch	A Programmer's Guide to Jini Technology
1-893115-58-5	$49.95	Oellermann	Architecting Web Services
1-893115-81-X	$39.95	Pike	SQL Server: Common Problems, Tested Solutions
1-893115-20-8	$34.95	Rischpater	Wireless Web Development
1-893115-93-3	$34.95	Rischpater	Wireless Web Development with PHP and WAP
1-893115-89-5	$59.95	Shemitz	Kylix: The Professional Developer's Guide and Reference
1-893115-40-2	$39.95	Sill	An Introduction to qmail
1-893115-24-0	$49.95	Sinclair	From Access to SQL Server
1-893115-94-1	$29.95	Spolsky	User Interface Design for Programmers
1-893115-53-4	$39.95	Sweeney	Visual Basic for Testers
1-59059-002-3	$44.95	Symmonds	Internationalization and Localization Using Microsoft .NET
1-893115-29-1	$44.95	Thomsen	Database Programming with Visual Basic .NET
1-893115-65-8	$39.95	Tiffany	Pocket PC Database Development with eMbedded Visual Basic
1-893115-59-3	$59.95	Troelsen	C# and the .NET Platform
1-893115-26-7	$59.95	Troelsen	Visual Basic .NET and the .NET Platform
1-893115-54-2	$49.95	Trueblood/Lovett	Data Mining and Statistical Analysis Using SQL
1-893115-16-X	$49.95	Vaughn	ADO Examples and Best Practices
1-893115-68-2	$49.95	Vaughn	ADO.NET and ADO Examples and Best Practices for Visual Basic Programmers, Second Edition
1-59059-012-0	$34.95	Vaughn/Blackburn	ADO.NET Examples and Best Practices for C# Programmers
1-893115-83-6	$44.95	Wells	Code Centric: T-SQL Programming with Stored Procedures and Triggers
1-893115-95-X	$49.95	Welschenbach	Cryptography in C and C++
1-893115-05-4	$39.95	Williamson	Writing Cross-Browser Dynamic HTML
1-893115-78-X	$49.95	Zukowski	Definitive Guide to Swing for Java 2, Second Edition
1-893115-92-5	$49.95	Zukowski	Java Collections

Available at bookstores nationwide or from Springer Verlag New York, Inc. at 1-800-777-4643; fax 1-212-533-3503. Contact us for more information at sales@apress.com.

Apress Titles Publishing SOON!

ISBN	AUTHOR	TITLE
1-893115-91-7	Birmingham/Perry	Software Development on a Leash
1-893115-39-9	Chand	A Programmer's Guide to ADO.NET in C#
1-893115-42-9	Foo/Lee	XML Programming Using the Microsoft XML Parser
1-893115-55-0	Frenz	Visual Basic for Scientists
1-59059-009-0	Harris/Macdonald	Moving to ASP.NET
1-59059-016-3	Hubbard	Windows Forms in C#
1-893115-38-0	Lafler	Power AOL: A Survival Guide
1-893115-43-7	Stephenson	Standard VB: An Enterprise Developer's Reference for VB 6 and VB .NET
1-59059-007-4	Thomsen	Building Web Services with VB .NET
1-59059-010-4	Thomsen	Database Programming with C#
1-59059-011-2	Troelsen	COM and .NET Interoperability
1-893115-98-4	Zukowski	Learn Java with JBuilder 6

Available at bookstores nationwide or from Springer Verlag New York, Inc. at 1-800-777-4643; fax 1-212-533-3503. Contact us for more information at sales@apress.com.

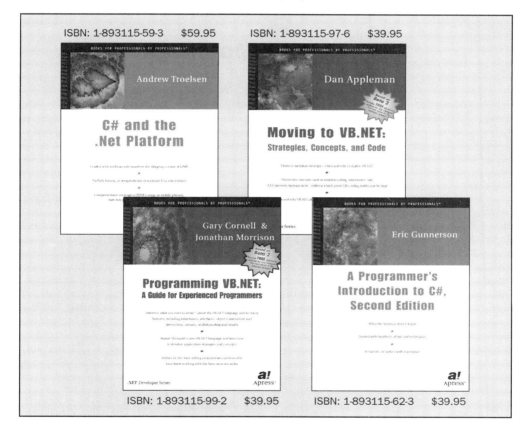

books for professionals by professionals™

apress™

About Apress

Apress, located in Berkeley, CA, is an innovative publishing company devoted to meeting the needs of existing and potential programming professionals. Simply put, the "A" in Apress stands for the "Author's Press™." Apress' unique author-centric approach to publishing grew from conversations between Dan Appleman and Gary Cornell, authors of best-selling, highly regarded computer books. In 1998, they set out to create a publishing company that emphasized quality above all else, a company with books that would be considered the best in their market. Dan and Gary's vision has resulted in over 30 widely acclaimed titles by some of the industry's leading software professionals.

Do You Have What It Takes to Write for Apress?

Apress is rapidly expanding its publishing program. If you can write and refuse to compromise on the quality of your work, if you believe in doing more than rehashing existing documentation, and if you're looking for opportunities and rewards that go far beyond those offered by traditional publishing houses, we want to hear from you!

Consider these innovations that we offer all of our authors:

- **Top royalties with *no* hidden switch statements**
  Authors typically only receive half of their normal royalty rate on foreign sales. In contrast, Apress' royalty rate remains the same for both foreign and domestic sales.

- **A mechanism for authors to obtain equity in Apress**
  Unlike the software industry, where stock options are essential to motivate and retain software professionals, the publishing industry has adhered to an outdated compensation model based on royalties alone. In the spirit of most software companies, Apress reserves a significant portion of its equity for authors.

- **Serious treatment of the technical review process**
  Each Apress book has a technical reviewing team whose remuneration depends in part on the success of the book since they too receive royalties.

Moreover, through a partnership with Springer-Verlag, one of the world's major publishing houses, Apress has significant venture capital behind it. Thus, we have the resources to produce the highest quality books *and* market them aggressively.

If you fit the model of the Apress author who can write a book that gives the "professional what he or she needs to know ™," then please contact one of our Editorial Directors, Gary Cornell (gary_cornell@apress.com), Dan Appleman (dan_appleman@apress.com), Karen Watterson (karen_watterson@apress.com) or Jason Gilmore (jason_gilmore@apress.com) for more information.